HUMAN RIGHTS LAW AND THE MARGINALIZED OTHER

This groundbreaking application of contemporary philosophy to human rights law proposes significant innovations for the progressive development of human rights. Drawing on the works of prominent "philosophers of the Other," including Emmanuel Levinas, Gayatri Chakravorti Spivak, Judith Butler, and, most centrally, Argentine philosopher of liberation Enrique Dussel, this book advances an ethics based on concrete face-to-face relationships with the Marginalized Other. It proposes that this ethics should inspire a human rights law that is grounded in transcendental justice and framed from the perspective of marginalized groups. Such law would continuously deconstruct the original violence found in all human rights treaties and tribunals and promote preferential treatment for the marginalized. It would be especially attentive to such issues as access to justice, voice, representation, agency, and responsibility. This approach differs markedly from more conventional theories of human rights that prioritize the autonomy of the ego, state sovereignty, democracy, and equality.

Dr. William Paul Simmons is associate professor of political science and director of the MA program in Social Justice and Human Rights at Arizona State University. His interdisciplinary research employs numerous theoretical, legal, and empirical approaches to social justice and human rights issues. He is the author of *An-Archy and Justice: An Introduction to Emmanuel Levinas' Political Thought* and numerous articles and chapters on contemporary political thought. Dr. Simmons also has worked extensively on human rights issues in Mexico and at the U.S.–Mexico border. He is co-editing a volume on localizing human rights in the U.S.–Mexico context and conducted, with Michelle Telléz, groundbreaking ethnographic research on sexual violence against migrant women. He has also published law review articles and a book chapter on violence against women in Ciudad Juárez, Mexico, and has served as a consultant on human rights and social justice issues in The Gambia, China, Mexico, and the United States.

Human Rights Law and the Marginalized Other

WILLIAM PAUL SIMMONS

Arizona State University

Dear Norbert,

With great admiration for your work with marginalized groups!

Bill

CAMBRIDGE
UNIVERSITY PRESS

CAMBRIDGE
UNIVERSITY PRESS

32 Avenue of the Americas, New York NY 10013-2473, USA

Cambridge University Press is part of the University of Cambridge.

It furthers the University's mission by disseminating knowledge in the pursuit of education, learning and research at the highest international levels of excellence.

www.cambridge.org
Information on this title: www.cambridge.org/9781107671539

First published 2011
First paperback edition 2014

A catalogue record for this publication is available from the British Library

Library of Congress Cataloguing in Publication data
Simmons, William Paul, 1965–
    Human rights law and the marginalized other / William Paul Simmons.
        p.   cm.
    Includes bibliographical references and index.
    ISBN 978-1-107-01007-9 (hardback)
    1. Human rights – Philosophy.   2. Minorities – Legal status, laws, etc.   3. Other
    (Philosophy)   4. Marginality, Social.   I. Title.
    K3240.S5345   2011
    341.4'801–dc22   2011012051

ISBN 978-1-107-01007-9 Hardback
ISBN 978-1-107-67153-9 Paperback

Dedicated in humility, with love and pride, to Alfusainey Jarju

Brief Contents

Contents

Preface

This ambitious and complex work of both philosophy and human rights law seeks to make major advances in both fields and to develop a fresh dialogue between the two. I delve into a wide range of philosophical works in considerable detail, especially debates in recent philosophies of the "Other," and analyze many legal cases from disparate jurisdictions around the globe. In the philosophical chapters, I analyze concrete legal situations, and I suffuse the legal chapters with philosophical insights. To make this work more accessible to a range of readers, and not just philosophers and political theorists, this preface quickly lays out the overall argument of the work and provides a roadmap for the reader, especially those in nonacademic fields who may be attracted to the topic but might find some more densely theoretical sections relatively inaccessible.

In a nutshell, this book argues that human rights law should be *deconstructed* – that is, continuously examined and critiqued to expose existing dominant power relations – and *reinvigorated* by adopting a new theoretical orientation, one that privileges the voices of people who are excluded from social and political power, referred to in this work as the Marginalized Other. The two chapters in Part I make the case for critically examining or deconstructing the prevailing modes of thought that inform human rights law through detailed readings of works by political theorists Hannah Arendt and Seyla Benhabib. These chapters aim to show the resilience of dominant or hegemonic ways of thinking and the need to have a more radical deconstruction of these discourses to privilege the voice of the Marginalized Other. I argue that to conduct the necessary deconstruction of hegemonic ways of thinking requires a new way of thinking about the Other, one that is founded in transcendence – that is, beyond the hegemonic discourses – but that also can be made concrete to affect the political and social realms in a profound way. The two more theoretically rich chapters in Part II develop my phenomenology of the Saturated Other by combining insights from the philosophies of Emmanuel Levinas, Jean-Luc Marion, and Enrique Dussel. Note: When referring to my phenomenological account of the Other that is excluded from power, I will use the term "Saturated," because the ego owes a deeper, more saturated responsibility to this Other than to those within the system. When referring to the resulting application of this phenomenology to human rights and human rights law, I will refer to the "Marginalized" Other. The two are interchangeable, but the term "Saturated" has more of a technical philosophical meaning. The three chapters in Part III further develop this phenomenology, especially through the writings of feminist scholars Gayatri Spivak and Judith Butler. This part also shows how scholars and activists can concretely reinvigorate contemporary human rights law by analyzing such critical issues as environmental displacement in India, asylum law in the United States, aboriginal rights cases from Canada, reparations in the Inter-American Court of Human Rights, and the right to mental health in the African Commission on Human and Peoples' Rights. Throughout the work, the theoretical insights are made concrete through the case law, and the case law is deconstructed and reinvigorated by theoretical insights.

Several common themes stand out in the legal analysis. We encounter a number of well-meaning theorists, judges, and other legal players who failed to push past varieties of hegemonic discourses and in the process further marginalized the Other, the people actually seeking redress for human rights violations. We also encounter a number of progressive judges who managed to suspend the violence of the hegemonic discourses and patiently listened to the voices of the Marginalized Other, as well as a series of progressive tribunals that have modified their procedural rules to give voice to the Other and crafted new rights or given progressive new meanings to existing rights to better serve the Marginalized Other.

The theoretical insights of this work are drawn mostly from phenomenology, postmodernism, post-colonialism, and deconstruction – precisely those fields usually considered most opaque to non-philosophers, and even to some philosophers. I hope to persuade the reader that these seemingly obscure lenses are especially fitting for developing the necessary sustained deconstruction of hegemonic systems and for developing an alternative framework for reinvigorating human rights law. In particular, phenomenology, which seeks to "bracket" or suspend pre-existing theoretical insights to better dwell on experiences or phenomena, can be particularly beneficial when examining what types of knowledge have been privileged in human rights law. Post-colonialism, which takes the side of the marginalized and uncovers oppressive structures, is especially apt for identifying those voices that should be privileged.

The phenomenology in Part II is quite meticulous so that it will stand up to the scrutiny of philosophers and political theorists. Those who are mostly interested in legal analysis might want to skim through the intricate phenomenology in Part II and focus on Parts I and III. Similarly, readers with less facility in legal issues may struggle with the terminology and institutional intricacies in the discussions of case law and might focus on Parts I and II. Of course, my hope is that those who initially focus on only parts of the work will be drawn back to the remaining sections, as the theoretical insights and case examples are meant to complement each other.

It is heartening that an increasing number of theorists are taking on issues in current human rights law and some legal scholars are taking seriously the insights of contemporary debates in philosophy. Of course, scholars from a variety of disciplines and theoretical orientations embrace theories and methods that privilege marginalized communities, including many in cultural anthropology, critical race theory, critical legal studies, feminism, and postcolonialism. This book, heavily indebted to scholars in these fields, proposes something of an overarching theoretical framework that could be fruitfully applied in each of these areas.

I am thrilled by just how far this work has evolved from its initial conception several years ago and how many diverse voices have shaped and reshaped it. Of course, I alone remain responsible for its remaining limitations, many of which undoubtedly are the result of my failure to listen patiently enough to my mentors.

Many gifted scholars have informed my thinking through their comments on earlier drafts or through their encouragement, including Bill Conklin, James Hatley, Randy LeBlanc, Diane Perpich, and Devorah Wainer. Special thanks to Todd Landman, Rhona Smith, and the groundbreaking Chinese human rights scholars and practitioners who worked with us during the Training on Multi-Disciplinary Human Rights Research funded by the Norwegian Centre for Human Rights and the Raoul Wallenberg Institute for Human Rights and Humanitarian Law. Todd's and Rhona's published works have for many years been insightful and faithful companions in my human rights research. Numerous thinkers have also inspired me through their brilliant writings, including Upendra Baxi, Bill Conklin, and Gayatri Spivak. Two anonymous reviewers for Cambridge University Press offered helpful advice, especially for clarifying my central arguments and for making the work as a whole more accessible. Special thanks to Enrique Dussel for being a role model of infinite hospitality and radical deconstruction of hegemonic systems. A lively conversation with Professor Dussel over dinner at Purdue University enlightened and encouraged me at a critical point in the manuscript's evolution.

I thank my colleagues at Arizona State University who have taught me so much about the themes covered in this book, including Duku Anokye, Gloria Cuadraz, Julie Murphy Erfani, Alejandra Elenes, Anna Guevara, Richard Morris, Carol Mueller, Charles St. Clair, and Michelle Téllez. My students past and present, especially those in the MA program in Social Justice and Human Rights at ASU, as well as Becky Coplan, Grace Daniels, Dan Hoffman, Imran Kirkland, and Emily Taylor, were patient while I developed these ideas, and they challenged and shaped my thoughts on working with the Marginalized Other. Parts of this manuscript were made possible through two Scholarship, Research, and Creative Activity grants from ASU and a sabbatical in spring 2010.

This book is inspired in countless ways by my many role models in the community, whose love and guidance have sustained me much more than they could ever know or I could ever repay. These include Marco Albarran, Peggy Bilsten, Judy Butzine, Deb Carstens, Elsa Chyrum, Stella Pope Duarte, Jean Fairfax, Semere Kesete, Jack Lunsford, Elaine Maimon, Melanie Ohm, Vicky Ortiz, Dave Tierney, Steve Tracy, Libby Walker, Dr. C. T. Wright, and Mary Wright. They live the philosophy that I develop in this work. I am heavily indebted to the Institute for Human Rights and Development in Africa, especially Executive Director Sheila Keetharuth and Deputy Director Angela Naggaga, for allowing me to hang out with them and, in a small way, make a contribution to their wonderful work advancing human rights for marginalized communities across Africa. To those marginalized communities that I have been privileged to work with in several countries: Thank you for teaching me more about ethics than I can ever have imagined and showing that there is so much more work to do.

An infinite debt is owed to Monica Casper, my collaborator, co-conspirator, and life partner, for her wisdom and her uncanny editing ability, and for seeing promise in my work that often escaped me. To my daughters, Mason and Delaney: Thank you for teaching me new ways of listening and for giving me so much hope for the future.

Introduction

Deconstruction, Concrete Universalisms, and Human Rights of the Other

To call for a deconstruction of human rights law must seem both impudent and untimely. Impudent because deconstruction, having arrived uninvited and quite late to the human rights party, dares to undertake a criticism of human rights law's very foundations; untimely because this critique comes at the very moment that human rights law is struggling to maintain its newly gained prominence in legal, academic, and policy circles against the onslaughts of interminable wars on terror and their concomitant ideologies of realpolitik. Just when human rights law appears in its most robust state, deconstruction has the nerve to call for its reinvigoration. How could human rights law require reinvigoration today?

Furthermore, deconstruction must appear to be an odd candidate to assist in the reinvigoration of human rights law when it, along with its fellow traveler postmodernism, are infamous for their obscurantism, for "producing a scholarship" that is "conceptual, arid, and removed from experience" (Blumenson 1996, 527). More substantively, they have been censured for their rejection of any type of values or universalism, leaving behind a morass of relativism. As feminist legal scholar Catharine MacKinnon challenges:

> Can postmodernism hold the perpetrators of genocide accountable? If the subject is dead, and we are dealing with deeds without doers, how do we hold perpetrators accountable for what they perpetrate? Can the Serbian cultural defense for the extermination of Croats, Bosnian Muslims, and Kosovar Albanians be far behind? If we can have a multicultural defense for the current genocide, because that's how the Serbs see it, why not a German cultural defense for the earlier one? Anti-Semitism *was* part of German culture. (2000, 706)

We are told, in the *New York Times* no less, that postmodernism is so "ethically perverse" that it would even rule out condemnation of the terrorist attacks of 9/11. After all, the purported "rejections of universalist values and ideals leave little room for unqualified condemnations of a terrorist attack, particularly one against the West" (Rothstein 2001).

Deconstruction and postmodernism, in response to these critiques and to a series of historical events such as the Rwandan and Bosnia genocides, the fall of communism, and the growing entanglements of globalization, undertook a well-publicized ethical turn in the 1980s and 1990s. Their adherents searched, sometimes in vain, for theoretical grounds on which to make ethical and political judgments. Some, such as Stanley Fish and Richard Rorty, took the pragmatic way out and reveled in their newfound anti-foundationalism, holding that no adequate *theoretical* answers could be made to the cultural relativism challenge and theorists should just accept that fact. Others embraced pseudo-Nietzschean critiques, arguing that philosophy could only provide a questioning of all final answers and was incapable of providing any new ethical foundation on which to reconstruct human rights. Other thinkers abandoned postmodernism for, or supplemented it with, insights from Marxism, feminism, and post-colonialism. Other theorists, such as the current author, have found solace in various ethics of the "Other" such as that propounded by the Franco-Jewish philosopher Emmanuel Levinas. Levinas, while sharing many of the same philosophical foundations of the postmodernists, had been writing about "ethics as first philosophy" decades before the famous ethical turn. Indeed, Levinas' philosophy based on the ego's infinite responsibility for the Other, the other person, has recently gained cachet in a number of fields, but it has rarely been applied to human rights law.[1]

In this work, I move beyond Levinas' ethics of the Other and develop a phenomenology of the Saturated Other by supplementing Levinas' work with that of such theorists as Judith Butler, Enrique Dussel, Jean-Luc Marion, and Gayatri Spivak. I propose that a philosophy that begins with the ethical relationship with the Saturated or Marginalized Other, provides a much needed and timely deconstruction of human rights law, and opens fruitful avenues for its reinvigoration. This book's central premise is straightforward: Human rights law should find its inspiration from the Other, the marginalized person who, in most cases, has no other place to turn. This premise should be self-apparent. After all, the raison d'être of human rights law should be the protection and empowerment of those who have been most marginalized, "to give voice to human suffering, to make it visible, and to ameliorate it" (Baxi 2002, 4). Human rights law should privilege the "right to have rights" (Arendt's

---

[1] Notable exceptions include Douzinas (2000), Shepherd (2006), Burggraeve (2002), and Simmons (2003).

phrase) of those that have been marginalized in society. As Rene Cassin said of the Universal Declaration of Human Rights, in the drafting of which he played a large role: "[I]t is the voice of millions of human beings, victims of oppression, misery and ignorance, who aspire to live under conditions of greater justice, freedom and simple dignity" (Cassin 1970). Unfortunately, as I show in the discussion that follows, the voices that should be empowered by human rights law are often disregarded by human rights law and frequently even further silenced by it. They remain, in Aristotle's term, *aneu logou* (without a voice). Only when human rights tribunals, attorneys, and activists learn to patiently listen to the voices of the marginalized will the *aneu logou* realize their human rights.

DEDUCTIVE AND INDUCTIVE UNIVERSALISMS

Most previous human rights theories did not begin from the voices of the Marginalized Other. Instead, in an attempt to develop theories of rights with near-scientific certitude, many philosophers (from Hobbes to the present) have embraced a deductive approach that consciously parrots the methods of mathematicians and scientists. Most rights theories begin with first principles derived from the thought experiments of philosophers, political theorists, or theologians. Rights are deduced from self-preservation, reason, the laws of nature, freedom, or the categorical imperative. Often, to ensure objective first principles, these theorists attempt to "bracket" or set aside social or cultural influences by imagining abstract states of nature (Hobbes, Locke, Rousseau, etc.), or, more recently, through an "original position" stemming from an assumed veil of ignorance (Rawls) or an ideal speech situation (Habermas). Many political theorists and philosophers still embrace this method and have come up with a plethora of lists of basic rights that will presumably garner near-universal support. The debates then become whether this original list of rights can be expanded while maintaining universal or perhaps overlapping consensus (e.g., Beitz 2001; Talbott 2005).

In contrast to these endless searches for an abstract universalism, human rights attorneys, judges, and activists have employed an inductive approach to develop their own collections of rights. The rights found in international treaties and the decisions of international courts and quasi-judicial bodies are rarely framed in terms of general abstract principles. For instance, the drafters of the Universal Declaration of Human Rights (UDHR) consciously eschewed philosophical or religious justifications. The most important early draft of the UDHR was prepared by Canadian delegate John Humphrey and resembled a laundry list of rights derived from existing rights documents.

It was not so much a draft as a collation. When queried about the philosophy behind the document: "What principles did they adopt; what method did they follow? Is it their own idea; is it a collection of various principles?" Humphrey conceded, it "is based on no philosophy whatsoever" (Glendon 2001, 58).

While the abstract universalists are still debating first principles and whether a resulting specific right can obtain universal agreement, the human rights regimes, consciously avoiding debates about first principles, have developed a robust collection of rights that have proven surprisingly universal and justiciable. The universality of these rights is apparent in the near-unanimous acceptance of the UDHR and the current ratification status of the myriad UN human rights treaties, such as the Convention on the Rights of the Child, which has been ratified by every country except Somalia and the United States.[2] Even the 1993 Vienna Declaration, drafted in the midst of contentious cultural relativism–universalism debates, was signed by all 172 countries present and boldly proclaimed the universality of the existing human rights regimes:

> The World Conference on Human Rights reaffirms the solemn commitment of all States to fulfill their obligations to promote universal respect for, and observance and protection of, all human rights and fundamental freedoms for all in accordance with the Charter of the United Nations, other instruments relating to human rights, and international law. *The universal nature of these rights and freedoms is beyond question.* (emphasis added, but see Otto 1997)

These human rights norms have also proven to be widely justiciable as evidenced by the creation of the International Criminal Court (ICC); the ad hoc courts for Rwanda, Yugoslavia, and Sierra Leone; the enormous growth in caseload and prestige of the European and Inter-American courts of human rights; and other less publicized advances such as the growing use of universal jurisdiction laws in numerous countries, the incorporation of human rights

---

[2]   Not merely hortatory, these treaties often require extensive intrusions into state sovereignty. For example, the most recently drafted human rights treaty, the Convention on the Rights of Persons with Disabilities, requires ratifying states, inter alia, to "modify or abolish existing laws, regulations, customs and practices that constitute discrimination against persons with disabilities," "to take into account the protection and promotion of the human rights of persons with disabilities in all policies and programmes," and "to take all appropriate measures to eliminate discrimination on the basis of disability by any person, organization or private enterprise" (Article 4).

treaties into national laws, and the recent innovative uses of the Alien Tort Statute in the United States.

Significantly, this "human rights cascade" (cf. Lutz and Sikkink 2001) has proceeded with precious little conversation between the human rights community and the deductive theorists of human rights. This was made evident to me several years ago when I attended a Salzburg Seminar on International Human Rights Law. Spending one intensive week discussing human rights with some of the leading practitioners from around the world gave me wonderful insight into the myriad recent advances in human rights law. Yet I was struck by how little attention was paid to philosophical arguments. In fact, not once during the sessions was any political theorist or political scientist mentioned, and philosophers were only mentioned in the most cursory fashion.[3]

So we are confronted with an extensive theoretical discussion of human rights that rarely, if ever, is applied by human rights workers and a wide-ranging application of human rights that rests on little philosophical justification. Not surprisingly then, the participants in the human rights cascade have been mostly unaware of several important recent philosophical critiques, most notably – for the present work – of the extent to which human rights may be founded on an invisible ideology that conceals an original violence (cf. Lefort 1986, 224; Derrida 1992).[4] John Humphrey claimed that his collation of rights was based on "no philosophy whatsoever," and yet it is quite clear that it, like all human rights documents of the post–World War II era, was steeped in a particular way of looking at the world based on Enlightenment values, the state sovereignty of the Westphalian system, and various manifestations of colonialism. Each of these biases privileges a certain type of human rights, applicable only in certain situations and for

---

[3] Similarly, Hopgood (2006) expresses surprise that few, if any, staff at Amnesty International's International Secretariat were aware of the death of John Rawls or even could identify Rawls (6–7).

[4] Many other theoretical critiques are germane to the general thrust of this book. Baxi (2002) argues against the commodification of human rights by non-governmental organizations (NGOs). "Human rights violations must be constantly commoditized to be combated. Human suffering must be packaged in ways that the mass media markets find it profitable to bear overall" (125). Macdonald (2004) argues that any human rights regime that lacks such theorization "loses much of its critical potential, and is thus far more susceptible to being appropriated by the powerful in order to sustain the global relations of domination prevailing today" (970). Otto (1997) goes further and claims that the universalism–cultural relativism debate itself is, at its core, about "global economic dominance" between the global North and the growing economies of Asia. "The debate is serving a variety of elite macroeconomic interests, and will continue to do so while articulated in modernity's dualistic terms" (4). The merits of these positions reinforce my call for a continuous deconstruction of human rights law (see Chapter 3 in this volume).

specific individuals. Women's rights and indigenous rights were marginalized while the horrors and brutality of colonialism and the proxy wars of the Cold War were almost completely absolved. Economic, social, and cultural rights were relegated to "second-generation rights," groups and "peoples" had little or no rights of their own, and states had little or no affirmative duties, especially for the actions of non-state actors. Human rights regimes to this day, unbothered by the works of philosophers, retain and reinforce what Jacques Derrida would call the "original violence" of this founding moment. Some progressive development in the meaning of human rights has taken place, but jurists have often been reluctant to challenge this original violence and its effects. Attorneys and activists have met great resistance when pushing for such advances as state responsibility for non-state actors, the justiciability of economic, social, and cultural rights, or gendered interpretations of treaties such as the Convention against Torture (cf. Simmons 2007). As human rights law becomes more robust, as its foundations become more widely accepted, as a human rights triumphalism sets in, the original violence risks becoming further obscured and thus more pernicious. Human rights workers may question less and less their very assumptions, especially the extent to which their very work may be perpetrating a type of violence by privileging a specific conception of rights. And here, we begin to glimpse the timeliness of a deconstruction of human rights law.

CONCRETE UNIVERSALISMS

This is not to say that human rights regimes have not been subject to, and conscious of, extensive critique. Both sets of universal rights – the one more legal and practical, the other more abstract and philosophical – have had their share of detractors, especially in the famous universalism–cultural relativism debates that for many years unduly dominated much of human rights discourse at both the legal and theoretical levels. In response, both types of universalisms have tempered their claims; they have both been drawn to what have been called concrete universalisms.[5]

---

[5]   The term "concrete universal" has a long history, made most famous in Hegel's work where the modern German state concretely realized the abstract idea of the state. Most recent uses of this term depart from Hegel's emphasis on unity (see, for example, Hanssen [2000] who argues for "a situated universalism, where provisional universalist programs are tested and corrected as seen fit" [74]). For other relevant uses of this term, see Cohen (2003; "the elevation demanded by ethical universality is rooted in the particular, just as the aspiration of particularity requires and demands universality" [138]), Gould (1976), Levinas (1990, 6; in reference to "Israel's vocation"), Peperzak (1997, 84–87), and Simmons (2003, 82–85).

In the case of the human rights regimes, their concrete universalisms frequently mix the universalism of law with the concrete aspects of particular cases and the plurality of conditions confronted when applying the law.[6] Human rights judges grapple daily with questions of relativism and universalism, and very few can be human rights absolutists or unqualified relativists. They must weigh the application of universal standards with the rights of defendants, the sovereignty of nations, political exigencies, and claims of victims and their families, as well as social and cultural norms. Despite this need to concretize or contextualize human rights laws, jurists have been surprisingly willing to make universal pronouncements. Even on those issues that universalism's detractors often trot out as its Achilles' heel, jurists and other human rights practitioners have increasingly sided with universalism. For example, the recent protocol on the Rights of Women in Africa takes an unexpectedly strong stand against female genital mutilation and other "harmful traditional practices," and the African Commission on Human and Peoples' Rights has made significant rulings curtailing the application of Sharia law. Further, the Inter-American Court of Human Rights has overruled elected bodies and the judiciary in Chile, an overwhelmingly Catholic country, in rejecting the censorship of the allegedly blasphemous film *The Last Temptation of Christ* (*"The Last Temptation of Christ" Case*, 2001), and the European Court of Human Rights acted in a similar manner in overturning Northern Ireland's anti-sodomy law (*Dudgeon v. United Kingdom* 1981).

At the same time, many theorists have developed concrete universalisms without relying on deductions from abstract first principles. These theorists have often found Nietzschean formulations of the death of God – that is, the death of abstract ideals – to be compelling, but at the same time, they have been fearful of embracing any sort of strong ethical relativism. These theorists have often turned to philosophers such as Aristotle and Hegel for guidance in constructing concrete universalisms using an inductive approach beginning from concrete experiences. They often heed phenomenologist Edmund Husserl's famous exhortation, "back to the things themselves" – that is, a theorist should attempt to bracket any a priori theoretical framework and focus on phenomena as they appear as opposed to how they are categorized by the speculations of contemplative philosophers. For instance, the twentieth-century émigré philosopher Hannah Arendt wrote that "thought itself arises

---

[6] Cf. Donoho (2001): "Ultimately, the real issue is not legitimacy of relativism but rather the degree to which diversity, pluralism, self-governance, and autonomy values will be accounted for within the international human rights system" (3). See also An-Na'im (1992).

out of incidents of living experience and must remain bound to them as the only guideposts by which to take its bearings" (1968, 14). From this emphasis on concrete experience, a major role of philosophy becomes a questioning of what Arendt calls *banisters*: "categories and formulas that are deeply ingrained in our mind but whose basis of experience has long been forgotten and whose plausibility resides in their intellectual consistency rather than in their adequacy to actual events" (Arendt 2003, 37). These banisters or artificial typologies categorize (etymologically; to accuse) phenomena and deny them their full reality. When applied to human affairs, such typologies risk reducing individuals to preconceived categories based on race, gender, nationality, and so forth.

Arendt and other concrete universalists do not defend some type of casuistry where each case or set of facts must be treated as isolated and absolutely unique. They trudge on and make judgments that can be generalized or universalized, but these judgments are grounded in concrete experience. How is it possible for jurists or philosophers to make universal judgments from concrete experiences without slipping into casuistry or relativism? Recall that a good number of philosophers, from Plato to Hobbes to the present day, deride the "truths" of such inductive thinking as mere "illusion and opinion" (Arendt 1968, 232) because of their contingent nature. If we are to found truths on facts, then we must navigate what Kant called the "melancholy haphazardness" of facts, "the intractable, unreasonable stubbornness of sheer factuality" (Arendt 1968, 243). In other words, if we do not subscribe to a teleology or "divine" plan in history, we must admit that there could just as easily have been other facts. If the universal human rights that we hold so dear are drawn from the current concrete facts, we must ask whether the same universalism would have evolved under a different set of facts, such as a hypothetical victory of Nazism or Stalinism. Likewise, if the UDHR had been drafted 150 years earlier, would it have included Article 4's denunciation of slavery or Article 2's prohibition of discrimination based on "race, color, sex, language, religion, etc."? And so, removing the banisters of abstract philosophers quickly leads us to the indictments of postmodernism's relativism posed by Catharine MacKinnon and discussed earlier in this book. This is not to say that supposedly universal principles cannot be created inductively. After all, the drafters of the UDHR and subsequent treaties have created universally recognized principles without such abstract truths. But their ultimate formulations are surely subject to the melancholy of haphazardness and the related charges of relativism.

Along with the interrogations of the founding violence of human rights law, we now begin to see the need for a new foundation for human rights, a way to ground the concrete universalisms of philosophers and human rights regimes.

Can we find a new (nonabstract) foundation for human rights that critiques all foundations or banisters of thought, including its own, but avoids the charges of casuistry and relativism? Would not such a new foundation reinvigorate human rights law and open new avenues for its progressive development?

TOWARD A CONCRETE UNIVERSALISM OF THE OTHER

After its ethical turn, postmodernism and deconstruction offer much more than the endless critique or "desedimentation" (Derrida 1992, 13) of law for which they are most famous. Postmodernism's growing emphasis on the marginalized Other, inspired in large part by Levinas' work, can provide a new foundation or a "new normative map" (Benhabib 2004, 6) that can lead to a reinvigoration of human rights.

Levinas' thought begins not from abstract principles but from the infinite ethical responsibility that originates in the ego's exposure to the face of the human Other. The ego is commanded to respond to the Other to the point of substituting oneself for the Other; that is, "bringing comfort by associating ourselves with the essential weakness and finitude of the Other" (Levinas 2001, 228). The ego must incessantly question its actions: Has it really done enough for the Other? Levinas insists that this original commandment of the Other must be universalized into laws and political institutions to be most effective. The crucial point is that laws and institutions must find their inspiration in the original ethical relationship with the Other. Applied to human rights law, the raison d'être of human rights institutions must be to respond to the ethical demands of the Other, and this response requires a continuous questioning as to whether the institutions have done enough for the Other. Any original violence that would further silence the Other must be continuously deconstructed.

To begin with the ego's exposure to the Marginalized Other would appear to open Levinas' thought to the vicissitudes of the melancholy haphazardness of facts that Kant bemoans. After all, the Other that confronts the ego could very well be someone different, could be marginalized in some different way. Therefore, the ego's infinite responsibility would differ depending on the contingency of facts. MacKinnon's accusations about cultural relativism would remain valid.

Levinas argues, however, that by rooting this very concrete experience of exposure to the Other in *transcendence*, his thought is not tied to the contingency of facts and therefore allows for judgment that surpasses cultural relativism. For Levinas, the face of the Other points to a transcendence beyond the comprehension or categories of the ego and resists the creation of all typologies in its name. Levinas calls this transcendence a "return to Platonism in a new way" (Levinas 1996, 58, cf. Blum 2000), by which he means the establishment of an ethical standard that moves beyond cultural relativism and can call into question all ideologies or typologies. Indeed, the face of the Other rooted in transcendence calls into question all institutions, even those created for the Other. All institutions must be constantly interrogated as to whether they are truly serving the Other.

CAUTERIZATION OF THE OTHER

Most human rights theories do not begin from the perspective of the Marginalized Other. In fact, most exclude – or, more accurately, "cauterize" – the Marginalized Other. The term "cauterize" aptly describes the comprehensive way that the Other has been excluded by most rights thinking, be it philosophical, political, or legal. I identify three aspects of cauterization (see Figure I.1) that correspond to the term's three interrelated meanings (cf. *Oxford English Dictionary*). The first meaning comes from its roots in the Greek verb *kauteriazein*, which means to burn with a *kauter* or a branding iron. Such branding was historically done to physically mark a slave or criminal as rightless. Second, cauterization refers to a medical procedure in which burning is used to seal off or remove part of the body. This procedure is most often used to stop bleeding, but it can also seal a wound to stop the spread of infection. Finally, in its most metaphorical meaning, cauterization means to deaden feelings or make one callous to the suffering of another.

Previous rights theories, whether philosophical or legal, often cauterize the Marginalized Other. The Other is branded as beneath humanity, below those who deserve rights. Then, those that are deemed inferior or rightless are sealed off from the polis or the courtroom, in effect treating the voice of the rightless as an infection that must be stopped from spreading. This meaning is suggested by Adolph Eichmann's attorney when describing the extermination camps as a "medical matter" (Arendt 2003, 43). Finally, those with rights, the full members of the polis, deaden their feelings toward the suffering of those who are branded as rightless.

Of course, this logic lurks behind almost every ideology that has supported genocide, colonization, or slavery. Examples abound. African slaves brought to the Americas were often physically branded on their faces or shoulders. Even after that practice was banned in much of the United States, less physical, but very real, legal branding was perpetrated by legislation and legal opinions. African Americans were famously branded as "so far inferior that they had no rights which the white man was bound to respect," and therefore, they "might

Cauterization		Reversal of cauterization Through the creation of an anti-hegemonic community with the marginalized Other	
Three aspects of cauterization	Representative quote	Reversal of cauterization	Representative quote
Branding the Other as inferior and rightless, like a slave or fugitive	African Americans are "so far inferior that they had no rights which the white man was bound to respect," and therefore, they "might justly and lawfully be reduced to slavery for his benefit" (*Scott v. Sandford*, 1857).	The right for the Other to self-ascribe her identity and define her rights, including which rights are most fundamental	"Equality and non-discrimination are subjective rights which must remain under the control of those who are entitled to benefit from them" (Judge Tulkens of the European Court of Human Rights).
Sealing the Other and Her Voice from the Polis	During the French "headscarf" debates, "the voices … are exclusively those of men – politicians, school principals, editorialists, and religious leaders. The only female voice acknowledged is Danièle Mitterand, wife of the former President of France. As for the young Muslim women, they are quoted only once and very briefly (Ardizzoni 2004, 634).	Restore Voice through a Patient Listening (Dussel); Learning to Learn from Below (Spivak)	A "self-suspending leap into the other's sea" (Spivak 2004a, 207–8) is an embrace of a different episteme, which requires a suspension of the hegemonic language and "a sustained institutional practice of diversified language learning in imaginative depth" (Spivak 2006, 1612).
Deadening Feelings for the Other and Her Suffering	As James Field Stanfield described one slave ship captain: "Because of his debility, he ordered anyone to be flogged tied to his bedpost so he could see the victims face-to-face, "enjoying their agonizing screams, while their flesh was lacerated without mercy" (Rediker 2007, 149).	Responding concretely to the Other (Levinas), working in Solidarity with the Other (Spivak)	Solidarity is "the affirmation of the exteriority of the other, of his life, his rationality, his denied rights" (Dussel 2004, 330) and this is a call for the ego to work "with the victim in order to stop him or her from being a victim" (2004, 332).

FIGURE I.1.The cauterization of the Other and its reversal.

justly and lawfully be reduced to slavery for his benefit" (*Scott v. Sandford*).[7] Once branded as rightless, as beneath rights, those marginalized would no longer be granted access to the courts and could not even testify in the courts in any state, as if their voices, their perspectives, literally did not exist (see, for example, Cogan 1989). Of course, such branding and exclusion contributed in no small part to the brutality suffered at the hands of genteel slave owners and "courageous" captains of death boats who were deadened to the immense suffering of the rightless. As British seaman James Field Stanfield described one ship captain: "Because of his debility, he ordered anyone to be flogged tied to his bedpost so he could see the victims face-to-face, "enjoying their agonizing screams, while their flesh was lacerated without mercy" (Rediker 2007, 149).

We would expect that such pernicious attitudes would wither away with the embrace of the eighteenth-century "rights of man," the ratification of the Civil War Amendments, or in the wake of the horrors of the twentieth century, but we still find evidence of cauterization operating even within human rights regimes themselves.[8] Liberal formulations of human rights, including

---

[7] Baxi (2002) similarly quotes a privy council decision that some "natives" may be "so low in the scale of social organization as to render it idle to impute to such people a shadow of rights known to our law" (33).

[8] For an excellent discussion of how modern human rights theories (such as those of Locke and Mill) "were devices of exclusion" through imperialism and slavery, see Baxi (2002). He writes, "the Other in many cases ceased to exist before the imperial law formations as the doctrine of terra nullius…illustrates with vivid cruelty" (30).

those of Locke and Mill, have been condemned for providing an imprimatur for colonization: "Suffering was made invisible because large masses of
colonized peoples were not regarded as human or because a considerable
number of human beings were regarded as not fully human, in need of tute-
lage" (Baxi 2002, 33, cf. Finkielkraut 2000). Even the drafting of the UDHR
evinces a pattern of cauterization. The cloak of universality concealed the
exclusion of sub-Saharan Africans and all indigenous and colonized peoples
from the drafting process – just those who were most in need of the protection
of human rights.

   Cauterization of the Other continues to haunt human rights regimes today.
Consider, for example, the rules of procedures for the generally progressive
Inter-American Court of Human Rights. Only in 1997, two decades after its
inception, did the Court allow victims to directly address the Court, and then
only during the reparations phase of the proceedings. Only in the past few
years has the Court allowed the victims to address the Court at all stages of
the proceedings.[9] Even with such institutional advances and a growing awareness of the need to include the voice of the Other, the cauterization process
continues to operate even in liberal democracies. During the recent headscarf
affair in France (discussed in Chapter 2), the voices of the young Muslim
women who wore headscarves were mostly cauterized from the lengthy political debate. An analysis of the voluminous newspaper coverage showed that
"the voices heard in the articles are exclusively those of men – politicians,
school principals, editorialists, and religious leaders....As for the young
Muslim women, they are quoted only once and very briefly" (Ardizzoni 2004,
634). Even the national commission that examined the issue "only invited one
French Muslim woman who wears a headscarf to give testimony out of 150
witnesses" (Wing and Smith 2006, 784). Young Muslim women were often
branded as victims of patriarchy or as uneducated immigrant girls, and thus
their voices needed to be sealed off or cauterized from the debates.

   Any deconstruction of human rights law must be especially sensitive to
the multitude of ways in which Others and their voices continue to be cauterized.[10] I argue that patiently listening to the voice of the Other is a precon-
dition for deconstructing the original violence inherent to any human rights
regime. Likewise, any reinvigoration of human rights must find a prominent
place for the voice of the Other. As Indian attorney Upendra Baxi (n.d.) wrote

---

[9] The former President of the Court notes that this change "marks a major milestone in the
     evolution of the Inter-American system for the protection of human rights" (Trindade 2002,
     11). This change is discussed in much greater detail in Chapter 7 in this volume.
[10] Indeed, cauterization may be endemic to any type of theorization or law (see Chapter 5 in
     this volume).

of the urgent need to reform human rights education (HRE) from the perspective of the Other:

> Perhaps, the first step in the activist journey of huper solidarity is for HRE activists to *learn* from the victims of the perfidies of power *rather than to presume to educate them in the struggle for survival and justice. Which victim of land mines in today's world does not know the meaning, method and message of state terrorism? Which victim of ethnic cleansing and contemporary genocides needs to be educated in the HRE Decade Plan of action? Do the victims of militarized rapes need education in the CEDAW? Humility before the victims of gross and flagrant violations of human rights*, I believe, is critically indispensable for the would be HRE communities of the future. I hope I am wrong in saying this but from what I have seen of the evangelical militancy of some HRE endeavor [sic] makes me think and *feel* anxious concerning what I must name *faute de mieux* as HRE "imperialism." If this is a proper diagnosis, the problem then becomes one of *how may we educate the HRE educators, rather than the people whom they so ardently wish to serve?*

BOOK OUTLINE

An ethics of the Marginalized Other cannot be applied formulaically to human rights law. It cannot provide a step-by-step recipe for making judicial decisions. Nor is a human rights of the Marginalized Other the last answer to current controversies in human rights law. This book's claim is that the phenomenology of the Saturated Other developed here can assist in the deconstruction of the original violence within current human rights law and further its progressive development.

This book is divided into three major parts. The first part examines the well-known theoretical concrete universalisms of Hannah Arendt and Seyla Benhabib. I argue that despite their emphases on minority rights and pluralism derived from their adherence to deliberative democracy, both theories ultimately cauterize the Other. This is most apparent in their respective analyses of the 1957 desegregation crisis in Little Rock, Arkansas, and the recent headscarf affairs in France and Turkey. Whereas Arendt's theory of judgment overtly cauterizes the Other, Benhabib's theory of discursive democracy is much more sensitive to the Other's voice. However, because it relies on a theoretical typology founded in procedural deliberative democracy, Benhabib's work ultimately also risks silencing the Other. I conclude that human rights law requires a continuous deconstruction of such institutions and typologies, including democracy and human rights tribunals and treaties. The first part ends by employing Derrida's writings, especially his famous essay, "The Force of Law," to outline such a deconstruction of human rights law and what types of aporiai or questions any such deconstruction must address.

In the second part, I develop a concrete universalism of the Marginalized Other, drawing primarily on the writings of Levinas, Enrique Dussel, and Jean-Luc Marion. Levinas' "ethics as first philosophy" has been called a Copernican Revolution in philosophy because it places a concrete ethics before abstract first principles but is still transcendent enough to make ethical judgments. The exposure to the face of the Other is both concrete and transcendent. However, many commentators, including the present author, have labored to develop a political theory or any type of universalism from his ethical thought. Two other critiques of Levinas' ethics as first philosophy are especially relevant to this work. First, by rooting the exposure to the Other in transcendence, Levinas' philosophy risks falling into an abstract universalism grounded on some foundational theological principle. Second, by claiming that all individuals have a face, that the ego owes an infinite responsibility to the exposure of any Other, Levinas risks minimizing the differences between the ego's responsibility to, say, the street child in Guatemala City or São Paulo and the prison guard at Auschwitz. I draw heavily on the writings of the philosopher of liberation Enrique Dussel and the French phenomenologist Jean-Luc Marion, especially the latter's phenomenology of "saturated phenomena," and argue that the Marginalized Other affects the ego in a more saturated or comprehensive way than Levinas' conception of the Other. This framework supplements Levinas' phenomenology of the Other and develops an ethical philosophy that begins with the very concrete exposure to the face of the Other, which is founded in a type of transcendence that does not slip into relativism or theology and allows differentiation between the faces of the Others. This phenomenology concretizes the Other but maintains the transcendental aspect of the Other without losing the anti-foundational character of Levinas' thought. From this phenomenology of the Marginalized Other as a "Saturated" Other, I argue for a reinvigorated conception of human rights law where the Marginalized Other will have a right to have a privileged voice in the polis, the right to define their own identity, and the right to define their own rights. All apparatuses of the system, such as the state and judges, and the ego then have corresponding duties: to patiently listen to the Other, to work to deconstruct the interpellation of the Other's identity that has led to the marginalization, and to work with the Marginalized Others to realize their life projects (*proyectos de la vida*).

In the third part, I employ the insights of such prominent thinkers as Gayatri Spivak, Judith Butler, and Jacques Rancière to further elaborate on the three sets of rights and duties that I derive from Dussel's work. I also apply the human rights of the Marginalized Other to a wide variety of concrete cases in human rights law from a variety of jurisdictions around the globe. In many cases, judges, attorneys, and activists are increasingly giving preference to the perspective of the Marginalized Other, but I show that some of the innovations intended to give voice to the Other have been co-opted by the hegemonic system and further cauterize the Marginalized Other.

More specifically, a human rights of the Other will focus much more on restoring the voice and agency of the Other. I discuss the voice of the Other in Chapter 5 in relation to recent, generally progressive, social action litigation (SAL) cases in India. Ultimately, however, in the most infamous SAL case, the Indian Supreme Court further silenced the voices of the marginalized Others who were affected by the building of the Sardar Sarovar dam. The Other should also be able to self-ascribe their identity, which I discuss in relation to the self-ascription of particular social groups in U.S. asylum law in Chapter 6. The Marginalized Others should define their own rights and decide which rights are most fundamental to them. I discuss such heteronomic rights in Chapter 7 in the context of recent aboriginal rights cases in Canada. There I call for "heteronomic tiered scrutiny" where the determination of which rights are most fundamental are defined, not by a distant tribunal, but by the Marginalized Other. Such an approach will have a pronounced effect on recent indigenous law cases in Canada and elsewhere. Finally, I consider the case of the Moiwana village in Suriname where the judges of the Inter-American Court of Human Rights patiently listened to the voice of the Other, allowed the marginalized community to define their own identity and their own rights, and then ordered the state to work with them to realize their *proyectos*. I end with a call for human rights law to be continuously deconstructed and reinvigorated by working with the Marginalized Other.

THE MARGINALIZED OTHER DOES NOT APPEAR HERE

Although this book calls for a deconstruction and reinvigoration of human rights law from the perspective of the Marginalized Other, the Marginalized Other does not appear in its pages. The work is sprinkled with quotations and rich descriptions from those who suffer human rights abuses, but I cannot pretend to have captured the voices of the Marginalized Other. As Spivak writes, the Other is "irretrievably heterogeneous" (1988, 284); any author would be unable to accurately represent or do justice to the voice of the Other through a work such as this. In a similar vein, anthropologist Leslie Butt has recently warned against using truncated narratives of suffering as an "ornamental illusion" that "masks the real absence of the voices of the poor and their suffering on the world stage" (Butt 2002, 1). Legal or theoretical works like the present one risk mobilizing the Marginalized Other merely as a tool to support their pre-derived theoretical points.

The present book is not immune to these critiques. The reader will be presented with detailed narratives of a number of human rights situations from a range of jurisdictions and contexts, many of which include truncated *testimonios* from marginalized individuals. I am under no illusion that I have presented the voice of the Marginalized Other here, that the Marginalized Other is truly speaking in its pages. Indeed, I would echo Butt's concerns and take them one step further. She is correct, theory does cauterize the Other, and perhaps all works, even the most extensive and sensitive ethnographies, must rely on truncated voices of the Other and merely present the author's own representations of the Marginalized Others' lives and sufferings. Such dilemmas in writing about the Other do not invalidate the conclusions of this work, but further confirm the need for a human rights of the Marginalized Other. Such work calls for a learning to learn from below, a need for institutions to be transformed and reinvigorated to be sensitive to the voice of the Other, and to take on a duty to work with the Other to realize their life project.

PART I

Deconstruction of Human Rights Law

Arendt, Little Rock, and the Cauterization of the Other

The human rights of the Marginalized Other developed in this book owes a great deal to recent attempts to develop a theoretical concrete universalism by prominent proponents of discursive democracy such as the political theorists Hannah Arendt and Seyla Benhabib. However, it questions the extent to which these prominent concrete universalisms are able to shed artificial typologies that cauterize the Other. Whereas the present work argues for extraordinary measures to patiently listen to the voice of the Other, Arendt's account of deliberative democracy urged the exclusion of the voiceless from the polis. Arendt also urged members of the polis to eschew such private emotions as pity and compassion for the marginalized while in the public realm and that they only cautiously take up solidarity with the marginalized Other. These forms of cauterization are most apparent in Arendt's famous theory of judgment, especially as it is applied in her analysis of the Little Rock School Crisis in 1957.

Arendt's theory of judgment is an exemplar of a concrete universalism and has been recently embraced by a number of political theorists. Whereas Arendt attempts to dismiss the banisters of thought and to develop a universalism based on concrete experience, her theory of judgment ultimately relies on artificial typologies that for the most part remain un-interrogated. I argue that this lack of questioning is directly related to her deliberate cauterization of the Other from political judgment. Without the voice of the Other, the rulings of an Arendtian judge are never seriously questioned. Arendtian judgment resembles groupthink, where like-minded judges make decisions that reinforce their privileged position. This chapter argues that Arendt's reliance on her own theoretical typologies and the silencing of the Other explain her ill-fated essay on the Little Rock Central High School crisis in 1957 in which Arendt famously sided with many of the arguments of the segregationists. We may be tempted to label Arendt's Little Rock essay as an anomaly by a normally sensitive writer, or representing a type of judgment that has been since discounted, but the problems inherent to Arendt's analysis run through the very foundations of human rights law and are frequently seen in a number of other human rights cases, as we shall see in subsequent chapters.

ARENDT'S "REFLECTIONS ON LITTLE ROCK"

In a justly infamous essay, Arendt reflected on the case of the "Little Rock Nine," the nine African-American children who, in 1957, were the first students in the South to attempt to attend desegregated public schools after the landmark *Brown v. Board of Education* decision of 1954. In *Brown*, the U.S. Supreme Court had emphatically declared, "[I]n the field of public education, the doctrine of 'separate but equal' has no place. Separate educational facilities are inherently unequal." By 1957, much of the political establishment in Little Rock favored the gradual desegregation of public schools, but in the weeks before the school year, Governor Orvall Faubus bowed to the political pressure of an election cycle and took steps to oppose the desegregation plan. On the first day of class, the state's National Guard was sent to prevent the African-American children from entering Central High, directly contravening the decision of the U.S. Supreme Court. Fifteen-year-old Elizabeth Eckford was the first of the nine children to arrive that morning. The National Guard turned Ms. Eckford away, leaving her and her precious few escorts to confront an increasingly angry mob outside of the school. Local photographer Will Counts snapped a now famous picture of Eckford, understandably shaken as she was verbally assaulted by "a jeering and grimacing mob of youngsters" (Arendt 1959a, 50). Seeing this snapshot, Arendt was spurred to write as the image conjured up memories of similarly desperate children in Europe during World War II. After a lengthy and controversial dispute, Arendt's Little Rock essay appeared in the journal *Dissent* in 1959 with a highly unusual preface penned by the editors: "We publish it not because we agree with it – quite the contrary! – but because we believe in freedom of expression even for views that seem to us entirely mistaken" (Editors 1959, 45).

I read Arendt's Little Rock essay as a quasi-legal opinion.[1] One can imagine a white segregationist, perhaps one of those jeering at Ms. Eckford that fateful morning, bringing a petition to an international court alleging that the eventual federally enforced desegregation of Little Rock Central High

---

[1]   Failinger (1987) appears to be the only other scholar that treats Arendt's essay as a quasi-legal opinion. She deftly compares Arendt's balancing of rights claims with 1980s U.S. case law on the rights to association and gender equality.

School violated his human rights, especially those Arendt says "clearly belong to them [parents] in all free societies – the private right over their children and the social right to free association" (Arendt 1959a, 55). In her essay/legal opinion, Judge Arendt took hypothetical testimony first from an African-American mother asking "What would I do if I were a Negro mother?" and then from a white mother asking "What would I do if I were a white mother in the South?"[2] Judge Arendt then crafted her opinion, weaving this testimony and the facts of the case with theory and precedent to weigh the conflicting rights claims.

Before considering her judgment, we must ask whether Arendt is well placed to serve as judge in this case. In her "Preliminary Remarks," she claimed that she is an "outsider" as she had spent little time in the South "because that would have brought me into a situation that I personally would find unbearable" (Arendt 1959a, 46). For Arendt, this lack of on-the-ground perspective is not grounds for recusal; instead, it seems to enhance her qualifications as judge. She knows, for example, that her abstract position is better than that of the oppressed (the children) and their representatives (the parents and the NAACP). Against the NAACP's claim that the desegregation of schools should be their highest priority, Arendt condescendingly remarks that "this is understandable: oppressed minorities were never the best judges on the order of priorities in such matters" (Arendt 1959a, 46). However, we expect our human rights jurists at minimum to be on the side of human rights and the oppressed. Arendt writes, "As a Jew I take my sympathy for the cause of the Negroes as for all oppressed or underprivileged peoples for granted, and should appreciate it if the reader did likewise" (Arendt 1959a, 46). Here Arendt has taken on the role of most human rights jurists: She has objective distance and she is on the correct side – that is, she is sympathetic to the oppressed and thus she should be given some latitude by the reader.[3] From this ideal vantage point, this "Olympian authority" as Ralph Ellison (1995, 156) would later describe it, Arendt can act as Ronald Dworkin's ideal of a Judge Hercules who labors to apply abstract laws and judicial rules to specific claims of abuses to craft the perfect opinion.[4] We may be concerned by Arendt's condescending attitude,

---

[2] Arendt describes her method in this way in her reply to her critics (Arendt 1959b, 179–181).

[3] For Norton (1995) such a claim signals that Arendt never calls her own privilege into question: "In claiming that she, as author, can declare where her sympathies lie, she reveals that the texts she has already authored do not accomplish this end" (248).

[4] For Dworkin (1977) the ideal judge delves through all of the rules and principles that have founded the society and understands the moral fabric and political theory of the society. Even in hard cases, there is a right answer that can be reached by the Herculean judge without relying on his or her discretion in a strict sense.

but judges rarely, if ever, recuse themselves for arrogance. So Judge Arendt will hear the case.

It then becomes a matter of weighing various rights claims, which should be done according to the "Constitution and not by public opinion or by majorities" (Arendt 1959a, 46). One does not have to be a Critical Legal Studies scholar to ask whether a judge's background will affect his or her interpretation of the Constitution. Judge Arendt does not begin her deliberations from a blank slate. She brings her theoretical preconceptions, such as her famous distinction between the private, social, and political realms, to bear on this case. This typology has served her well in making sense of the rise of twentieth-century totalitarian regimes and had been compelling enough to spur a legion of followers, but it does not serve her well in this context. Judge Arendt's judgment is terse:

> It seems highly questionable whether it was wise to begin enforcement of civil rights in a domain where no basic human and no basic political right is at stake, and where other rights – social and private – whose protection is no less vital, can so easily be hurt. (1959a, 56)

Not only does Arendt side with our segregationist plaintiff, she berated the hypothetical co-defendants (the NAACP and the parents) for placing children on the front lines of intractable political questions about race while they sat idly by as spectators. Ms. Eckford "obviously, was asked to be a hero, that is, something neither her absent father nor the equally absent representatives of the NAACP felt called upon to be" (1959a, 50). As judges are inclined to do, Arendt suggests how she will view subsequent cases. She will look more favorably on cases involving a private right, namely "the right to marry whoever one wishes" because it "is an elementary human right compared to which 'the right to attend an integrated school, the right to sit where one pleases on a bus, the right go into any hotel or recreation area or place of amusement, regardless of one's kin or color or race' are minor indeed" (Arendt 1959a, 49). Further, "even political rights, like the right to vote…are secondary…to the right to home and marriage" (Arendt 1959a, 49).

The U.S. Supreme Court's opinion on the Little Rock crisis, issued several months before the publication of Arendt's essay, offers an equally terse but sharply divergent judgment. The Court found that the desegregation of schools was fundamental to the Equal Protection Clause of the Fourteenth Amendment to the U.S. Constitution:

> The controlling legal principles are plain. The command of the Fourteenth Amendment is that no "State" shall deny to any person within its jurisdiction

the equal protection of the laws.... In short, the constitutional rights of children not to be discriminated against in school admission on grounds of race or color declared by this Court in the Brown case can neither be nullified openly and directly by state legislators or state executive or judicial officers, nor nullified indirectly by them through evasive schemes for segregation whether attempted "ingeniously or ingenuously." (*Cooper v. Aaron* 1958)

The Supreme Court found fault with Governor Faubus and the state government's elaborate efforts to contravene the rights of the children as enshrined in the U.S. Constitution as interpreted through the *Brown* decision. Arendt, from her Olympian authority, placed the blame for the crisis on the parents and the NAACP for putting the children in harm's way and for privileging the wrong set of rights. Judge Arendt's human rights court would rule the 1958 judgment of the U.S. Supreme Court be REVERSED.

ANALYSIS OF ARENDT'S "REFLECTIONS ON LITTLE ROCK"

Arendt's essay provoked a plethora of responses immediately after its publication, and there has been a recent resurgence of interest in the essay. Some scholars have tried to exonerate Arendt and explain away how one of the twentieth century's most astute writers on totalitarianism could critique one of the cardinal moments of non-violent resistance to an unjust public policy.[5] Much less forgiving commentators have charged Arendt with racism (Norton 1995; Steele 2002, 186) whereas others have argued that she too strictly applied her theoretical writings to a dissimilar political reality (e.g., Benhabib 1996; Bernasconi 1996), and still others have used the essay as a springboard to discuss pivotal Arendtian themes such as the need for social plurality (Bohman 1997). Several commentators (e.g., McClure 1997) have tried to salvage Arendt's work by contending that it exemplifies a practical application of her theory of judgment. In contrast, I maintain that it is her theory of judgment, increasingly in vogue among political theorists, which leads to her misinterpretation of the Little Rock situation. Moreover, Arendt's essay spotlights problems common to a specific manner of judgment that has predominated "western" thought for millennia, namely the abstract judgment of like-minded elites that base their decisions on artificial typologies with little regard for the voice of the marginalized. This type of judgment is typical of an entire line of thought

---

[5] For example, Kohn (2003) belittles Arendt's contemporaneous critics and inexplicably concludes: "The desegregation of schools has not achieved its intended goals; many of Arendt's warnings have been realized, and the entire question remains open to judgment" (xxxv).

back to at least Aristotle and continues to haunt much thinking about human rights law, as we will see throughout this book.

Arendt's Misapplied Typology of the Private, Social, and Political

As numerous commentators (e.g., Benhabib 1996, 56; Bernasconi 1996, 4) have noted, Arendt's essay hinged on typologies that she developed, and that served her well, in other contexts, most notably the rise of totalitarianism in Europe in the 1930s. Of these typologies, the most evident is her well-known distinction between the private, social, and political spheres that she developed in *The Human Condition.* This typology not only guides her thinking on the Little Rock crisis, it is also pivotal for her theory of judgment.

Arendt argued that the rise of twentieth-century totalitarianism could be traced to the rise of the homogenizing social sphere in the modern state. With the rise of the social sphere, the distinction between the private and the public, which was a hallmark of the ancient Athenian polis, became blurred. In the private household realm of ancient Athens, individuals were united out of necessity and they were predominately focused on applying their labor to meet their necessity. Some "men" would emerge from this realm of necessity, often with the aid of slaves who would take care of their needs, and enter the political realm, where they were free to initiate action. Whereas the household was a realm of inequality based on a clearly delineated hierarchy, the realm of the polis, the realm of action, was a realm of equals. Of course, Athens as a whole was not built on equality. The equality found in the polis "presupposed the existence of 'unequals' who, as a matter of fact, were always the majority of the population in a city-state" (Arendt 1958, 32).

Arendt pines for the Athenian polis because it nurtures pluralism in the private and public spheres, which could serve as a bulwark against the conformity of modern society and totalitarianism. The seeds of pluralism would be sown in the insulation of the private realm with its "atmosphere of idiosyncratic exclusiveness" (Arendt 1959a, 55). These idiosyncrasies would then blossom as a healthy pluralism through the open expression of a wide range of competing ideas in the political sphere. In the modern world, the important distinction between the private and public spheres became blurred with the rise of mass society. The necessity of life, a private concern, became a matter for society through the rise of economics (etymologically: the rule of the household). At the same time, politics became focused on political economy (etymologically: an oxymoron for Arendt). With an increasing concern for the common good and welfare, the political became involved in all aspects of our lives. This led to an equalizing, or flattening, of the political. Instead of political action serving as a means for distinguishing oneself, the political sphere became a realm of conformity as it assumed the characteristics of mass society, which "expects from each of its members a certain kind of behavior, imposing innumerable and various rules, all of which tend to 'normalize' its members, to make them behave, to exclude spontaneous action or outstanding achievement" (Arendt 1958, 40). The conformity of the social realm swallowed up "the only place where men could show who they really and inexchange-ably were" (Arendt 1958, 41). The public realm, made up of those who had escaped the necessity of the household realm, became driven by the concerns of the household realm, namely, consumerist wants and needs where society's "members act as though they were members of one enormous family which has only one opinion and one interest" (Arendt 1958, 39). This conformity of thought, Arendt argues, allowed totalitarianism to take root in Germany and elsewhere. For her, it was crucial that the private, social, and political spheres remain distinct so that pluralism could check totalitarianism.

Arendt was well aware that unrestrained pluralism in the social sphere would most likely engender social inequality and discrimination as part of the organic process of group formation. This inequality and discrimination should be tolerated or even welcomed as it would check the rise of conformity and totalitarianism. As she writes, "Without discrimination of some sort, society would simply cease to exist and very important possibilities of free association and group formation would disappear" (Arendt 1959a, 51). Such social discrim-ination could only be "legally abolished" at the risk of violating the "freedom of society" (Arendt 1959a, 53). From this analysis and her fear of social con-formity, Arendt vehemently opposed any form of hegemonic national govern-ment or any laws that infringed on the freedom of association.

Judge Arendt's Little Rock opinion is rooted in a "hierarchy of rights" (Benhabib 1996, 150) that preserves pluralism by maintaining the distinctions between the private, social, and political spheres. Anti-miscegenation laws in which the government interfered with an individual's right to marry were clearly an involvement of the government in the private sphere and were deemed by Arendt the "most outrageous law(s) of Southern states" (Arendt 1959a, 49).[6] The education system as part of the social sphere should be a realm of pluralism or free association where parents choose their children's classmates. Here, Arendt's conclusions echo President Eisenhower's regretta-ble comments to Chief Justice Warren about segregationists during the Little Rock crisis: "These are not bad people. All they are concerned about is to see

---

[6] Sidney Hook (1958) scoffs that Arendt was asking for African Americans to agitate for "equality in the bedroom rather than... equality in education" (203).

that their sweet little girls are not required to sit in school alongside some big overgrown Negroes" (Warren 1977, 291). Judge Arendt then wanders outside the scope of the case to argue that any form of social discrimination must be beyond the scope of the government. "There cannot be a 'right to go into any hotel or recreation area or place of amusement' because many of these are in the realm of the purely social where the right to free associate, and therefore to discrimination, has greater validity than the principle of equality" (Arendt 1959a, 52).[7] Finally, even though not everyone will emerge into the political sphere, it is important that all have the potential right to exercise political action (Arendt's famous "right to have rights," discussed in Chapter 3) such as the right to vote. However, "even political rights, like the right to vote...are secondary...to the right to home and marriage" (Arendt 1959a, 49). From this hierarchy of rights, Judge Arendt sides with the segregationist and his "private right over [his] children and the social right to free association" (Arendt 1959a, 55).

Arendt was so intent on establishing the separation of the private, social, and political spheres that she underestimated the multitude ways that they bleed into one another.[8] Social discrimination will infringe on the private sphere when it leads to economic deprivation or when it sanctions domestic violence. As many feminist scholars have argued, permitting a strict dichotomy between the public and private spheres "in effect tolerates violence against women, especially in the legal and juridical realm, depoliticizing and relegating violence to the domestic private sphere and narrowly portraying it as personal in nature, rather than as a 'systemic historical and political event'" (Fregoso 2006, 18; cf. Simmons 2007). Moreover, often social discrimination is so extreme it will interfere with meaningful participation in the political realm (cf. Bohman 1997). However, Arendt resists using political means for solving such social questions as persistent poverty and pervasive

---

[7] The U.S. Supreme Court saw this issue much differently and creatively interpreted the Equal Protection Clause of the Fourteenth Amendment and the Commerce Clause to uphold the Civil Rights Act of 1964 ending social discrimination in public accommodations. The U.S. Congress, through the Civil Rights Act of 1964 and the Elementary and Secondary Education Act of 1965, also failed to pay heed to Arendt's warning that "it would be very unwise indeed if the Federal government...were to use its financial support (of education) as a means of whipping the states into agreement with positions they would otherwise be slow or altogether unwilling to adopt" (Arendt 1959a, 211). Of course, these laws and the interpretations of the Supreme Court proved to be major factors in finally ending the massive Southern resistance to desegregating public schools (Mazmanian and Sabatier 1983).

[8] Arendt wrote: "The question is not how to abolish discrimination, but how to keep it confined within the social sphere, where it is legitimate, and prevent its trespassing on the political and personal sphere, where it is destructive" (Arendt 1959a, 51).

discrimination. From her analysis of the French Revolution, she claims flatly that "every attempt to solve the social question with political means leads into terror" (Arendt 1963b, 112).

Arendt's Misreading of the Little Rock Context

Arendt's over-reliance on the private, social, political typology – a lens "crafted in another context" (Benhabib 1996) – combined with her lack of personal experience and her Olympian authority, prevented her from fully appreciating the social, economic, and historical context of the South in the 1950s. The segregation of Little Rock Central High should not be seen in isolation, but was part of a comprehensive structural violence that ensured African Americans were treated as second-class citizens. Arendt failed to see that this structural violence was supported by a vast majority of Southern citizens and government officials and that it touched every aspect of life for African Americans.

Elizabeth Eckford would not have been outside of the high school if the governor had not ordered the Arkansas National Guard to refuse entry to any African-American children, and he would not have made that order if he was not responding to a populist states' rights current during a contentious election cycle. Arendt fails to mention that many of the members of the mob demanding their rights were also carrying ropes and other weapons. The violence of the mob was part of the everyday reality and was sanctioned by state and local law enforcement officials. It is difficult to imagine the helplessness that Ms. Eckford felt when she "turned back to the guards but their faces told me I wouldn't get help from them" (Lebeau 2004, 52, citing Bates 1962, 408–409). We also must remember that Ms. Eckford would not have been alone outside of the high school that fateful morning if she had received the phone call the night before to meet with the other children and approach the school as a group with a large number of escorts. But, alas, the Eckford family did not have a phone (Beals 1994, 52; Lebeau 2004, 52).

Arendt also selectively reads much of the civil rights movement and the massive Southern resistance. In her strong desire for political plurality, she embraces the states' rights claims of the segregationists because "states' rights in this country are among the most authentic sources of power, not only for the promotion of regional interests and diversity, but for the Republic as a whole" (1959a, 54). She fails to see the context of the states' rights claims, including the extreme measures that the Southern states were willing to take to resist the implementation of *Brown*. To subvert the federal government's mandates, Governor Faubus would shut down all Little Rock high schools for the entire 1958–1959 school year, and desegregation efforts were met with violence in numerous Southern cities (e.g., Baker 1996). Ten years after *Brown*, this massive resistance ensured that legalized segregation was still a fact of life in the overwhelming majority of Southern schools.

Most dramatically, Arendt failed to comprehend the experience of being an African American in the South in the 1950s. Judge Arendt begins with the photograph of Elizabeth Eckford, but her essay discusses everything else but Elizabeth Eckford and the plight of African Americans. Arendt's failing is succinctly summed up by Ralph Ellison: Arendt "has absolutely no conception of what goes on in the minds of Negro parents when they send their kids through those lines of hostile people.... The child is expected to face the terror and contain his fear and anger precisely because he is a Negro American" (Warren 1965, 343). In response to Ellison's charges, Arendt issued her only retraction to her essay, but it has been most aptly described as a "cryptic concession that takes little back" (Steele 2002, 187). In a letter to Ellison, Arendt concedes that she

> hadn't grasped the element of stark violence, of elementary bodily fear in the situation...your remarks seem to me so entirely right, that I now see that I simply didn't understand the complexities in the situation...it is precisely the ideal of sacrifice that I didn't understand. (Quoted in Bernasconi 1996, 15)

To say that she did not understand the "ideal of sacrifice" of the parents or the daily travails of the children is a vast understatement. Of course, this was not an "ideal of sacrifice" in the sense of being abstract, but a very real sacrifice with numerous moments of sheer terror as shown by this poignant recounting of that fateful September morning by Melba Beals, another member of the Little Rock Nine. Beals and her mother arrived at Central High as the mob berated Elizabeth Eckford. A small part of the mob turned their attention to the Beals saying: "We got us a nigger right here!" Beals recalls that as she and her mother fled in terror, "the men chasing us were joined by another carrying a rope." As one man grabbed at her mother,

> "Melba,...take these keys...get to the car. Leave without me if you have to."
>
> "No, Mama, I won't go without you."
>
> Suddenly I felt the sting of her hand as it struck the side of my face. She had never slapped me before. "Do what I say!" She shouted. (Beals 1994, 50)

Arendt does not discuss this very real and palpable sacrifice, or the bravery required to return to school each day for an entire academic year despite persistent and immediate threats. Nor does she consider what it must have meant for a 15-year-old child to hear: "Drag her over to this tree! Let's take care of the nigger" (Bates 1962, 75) or what terror must have resonated the morning of the first day of class when Melba Beals' younger brother casually reminds her of the famous lynching of 14-year-old Emmett Till in neighboring Mississippi only two years previously.

Even conceding this fundamental misunderstanding, Arendt does not "take back" any of the rest of the essay. She never backed away from her insistence on the validity of states' rights claims or her adherence to a typology "crafted in another context." Arendt, the advocate of practical reason and critic of speculative reasoning, stuck to her "penchant for the abstract classification of historical events according to her own philosophical categories" (Bohman 1997, 53).

ARENDT ON JUDGMENT

Many apologists for Arendt's Little Rock essay and for her equally controversial *Eichmann in Jerusalem* stress that these are examples of her "enactment of public judgment" (McClure 1997, 63). They claim that until her theory of judgment is understood, one should not be too critical of her conclusions.[9] However, I argue that it is her theory of judgment that is most problematic; it points to a problem with theories of judgment all the way back to Aristotle, namely, the cauterization (in its three facets) of the marginalized Other. An in-depth analysis of her theory of judgment is warranted as it will reveal how even a concrete universalism developed in the context of the fight against totalitarianism can further marginalize the Other. In subsequent chapters I borrow from Arendt's corpus such political ideas as the right to have rights, but I remain wary of this propensity for marginalization.

Although Arendt never wrote her planned treatise on judgment, the outlines of her theory are fairly clear and have been further illuminated by numerous excellent commentaries. Arendt draws on Kant's discussion of aesthetic taste in the *Critique of Judgment*, which she surprisingly concludes "contains perhaps the greatest and most original aspect of Kant's political philosophy" (1968, 219), but she admits that to include a discussion of aesthetic taste in a political discussion "sounds so strange" (1968, 223). It is also strange that

[9] McClure summarizes, "We might characterize Arendt's writings on Little Rock as one prominent public face on this process of judging. As an exemplar of the proprieties of judging that she identified with political thinking, their claim on the reader is an invitation to engagement rather than an appeal to truth…these writings present themselves as an attempt 'to communicate and expose to the test of the other' what she discovered in the solitude of thought" (1997, 76–77, cf. Parvikko 2003, 201–202).

Arendt, for the most part, eschews Kant's better-known discussions of ethics and politics including his more famous (and more deductive) formulations of the categorical imperative and perpetual peace. Instead, she finds in Kant's account of taste a theory of judgment that eschews the speculative thought of deductive philosophers but crucially retains a form of communal or even universal validity.

This concrete universalism is intimately connected to the private-public typology discussed earlier in this chapter. Judgment is the distinctly political faculty, or as she says, it is "one of the fundamental abilities of man as a political being" (Arendt 1968, 221). The free citizen employs judgment, working with others to gain a practical truth that could lead to political action. Indeed, "it is the most important way in which sharing the world with others comes to pass" (Arendt 1968, 241). However, as we will see, this "sharing the world" is restricted to similarly/hierarchically situated judges. Arendt insists on cauterizing the Other from the political sphere in order to ensure proper judgment.

The Stages of Judgment

Arendtian judgment begins with the concrete experiences of the subject and those around him or her. The judge should gain as much perspective on the situation as possible.[10] From these concrete experiences, judgment proceeds in three steps. The first two are "mental operations" (Arendt 1982, 68), and the third involves communal validity. The first mental operation is imagination, "in which one judges objects that are no longer present" where the object "becomes an object for one's inner senses." This is the closing of the external senses so that the object can be considered by the mind's eye. Ideally, this would be a perception of the object without the biases of sense perception and without any theoretical biases. "By closing one's eyes one becomes an impartial, not a directly affected, spectator of visible things. The blind poet" (Arendt 1982, 68). Imagination "prepares the object" for the second step in judgment, "the operation of reflection" (Arendt 1982, 68).

In reflection, the second mental operation, the judge applies her own taste to the object that is being considered by the mind's eye. She decides whether

[10] Arendt insisted that the judge need not be an active participant or even present in a given situation in order to pronounce judgments. Critics of her Eichmann essay claimed that she could not judge the actions of Jewish elders during the Holocaust because she did not walk in their shoes. Arendt responded: "The argument that we cannot judge if we were not present and involved ourselves seems to convince everyone everywhere, although it seems obvious that if it were true, neither the administration of justice nor the writing of history would be possible" (Arendt 1963a, 295).

she approves or disapproves of the object. Although this is a mental operation, it is not entirely subjective but relies on what Kant calls communal sense. We anticipate that our judgment will be subject to communal validity, and so we try to "put ourselves in the minds of other men." Or as Kant writes, "this is done by comparing our judgment with the possible rather than the actual judgments of others and by putting ourselves in the place of any other man" (quoted in Arendt 1982, 71). Through reflection we "liberate ourselves from the 'subjective private conditions'" (Arendt 1968, 220), and we begin to develop "an enlarged mentality" by thinking "in the place of everybody else" (Arendt 1968, 220).

When we apply our taste in reflection, we often rely on examples, what Kant called "the go-cart of judgments." Examples aid in moving from our concrete experiences to the general[11] because "the example is the particular that contains in itself, or is supposed to contain, a concept or a general rule." For instance, when an Athenian spoke of courage, they most likely would have in "'the depths of one's mind' the example of Achilles" or when Christians speaks of goodness "we have in the back of our minds the example of Saint Francis or Jesus of Nazareth" (Arendt 1982, 84). Examples themselves are subject to the communal sense. They must resonate with others who will have shared our similar experiences (Arendt 1982, 84–85). Just as imagination prepares the way for reflection, reflection grounded in communal sense and examples paves the way for the third step of judging, communal validity. "One can communicate only if one is able to think from the other person's standpoint; otherwise one will never meet him, never speak in such a way that he understands" (Arendt 1982, 74).

The third step in judgment is the actual appeal to communal validity in the political sphere. "The very faculty of thinking depends on its public use; without 'the test of free and open examination' no thinking and no opinion formation is possible. "Reason is not made 'to isolate itself but to get into community with others'" (Arendt 1982, 39–40). In this way, the judging person must in Kant's famous formulation, "woo the consent of everyone else" (Arendt 1968, 222).[12]

Arendt's theory of judgment tracks nicely with her typology of the private, social, and political spheres. Judgment that begins with the concrete

---

[11] Imagination "provides examples for judgment" (Arendt 1968), but it must be in reflection that the examples are compared to the object.

[12] It is far from clear that Kant took this third step. As Beiner (1992) points out, Kant's concepts in the Critique of Judgment are "transcendental categories: they do not connect judgments of taste to any empirical sociability" (26).

experiences and the subjective, private viewpoint of the judge is ultimately a political act as any individual judgment must stand the agonistic test of discussion in the polis. The individual will emerge from the private realm as an individual with specific tastes and judgments. Free association in the social and political spheres will then lead to a communal or political judgment among citizens. Individual predilections are nurtured in the private sphere, but they are subject to validity through interaction with the community of equals in the political realm. Or, to push the original analogy, Judge Arendt begins with concrete experience, taking testimony from a variety of perspectives before retreating to her private chambers – the act of imagination – and then she engages in reflection with the aid of the "enlarged mentality" of communal sense and examples. Her judgment is first rendered through imagination in private, before subjecting it to a communal validity in a conference room of other judges. In this way she ascends from the particular to the communal or universal without relying on the banisters of speculative thought.

Arendt's theory of judgment has recently received great attention for it seems to offer a fecund alternative to the stale cultural relativism–universalism debates. Her theory of judgment is a concrete universalism, an inductive method for creating norms and judgments without reliance on the abstract principles of speculative philosophy. Judgment's validity unfolds through political discourse. From Kant's account of aesthetic taste, Arendt finds the blueprint for an ethical thought that is both subjective and objective, that is both grounded in individual freedom and subject to communal validity. Arendt appears to be the perfect postmodern democrat, with her emphasis on performativity, pluralism, discourse, iterability, and interdependence of selves, but what about the maddening conclusions in her Little Rock essay?

Judgment of a Narrow Elite

I argue that in Arendt's theory the judge's initial opinions crafted in her chambers are rarely ever seriously interrogated in the conference room as she is rarely, if ever, exposed to any sort of otherness. The communal validity of the conference room resembles the mutual reinforcement of groupthink more than a true dialogue. Although she claims that judgment "is truly discursive, running, as it were, from place to place, from one part of the world to another, through all kinds of conflicting views," (Arendt 1968, 242) it actually rests on a very limited communal validity. The number of judges, and hence the number of viewpoints, is limited in at least two important ways. First, most people are branded as incapable of shedding their personal interests enough to serve as impartial judges; and second, only those who share a common worldview can be considered judges. Moreover, for Arendt, it is imperative that those who are not qualified to be judges are barred from the conference room.

Arendt's theory of judgment exemplifies what I call the "cauterization" of the Other. Recall that cauterization has three distinct but overlapping definitions. It is a branding or marking through burns, as in branding a human slave. It is a sealing off of a wound to protect the healthy part of an organism. Finally, to cauterize is to deaden feelings, to become callous to the suffering of another. For Arendt, those who remain tied to necessity or self-interest are incapable of serving as judges, and their viewpoints must be excluded or sealed off so they do not contaminate the healthy political realm. To seal them off, the judges must first brand these Others by accusing them as vulgar (*banausikos* in Greek) or base (*faulos*). And, finally, the judge or the political man must deaden any private feelings toward those who are excluded.

First, because judgment is a political activity, it is restricted to those few who have freed themselves from the necessity of the household and emerged into the political sphere. This freedom from necessity allows the judge to achieve a maximum of impartiality. The necessary objective or Olympian distance "cannot arise unless we are in a position to forget ourselves, the cares and interests and urges of our lives" (Arendt 1968, 210). If the common world is merely an object needed to sustaining life or out of self-interest, then we are not seeing the world or others from a sufficiently objective vantage point. We are not in a position to judge the world or to "woo the consent of everyone else." Arendt believed that most individuals would not be able to attain this esteemed position because most could not shed their personal interests enough to be judges. She writes: "The political way of life has never been and will never be the way of life of the many" (Arendt 1963b, 275).[13]

Arendt's surprising gloss of Aristotle's famous definition of man as a *zoon ekhon logon* (an animal having speech) is instructive. For Arendt, this definition does not refer to "man in general" or a declaration that the capacity of speech was the *specie differentia* of human beings. Instead, Aristotle refers to the empirical fact that only some humans will live the type of life that will allow them to exercise speech. Speech for Arendt is a particular form of

---

[13] It is then not surprising that Arendt embraces limited suffrage. She writes, "To be sure, such an 'aristocratic' form of government would spell the end of general suffrage as we understand it today; for only those who as voluntary members of an 'elementary republic' have demonstrated that they care for more than their private happiness and are concerned about the state of the world would have the right to be heard in the conduct of the business of the republic. However, this exclusion from politics should not be derogatory... would in fact give substance and reality to one of the most important negative liberties we have enjoyed since the end of the ancient world, namely, freedom from politics" (Arendt 1963b, 284).

communication that transcends mere utility. It is the disclosure of an individual in the course of action in the political sphere. Therefore, those individuals who could not emerge into the political sphere and are incapable of judging were literally not men and thus, *aneu logou* – without speech. Arendt explains, "Everybody outside the polis – slaves and barbarians – was *aneu logou*, deprived of course, not of the faculty of speech, but of a way of life in which speech and only speech made sense and where the central concern of all citizens was to talk with each other" (Arendt 1958, 27). The implications are clear: Without freedom from necessity, an individual could not participate in the political sphere and would thus be *aneu logou*.

Judgment excludes in another fundamental way. It is restricted to those who share a common understanding of the fundamental issues of the polis. As Canovan (1992) describes Arendt's view of the public space, "What unites the citizens of a republic is that they inhabit the same public space, share its common concerns, acknowledge its rules and are committed to its continuance and to achieving a working compromise when they differ" (227). Such an emphasis on like-mindedness may be surprising from a scholar who feared any homogenization of the public sphere such as twentieth-century totalitarianism or Rousseau's concept of a General Will, but it is actually pivotal to Arendt's embrace of pluralism. In Arendt's view, "citizens are held together not by a common will but by a common world" (Canovan 1992, 226). Citizens are "equal partners in a common world," but from this initial commonality, political action facilitates an "ever-increasing differentiation of citizens that is inherent in an agonal life" (Arendt 1990, 83).

Aristotle's discussion of *homonoia*, or like-mindedness, sheds light on what Arendt means by a common world and how it further limits the pluralism of the political sphere. In the *Nicomachean Ethics* in his famous argument for diversity in the polis against Plato's emphasis on unity, Aristotle writes that homonoia is the "chief aim" of lawmakers in order to eliminate factions and enmity (1999, 1155a, 25). This homonoia, which appears to be the highest level of political friendship, is "not merely agreement of opinion," and it is not just agreement "about any subject" but is an agreement among good men about the fundamentals of a society, "the realm of great matters" (*ta en megethei*). This like-mindedness is only possible among the good men who have shed personal interest as much as possible. "The base [*faulos*] on the other hand are incapable of homonoia except in some small degree, as they are of friendship, since they try to get more than their share of advantages, and take less than their share of labors and public burdens" (1999, 1167a, 10–15).

So, when Arendt praises the Greek polis where "the commonness of the political world was constituted only by the walls of the city and the boundaries of its laws, it was not seen or experienced in the relationships between the citizens" (Arendt 1990, 82), the essential point is how the good men understand the laws as common. The common world or public realm is famously described by Arendt "as a table is located between those who sit around it . . . [that] gathers us together and yet prevents our falling over each other" (Arendt 1958, 52). Conversely, the social realm of the base (*faulos*), who "try to get more than their share of advantages," lacks the "power to gather them together" (Arendt 1958, 52). This emphasis on a prior "common world" or homonoia in both Aristotle and Arendt reinforces the first type of exclusion in that only those who have shed self-interests will be able to appreciate the common world and have this type of friendship and thus be citizens.

Arendt's cauterization goes further; the good (disinterested) men who agree on the realm of great matters are charged with the crucial task of determining who or what should appear in the polis. As she says, the political man "renders" the "public realm" "politically secure" and "can be trusted to tend and take care of a world of appearances" (Arendt 1968, 218, 219). They must decide which individuals are capable of entering the political realm; that is, they must cauterize or seal off the polis from those who are unable to shed their selfish interests or lack the necessary homonoia about the great matters of the polis. The political man must "protect the island of freedom they have come to inhabit against the surrounding sea of necessity" (Arendt 1963b, 280).[14]

With such exclusion of the base or the banausic from the political sphere, Arendt's theory of judgment takes on the odor of groupthink. Her interpretation of Kant's passage that judgment is "valid for every single judging person" makes this clear. For Arendt, "the emphasis in the sentence is on 'judging'; it is not valid for those who do not judge or for those who are not members of the public realm where the objects of judgment appear" (1968, 221). This interpretation gives new meaning to her phrase that judgment includes "the ability to see things" from "the perspective of all those who happen to be present" (Arendt 1968, 221). To be present for Arendt means to be one of the few in the

---

[14] Arendt's elitism and its concomitant exclusion of the Other seems to be tempered by her famous right to have rights. Whereas she calls for "a self-selective process . . . that would draw together a true political elite in a country," she also believes "each person must be given the opportunity" to participate in the political realm (1969a, 233). All individuals must have the opportunity to exercise their political rights if they are able. So, Isaac (1998) is correct that Arendt did not a priori exclude any individuals from the political realm based on qualities such as race, gender, or wealth; and there would be no a priori exclusion of opinions (Bernstein 1986, 227). However, it would be quite rare for a person to shed his or her own necessity to break through into the political realm, especially when the political realm is monitored by those already present. These political actors would also be charged with excluding opinions that do not agree with theirs in fundamental respects.

public sphere. To be a judge means to consider the viewpoints of other judges. To be *aneu logou*, on the other hand, means not to be present in the political sphere, not to judge, and not to have your opinions considered when judgment on the basis of communal validity occurs.

ARENDT AND THE OTHER

So, we see that the judge is one who has freed herself from the necessities of life, shares a common world, and is tasked with maintaining the freedom of the political realm from the social and private spheres. Of what political import then are those who are deemed *aneu logou*, those who are without speech and thus cannot participate in the political realm?[15]

At first blush, the *aneu logou* resembles Giorgio Agamben's recent accounts of "bare life," that is, a person who is "politically irrelevant" (e.g., Agamben 2002). Unable to free himself or herself from necessity and initiate action in the political sphere, the *aneu logou* cannot properly be called "man" or even "human." Arendt writes, "A life without speech and without action . . . is literally dead to the world; it has ceased to be a human life because it is no longer lived among men" (1958, 176). Such a person would not strictly be a legal person with political rights and duties. They would be "a 'natural man' – that is, a human being or homo in the original meaning of the word, indicating someone outside the range of the law and the body politics of the citizens, as for instance a slave – but *certainly a politically irrelevant being*" (Arendt 1963b, 103, emphasis added).[16]

Nonetheless, the *aneu logou* are not irrelevant for Arendt's theory of judgment. As discussed earlier in this chapter, the opinions of the *aneu logou* as "politically irrelevant being" *would not* factor into the judge's calculations when anticipating the opinions of others from whom she would eventually have to woo consent. The judge would a fortiori not have to consider the

---

[15] Cf. "Speechless action would no longer be action because there would no longer be an actor, and the actor, the doer of deeds, is possible only if he is at the same time the speaker of words" (Arendt 1958, 158).

[16] Shockingly in some passages, Arendt even places slaveholders and slaves above those who are *aneu logou*, whose life is not human life. Slaveholders "may be unjust, but they certainly are human" (Arendt 1958, 176). In Arendt's idealized, mostly Greek, view of slavery, slaves had "a place in society – more than the abstract nakedness of being human and nothing but human" (Arendt 1951, 297). Arendt is far from consistent on this matter. She writes, "The two qualities that the slave according to Aristotle, lacks – and it is because of these defects that he is not human – are the faculty to deliberate and decide and to foresee and to choose. This, of course, is but a more explicit way of saying that the slave is subject to necessity" (Arendt 1958, 84 n.12).

potential discourse with those without speech. Yet the *aneu logou* would factor into the first step of judgment. Recall, it was imperative for the judge to begin with as many experiences as possible before she undertook the first formal operation of judgment. This gaining of as many standpoints as possible would presumably include all individuals, including the *aneu logou*. The judge must put herself in the position of the *aneu logou* but not adopt the (self-interested) views of the *aneu logou*. If the judge adopted the views of any other, including the *aneu logou*, she would not only lose her disinterestedness, she would lose her own identity, which was nurtured in the idiosyncrasies of the private realm. To lose oneself in the Other would risk bringing interests into the political realm and would promote social conformity. So, the judge "does not blindly adopt the actual views of those who stand somewhere else, and hence look upon the world from a different perspective" (Arendt 1968, 241).[17] Instead, the judge retains her identity but sees the world from the position of the *aneu logou*. Arendt sums this up nicely as "thinking in my own identity where I am not" (1968, 241). So when Arendt famously says the judge "trains one's imagination to go visiting" (1982, 43), her visiting with the *aneu logou* is not as a possible interlocutor but, in Kant's terms, as a "judging spectator" (1968, 219).[18] This judging spectator is one who "sees the play as a whole, while each of the actors knows only his part or, if he should judge from the perspective of acting, only the part of the whole that concerns him" (Arendt 1982, 68–69). So, here it becomes clear that Arendt's "Olympian authority," as Ellison called it, is part and parcel of Arendt's theory of judgment.

The Cauterization of Pity for the Other

The judge is well aware of the barely human status of the politically irrelevant *aneu logou* and their dire material conditions. However, Arendt insists that legal or political solutions should not be used to ameliorate their economic plight. "Nothing, we might say today, could be more obsolete than to attempt to liberate mankind from poverty by political means; nothing could be more futile and dangerous" (Arendt 1963b, 110). Moreover, following her

---

[17] "The trick of critical thinking does not consist in an enormously enlarged empathy through which one can know what actually [goes] on in the mind of all others…to accept what goes [on] in the minds of those whose 'standpoint'…is not my own would mean no more than passively to accept their thought, that is, to exchange their prejudices for the prejudices proper to my own station" (Arendt 1982, 43).

[18] Although Disch (1997) is correct to point out that visiting is "neither insistently egocentric nor self-effacingly empathic" (136), she does not distinguish the visiting with other political actors from visiting with the *aneu logou*.

private-public typology Arendt persistently attempted to seal off or cauterize the political realm from any sort of, what she categorizes as, private emotions, which include compassion as well as empathy, love, and (Christian) goodness.[19] Such emotions that "are located in the human heart" would be corrupted by being brought into the public realm. Arendt writes that "the qualities of the heart need darkness and protection against the light of the public to grow and to remain what they are meant to be, innermost motives which are not for public display" (Arendt 1963b, 91). Furthermore, from her analysis of the French Revolution she argues that such emotions, especially goodness, are destructive of the political realm. In fact, "absolute goodness is hardly any less dangerous than absolute evil" (Arendt 1963b, 77), and "every effort to make goodness manifest in public ends with the appearance of crime and criminality on the political scene" (Arendt 1963b, 93).[20] Goodness is "beyond virtue" (Arendt 1963b, 78), so it is not part of the human world of politics. It would be more for the saints and Jesus than for the political man.

This is not to say that a political man cannot feel compassion for the oppressed as a private man. But as a private emotion, compassion is unsuited for political means. If it is brought into the political sphere, it becomes pity, which is a "perversion of compassion." Pity is inimical to the political sphere because it lacks the patience to engage in the political arts of "persuasion, negotiations, and compromise." Instead, it will demand "swift and direct action, that is, for action with the means of violence" (Arendt, 1963b, 82). This demand for swift action and overwhelming pity leads to self-righteousness, to an appeal to ends by any means necessary despite laws and propriety. All can be sacrificed in the name of pity, even the pitiable. For instance, the French Revolution was "actuated by the limitless immensity of both the people's misery and the pity this misery inspired" but "from the sentiments of the heart whose very boundlessness helped in the unleashing of a stream of boundless violence" (Arendt 1963b, 87). The final and perhaps ultimate sin of the French Revolution was Robespierre's pity for the masses, which led to his demand to bring the sans-culottes or "the low people" (Arendt 1963b, 69–70) into the political realm.

Arendt opposes what she sees as the folly of the French Revolution with the American Revolution. While in France, pity overwhelmed the truly political

---

[19] Arendt's cauterization of pity helps to explain her impatience with the litany of survivors who emotionally testified in the Eichmann trial (see Mertens 2005).

[20] Arendt illustrates the unsuitability of Christian goodness for the public sphere through her analysis of Melville's *Billy Budd*. The title character represents goodness and innocence but is ultimately executed. Arendt concludes, goodness "must go into absolute hiding and flee all appearance if it is not to be destroyed" (Arendt 1963b, 75).

"feelings" of friendship and respect; the men of the American Revolution had "no pity to lead them astray from reason," so they "remained men of action from beginning to end, from the Declaration of Independence to the framing of the Constitution" (Arendt 1963b, 90). They did not try to solve the social question politically, but the American Revolution focused on preserving and fostering the political space in which a plurality could appear in political action. Their "republic granted to every citizen the right to become 'a participator in the government of affairs', the right to be seen in action" (Arendt 1963b, 127).

Solidarity with the Other

What then is the proper outlet for the private emotion of compassion? Arendt advocates "solidarity" with the *aneu logou*. Again, Arendt, as the great proponent of pluralism and fearful of political uses of private emotions, must advocate a very limited conception of solidarity or risk it becoming conformity or pity. Solidarity requires political men to "establish deliberatively and, as it were, dispassionately a community of interest with the oppressed and exploited" (Arendt 1963b, 84). The judging spectator observes suffering and is moved to action, not by the original suffering, but by solidarity or the community of interest (Arendt 1963b, 84). The judge creates such solidarity when she applies her practical reason to understand how the suffering fits in with the suffering of many others and thereby abstracts (etymologically "draws away from") the suffering of the oppressed. This suffering is translated then into political ideas, and therefore "compared with the sentiment of pity, it may appear cold and abstract, for it remains committed to 'ideas' – to greatness, or honor or dignity – rather than to any 'love' of men."

Because those who are *aneu logou* are unable to shed their own self-interest, they should not enter the political realm. Instead, their interests will be represented by someone else, someone who is able to shed their interests for them. When the judge enters the political realm to woo the consent of others, the judge does so in her own identity and is not overwhelmed by the feelings or interests of specific individuals who are *aneu logou*. As an example of how the judge will go visiting without adopting the viewpoint of the *aneu logou*, Arendt considers her relationship to the slum-dweller. Arendt as judge

> perceives the general notion...of poverty and misery. I arrive at this notion by representing to myself how I would feel if I had to live there, that is, I try to think in the place of the slum-dweller. The judgment I shall come up with will by no means necessarily be the same as that of the inhabitants, *whom*

time and hopelessness may have dulled to the outrage of their condition, but it will become for my further judging of these matters *an outstanding example to which I refer*…while I take into account others when judging, this does not mean that I conform in my judgment to those of others. I still speak with my own voice and I do not count noses in order to arrive at what I think is right. But my judgment is no longer subjective either. (Arendt 1982, 107–108, emphases added)

Arendt's judgment may be inspired by the "outstanding example" of the plight of the Other, but it is not taking on the Other's perspective or inviting the Other into the polis or into the courtroom. After all, they are perhaps, like the slum-dweller, unaware of the "outrage of their condition." So, Arendt's insistence on the cauterization of private emotions from the public sphere further cauterizes the *aneu logou*, who is unable to shed their private interests.

RETURN TO LITTLE ROCK

From the foregoing, Arendt's missteps in the Little Rock essay come sharper into focus, especially as a prime example of her theory of judgment. Emphasizing the cauterization of the Other adds several nuances to, and is in some ways more damning than, recent insightful critiques of Arendt's essay. For example, Bernasconi (1996) boldly points out that Arendt's plea that the reader take her sympathy for granted in the Little Rock essay is "of no value, because…she regarded such feelings as politically irrelevant and any intervention of them into politics as almost certainly disastrous" (16, cf. Arendt 1963b, 81). His statement may be a bit too strong. There is a modicum of value to Arendt's sympathy; it has the potential to lead to solidarity as well as an improvement in judgment as she puts herself in the shoes of the oppressed, thinks in her own identity where she is not, and ultimately speaks for the *aneu logou*.

Meili Steele (2002) has cogently argued that Arendt over-assumes a common world between the ego and the Other, between her and the African-American mother in Little Rock that would allow her "access to the self-understanding of African-American political thought that informs the judgment of the black families" (186). To speak for the Other would be to assume that this common world "is in good enough shape to articulate and draw together her own position and that of black mothers" (Steele 2002, 187). According to Steele, the problem with Arendt's account of Little Rock (besides its racism) is that she never interrogates the structural violence that girds this common world or the invisible ideology that supports the structural violence. As Steele concludes, the "imagination 'goes visiting' without interrogating the historical medium of language and culture" (Steele 2002, 187).

My analysis suggests that the flaw in Arendt's theory of judgment runs even deeper. The oppressed are not part of the common world. They are not invited into the conference room of judges. So, Norton (1995) rightly claims

> There is…a persistent asymmetry in Arendt's moral questioning. Arendt asks, "What would I do if I were a Negro mother?" She does not ask "What would I write if I were a Negro scholar?" or "What would the Negro mother write if she held this pen?" The strategy of moral metempsychosis is used to question the actions of the Negro mother. The writings of the white intellectual remain closed to the questions of the Negro mother. Arendt inserts herself into the mind of the Negro mother, but she does not invite that woman into hers. (258)

Inviting the *aneu logou* into the judge's realm as Norton suggests is not only unimaginable for Arendt, but it would be unconscionable, as it would repeat the mistakes of the French Revolution. The African-American mother has not shed self-interest enough to enter the political realm, so she cannot be an interlocutor among like-minded equals. Her interest should not be considered directly but must be filtered through the judge's reason. Here, Martin Jay (1997) asks the obvious question, "How could Arendt know that her thought experiment in imaginative visiting was more than the imposition of her own prejudices onto the others whose position she claimed to inhabit" (347). The obvious answer from Arendt's point of view is that the judge does, and should, impose her own prejudices, or what she calls individual idiosyncrasies nurtured in the private realm.[21] Arendt's essay on Little Rock is an exemplar of "thinking in my own identity where I am not."

CONCLUSION

Arendt's unfortunate claim that "oppressed minorities were never the best judges on the order of priorities in such matters" (Arendt 1959a, 46) is not a flippant comment, nor is it idiosyncratic to her analysis of the Little Rock crisis; but it is one of the lynchpins of Arendt's theory of judgment, a theory of judgment that cauterizes the Other from the political sphere.

Arendt's concrete universalism begins with a disdain of judgment from speculative ideals that she warned could become "fixed habits of thought, ossified rules and standards" that will close the judge to "the phenomenal richness of the appearances that make themselves available for our judgment"

---

[21] For example, she writes without hesitance, "If I were a Negro mother in the South, I would feel that the Supreme Court ruling, unwillingly, but unavoidably, had put my child into a more humiliating position than it had been in before" (Arendt 1959b).

(Arendt 1982, 111). Only by beginning with actual experiences and bracket-ing out theoretical preconceptions can the particular, in terms reminiscent of Husserl's phenomenology, "be apprehended as it truly discloses itself" (Arendt 1963a).

However, Arendt's theory ultimately over-relies on banisters, albeit banisters derived inductively from the examples of history. For her Little Rock essay, the most pertinent examples are drawn from the Greek polis, especially the private, social, and political typology, and from the French Revolution, espe-cially Robespierre's exaltation of pity.[22] These typologies became essential-ized and normativized. That is, they ultimately function in the same way as deductively derived principles of philosophers with the certainty that she dis-dained.[23] Because Arendt cauterizes or excludes the perspective of the Other, these typologies facilitate a self-reinforcing theory of judgment. Arendt's the-ory of judgment is a closed loop that is literally and etymologically a tautology; that is, it is a saying of the same thing. Despite her desire to oppose sameness, Arendt's theory of judgment cleanses the political sphere of all thinking that could (radically) challenge the judges' viewpoints. All those who have not shed self-interest and do not speak of the common world as determined by the judges are excluded. Even when the Other is taken into consideration through compassion, her voice will only be heard through the voice of the judge.

Before passing final judgment on this type of thinking, we need to strip it of its Arendtian elitism and its essentialized typologies. No theorist has attempted to realize the potential of a more democratized and more mod-ern Arendt than Seyla Benhabib.[24] In a series of works on Arendt's political thought, Benhabib has tried to "decenter" (1996, xxv) the *Human Condition* and its private, social, and political typology in Arendt's oeuvre. Benhabib also opens Arendt's account of judgment to the voice of the Other where enlarged

---

[22] Yet another typology "crafted in another context" further clouds Arendt's vision. Her dis-tinction between the parvenu and the pariah, developed in the context of post–World War I European Jewish society led her to argue that pride "is lost not so much by persecution as by pushing, or rather being pushed into pushing, one's way out of one group and into another" (Arendt 1959b, 179). Of course, the civil rights movement could be summarized as a group pushing themselves where they were told they originally did not belong, which led to an enormous sense of pride. For example, Ernest Green reflecting on his finally gaining entrance to Little Rock Central High in 1957 said, "Walking up the steps that day was proba-bly one of the biggest feelings I've ever had. I figured I had finally cracked it" (Hampton et al. 1990, 48).

[23] As Yar (2000) concludes, this leads Arendt "back to that which she first set out to overthrow, namely the supremacy of the *Bios Theoretikos*, the life of contemplation" (18).

[24] As Dana Villa (1998) writes, "Benhabib is a committed feminist, social democrat, and moral universalist (albeit one sensitive to the claims of difference). Arendt was none of these things (although Benhabib argues that she was an implicit universalist)" (818–819).

thought "enjoins us to view each person as one to whom I owe the moral respect to consider their viewpoint" (1992, 136). Their viewpoint is not derived from, or filtered through, the voice of the judge but is the "result of self-definition. It is the other who makes us aware of both her concreteness and her otherness" (Benhabib 1992, 168). The next chapter explores Benhabib's theory of discursive democracy within the context of the recent headscarf affairs in France and Turkey.

Democracy, Human Rights, and L'Affaire du Foulard

Political theorist Seyla Benhabib, like Hannah Arendt, develops a concrete universalism without deductive "banisters." She democratizes, modernizes, and further concretizes Arendt's theory of judgment and adds a cautious faith in international human rights law. More specifically, she has supplemented Arendt's work with the concerns of feminist scholars and insights from Jürgen Habermas' theory of discursive democracy. From her reading of feminist scholars, she is much more attuned to the ways that economic, social, and cultural conditions can silence the voice of the Other. From her reading of Habermas, she embraces a prominent role for wide-ranging and non-exclusionary discourse in the polis.

In her most recent works, Benhabib develops a theory of democratic iterations whereby "it is the people themselves who, through legislation and discursive will- and opinion-formation, must adopt policies and laws consonant with the cosmopolitan norms of universal hospitality" (2004, 177). Benhabib concedes that those who are excluded from the democratic/discursive space will most likely be those who are marginalized or silenced by politics and law, but "we can render these distinctions fluid and negotiable through processes of continuous and multiple democratic iterations" (2004, 177–178). In her most extensive practical treatment of democratic iterations, Benhabib argues that such iterations have characterized the French l'affaire du foulard (the headscarf affair).[1] Although there were some periods of the minority, particularly

---

[1]   The terms *foulard* and *voile* are often used interchangeably in the French press. Many commentators outside of France prefer the Arabic word "hijab," but it often refers to modesty in general or to any type of clothing that serves modesty. McGoldrick (2006) uses the neologism "headscarf-hijab." In the French context, I will use "foulard" over "voile" as voile or veil connotes the covering of the face, whereas foulard refers to a piece of clothing that only covers the neck and the hair. In the Turkish case, the term "türban" is used to describe the headscarves worn by educated, modern, and often Islamist women. The türban is usually longer and more colorful than the traditional headscarf worn by previous generations and

female, voice being silenced, the process itself, Benhabib argues, could serve as a model for working out the complex interplays between such issues as judgment, universalism, minority rights, voice, agency, and secularism.

It is safe to conclude that l'affaire du foulard has not turned out the way that Benhabib anticipated. After fifteen years of intense debate, the French people and politicians were galvanized in their opposition to the wearing of headscarves in public schools. In 2004 the national government, despite international protestations, overwhelmingly voted to ban Muslim headscarves in public schools. Benhabib, the committed cosmopolitan, though has still held out hope that the French law would be overturned by an appeal to the European Court of Human Rights. However, in November 2005 in a largely analogous case, the European Court overwhelmingly upheld the Turkish government's ban on the wearing of headscarves in public universities in *Leyla Sahin v. Turkey*. It is notable that the European Court framed its decision in "Benhabibian" terms. It praised the neutrality of the Turkish state as well as the extensive dialogue and participation that supposedly went into its policy. Indeed, the Court further accepted Turkey's reasoning that the ban frees women from the dictates of radical Islam and thus promotes gender equality, despite Ms. Sahin's repeated claims that she wears the headscarf of her own volition. In order to liberate women, the Court allowed a state to maintain a barrier that will prevent large numbers of women from continuing their education and thus has the potential to further cauterize their voices from the political sphere.

This chapter will analyze Benhabib's concrete universalism within the context of l'affaire du foulard and the *Sahin* case. Benhabib's discursive democratic theory will serve as an example of a concrete universalism based on democracy and human rights that, like Arendt's account of judgment, cauterizes, albeit in a much more subtle way, the voice of the Other. I will argue that any theory that relies on even a modicum of a typology, as Benhabib's ultimately does, risks silencing the Other. Likewise, the French and Turkish cases will serve as examples of how human rights law founded on democracy can still cauterize the Other. An appeal to a human rights court will often be unsuccessful when the court itself is grounded in an original founding violence and rests its decision making on artificial typologies. Human rights law requires a continuous deconstruction of such institutions and typologies,

still prevalent in rural areas (Secor 2005, 207). The turban is an essential part of the practice of tessetür, which often involves wearing long clothing that covers all of the hair as well as arms and legs. Often, a raincoat-type garment is also worn that serves to minimize the curvature of the body (İlyasoğlu 1998, 243–245). I will use the term "headscarf" for "turban."

including democracy. This chapter ends with a discussion of Jacques Derrida's famous essay "The Force of Law," which perhaps most clearly explores the important dilemmas or aporiai (plural of the Greek word *aporia*, often translated as "question") that result from attempts at deconstructing law by introducing some conception of transcendence as a check on law.

Both l'affaire du foulard and the *Sahin* case are rooted in complex social, historical, and cultural milieus that defy quick synopses. I will discuss each in turn in some depth and then analyze these in the context of recent writings by Benhabib.

L'AFFAIRE DU FOULARD

L'affaire du foulard began in 1989 in Creil when three young women, Leila and Fatima Achaboun and Samira Saidani, were asked by their middle school's headmaster to remove their headscarves while in classes. His justification was the official French policy of laïcité, which is a specifically French version of secularism that calls for religious neutrality in the public sphere. When they refused, the young women were threatened with expulsion. In the year of the French bicentennial, the issue took on great symbolic significance, evolving into a nationwide debate about French identity. The debate was often framed in apocalyptic terms, that French identity and Republican education must be saved from a rising immigrant population. For instance, five leading leftists, including the Levinasian Alain Finkielkraut, wrote an open letter warning "only the future will tell if the year of the bicentennial will also have been the Munich of the republican school" (Scott 2005, 107). The Conseil d'Etat, the highest French administrative court, quickly issued an *avis* (opinion) that allowed the wearing of headscarves unless they infringed on public order or the rights of other children. These determinations were to be made by local authorities. Over the next five years expulsion proceedings were begun against dozens of young women because of their headscarves, but they were almost always successfully challenged in school boards or the courts. Very few young women were banned from school for wearing the headscarf.

In 1994, the issue again emerged at the forefront of French politics with the appointment of politician François Bayrou as the Minister of Education. Bayrou issued an administrative ban on ostentatious religious symbols and famously said, "The school is designed to integrate, therefore it must exclude" (quoted in Ruchet 2006). The Conseil d'Etat struck down the Bayrou ban, and the issue once again receded for the most part from public debate. In 2003, the new Minister of Interior insisted that "Muslim women pose bare-headed for official identity photographs" (Scott 2005, 108). The ensuing controversy led President Jacques Chirac to create a commission to study the issue led by Bernard Stasi, a noted immigration expert. This twenty-person Commission made up of academics, politicians, lawyers, and educators heard testimony from approximately 150 people over the course of two months. Their final report, unanimous save for one abstention, was issued in December 2003. The first two parts of the Stasi report focused on the history of laïcité and its important place in French democracy. Part III of the report lays out current challenges to laïcité, focusing on the lack of assimilation of immigrants and how this affects various sectors of French life. By this time, much of the discourse on the headscarves was framed in terms of the oppression of women and girls under Islam, and this part included a litany of problems that some young Muslim women face, including sexual mutilation, polygamy, and forced marriages. It noted that the familial and social status of these girls did not permit them to effectively protest these conditions. The report concluded with a series of recommendations for buttressing laïcité and reconciling the needs of immigrants with the fundamental principle of laïcité. The most discussed recommendation and the one that eclipsed all the others in the ensuing discourse was the call for a law to ban the wearing of ostentatious religious symbols such as headscarves (*voiles*), large crosses, and yarmulkes in public schools.[2]

Soon afterward, on February 11, 2004, the French legislature overwhelming passed a law that prohibits the wearing of ostentatious religious symbols in schools (the vote was 494 to 36 in the Assembly and 276 to 20 in the Senate). The law reads in part: "In the schools, public secondary schools and high schools, wearing symbols or dress by which the students conspicuously manifest a religious affiliation is prohibited." Though this wording covers yarmulkes and crosses, it was quite clear that it was directed at headscarves of young Muslim women. The ban went into effect in the fall of 2005.

Not surprisingly, the headscarf debate has at times been acrimonious as it intersects with such timely and integral issues as French nationalism, attitudes toward immigrants, the war on terrorism, gender equality, French ideals of citizenship, and the French distrust of communitarianism.[3] The debate has created strange bedfellows, especially as it increasingly focused on gender equity in Islam. Many leading feminists were quite active in supporting the ban and

---

[2]   Other recommendations included adopting Jewish and Muslim days of observance as public holidays, the expansion of teaching languages from the Maghreb, and economic development programs for the banlieues.

[3]   An abhorrence to pluralistic politics that might undermine the unity of the state. It is because l'affaire touches on issues crucial to French identity and politics that I take exception to the tone of Alain Badiou's (2004) flippant commentary when he writes, "France has finally found a problem worthy of itself: the scarf draping the heads of a few girls."

sided with right-wing and nationalistic leaders. Religious leaders, socialists, and many leaders of the far right National Front opposed the ban for different reasons. The French public overwhelmingly supported the ban. It appears that Muslims were split on this issue – one study based on interviews with 300 Muslim girls found that 49 percent favored the ban and 43 percent opposed it (Thomas 2006, 240). Despite the overwhelming support for the ban in France, the global reaction was quite negative. For example, a British member of the European Parliament labeled the ban "a clear human rights violation" (Wing and Smith 2006, 757) and the U.S. State Department (2004) condemned it in its annual report on religious freedom.[4] The UN Human Rights Commission's special rapporteur on Freedom of Religion expressed strong concern that "the stigmatization of the so called Islamic headscarf has triggered a wave of religious intolerance" (United Nations 2005).

From an outsider's perspective, the report and its aftermath had fetishized the wearing of headscarves to the point that it was seen as the singular answer to the questions of how to better assimilate the recent waves of Muslim immigrants and how to improve the treatment of young Muslim women. As philosopher Alain Badiou wryly remarked, the young women are suffering from oppression "hence, they shall be punished" (Badiou 2004). From an outsider's perspective, these conclusions would not meet any type of heightened judicial scrutiny. In U.S. jurisprudence, a strict scrutiny analysis would require that in order for the state to interfere with a fundamental right such as the freedom of religion, it must have a compelling state interest and the proposed remedy must be narrowly tailored to meet that interest. Freedom of religion is a fundamental right guaranteed in the French Constitution, and laïcité and gender equity are compelling state interests in the French context.[5] However, the banning of headscarves would most likely not be considered narrowly tailored to meet those interests because other less insidious means are available for addressing these issues. Indeed, it can be argued that the ban will exacerbate the problems it seeks to address. It could lead to *less* assimilation of new immigrants by depriving young women of a public education overtly intended to assimilate them into French culture.[6] It could also worsen gender equality as

---

[4]   See Laborde (2005) for one of the few attempts outside of the French media to construct a "sympathetic, systematic and cogent case for the ban," and yet Laborde ultimately is "unconvinced" by her defense (307).

[5]   See, e.g., Article I of the French Constitution: "*La France est une République, unie, indivisible, laïque et sociale.*"

[6]   Cf. Balibar 2004, "One claims to defend young girls against religious fundamentalism, of which sexism is an intrinsic part, by banishing them from school, i.e., making them personally – in their lives, their futures, their flesh – bear the penalty for the injustice of which they are the 'victims', and sending them back to the communitarian space dominated by precisely

young women deprived of education will be less able to demand their rights. Another state interest, according to a member of the National Assembly, was to produce "good Muslims." He argued that "the law was not about the headscarf, it was about funneling Islam toward being a more acceptable religion for France." He added simplistically, "There are good Muslims and bad Muslims. In France, we want good Muslims" (Pantea n.d., 5). Of course, this justification would have difficulty meeting any type of heightened scrutiny, as there are numerous other ways of combating the rise of Islamic fundamentalism (*intégrisme*) if that is the problem to be addressed. Indeed, many commentators have stressed that this law may have the opposite effect: It could "promote the development of political-religious fundamentalist ideologies" (Balibar 2004, 355).

LAÏCITÉ AND L'AFFAIRE DU FOULARD

Discourse does not always lead to interrogation. Much of the voluminous public debate on this issue[7] was self-reinforcing, allowing little room for serious interrogation of the main issues. For instance, the term laïcité became a trump that often served to stifle debate,[8] and the Stasi report, though it focused on laïcité, did not analyze how its multi-faceted meanings had been determined by various social and historical contexts.

Laïcité is a uniquely French form of secularism that grew out of the nineteenth-century battles between Republicans and royalists. In the late nineteenth and early twentieth centuries, the victorious Republicans undertook a series of steps to cleanse entire segments of the nation from religious influences. This is an excellent example of Charles Taylor's "independent ethic" approach to secularism; that is, truths cleansed of religion will be used to govern society and will determine all questions of morality and politics (See Laborde 2005). This is perhaps most clearly evident with the banning of religious education from schools through the famous "Law of December 9, 1905 concerning the separation of Church and State," as well as the refusal to open theology departments in public universities. Instead, the public schools

---

this religious sexism" (354). A chapter of the French Council on the Muslim Religion concluded that the ban "is aimed at Muslims, stigmatizes their religion, practices exclusion, and condemns them to turning inward to their own community" (McGoldrick 2006, 97; cf. Freedman 2004).

[7] One study counted more than 1,200 articles on l'affaire du foulard between 1989 and 1998.

[8] This may have been a factor in the wide range of definitions of laïcité by teachers and students "who often gauge it according to their own belief systems rather than how the law is intended to work" (Keaton 2006, 187).

were given the affirmative role of creating citizens of a unified republic – they are charged with neutralizing the public sphere. Under laïcité, citizens will be defined by their sameness and not their differences, so assimilation is the mantra as opposed to pluralism. For the most part, new immigrants are expected to shed their particular socio-cultural public identities, including religion, in order to integrate into the French Republic.

In its strongest manifestations, as active secularism, laïcité will involve a sharp, even artificial distinction between the public and private spheres – à la Hannah Arendt's private-social-public typology – including the cleansing of the public sphere of any traces of religion, such as the banning of religious clothing by public servants. French laïcité then includes a citizen's responsibility to refrain from any form of proselytism, and this responsibility would take on added significance in public schools. At the same time, state interference in private expressions of religion would be considered abhorrent. Under this model, any attempt to cling to cultural identities in the public sphere would be seen as an attack on the very principles of the French Revolution and the Constitution. With active secularism and assimilation as its guiding principles, France could even claim in all seriousness that it "is a country in which there are no minorities."[9]

However, laïcité as a fundamental principle of the French Republic does not, by itself, explain the recent debates about the headscarf. After all, laïcité has been in place for more than 100 years, but headscarves were only recently banned. Laïcité does not explain why the headscarf became such an issue in the past fifteen years or why French attitudes shifted so much from 1989 to 2004 (see Thomas 2006). Laïcité "is an elastic rather than immutable concept" (Chadwick 1997, 48) influenced by historical, social, economic, political, and rhetorical factors with each also playing significant roles in the way the headscarf issue was framed. The mostly single-minded and often unsophisticated emphasis on laïcité and its use as a trump to end debates meant that these other factors went mostly unexamined. Sebastien Poulter (1997) points out that even though there is a long history of laïcité, "large-scale, post-1945 immigration only began to be perceived by some in France as a problem as increasing numbers of Algerians and other North Africans began to outstrip arrivals from Italy, Spain and Portugal by the end of the 1960s" (50). Similarly, he points out that the 1994 Bayrou controversy was spurred in part by the rise of disorder and fundamentalism in Algeria, which potentially could precipitate a surge

---

9   In a series of cases, the Human Rights Committee that oversees the International Covenant on Civil and Political Rights (ICCPR) has upheld France's position that it contains no minorities as a valid reservation to Article 27 of the ICCPR (see, e.g., *SG v. France* 1991, § 5.3).

in Algerian refugees.[10] Indeed, factors such as waves of immigration, political battles, and economic crises seem to periodically transform the meaning of laïcité along a continuum from a more passive secularism to a more active secularism, and it is these factors that need to be examined.

For instance, the Stasi Commission concluded that neutrality was an essential feature of laïcité, and in much of the debate there was an assumption of religious neutrality in French life and French public schools that is belied by French reality. An underlying premise of laïcité is that all should be encouraged to come to the public sphere, but they should leave radical ideas at home, especially in regard to religion. The Stasi report, adopting an even more active secularism, framed it this way: "Demanding state neutrality does not seem very comparable with the display of an aggressive proselytism, particularly within the schools. Being willing to adapt the public expression of one's religious particularities and to set limits to the affirmation of one's identity allows everyone to meet in the public space" (quoted in Thomas 2006, 242). One can speak freely in the public space, but one cannot aggressively proselytize. In reality, though, the state continues to fund the maintenance of religious buildings built before 1905, and not surprisingly these are overwhelmingly Catholic churches. Attempts to procure state funding to build Mosques "to remedy the radically insufficient provision of adequate Muslim religious facilities" (Laborde 2005, 314) have been rejected. Private schools, overwhelmingly Christian and Jewish, continue to be funded by the State (see Laborde 2005, 310), and it has been estimated that almost two million children still attend at least nominally Catholic schools (Idriss 2005, 265). Christian holidays are universally observed in schools, but students must attend class on almost all Muslim days of observance. Schools in the Alsace-Moselle region continue to require religious education (mostly Catholic) because the 1905 secularism law does not apply there.[11] In each of these cases, historical inequalities cannot be remedied by governmental action because it would be seen as an unacceptable government endorsement of religion, that is, a violation of procedural neutrality that must be maintained despite original substantive inequality. On a more nuanced level, the ideal of public neutrality and private practice of religion is better suited for specific belief systems, such as Catholicism,[12] that are more amenable to public-private

---

[10] Ironically, the fact "that those most likely to flee from Algeria would be middle-class 'secularists' seemed to be overlooked" (Poulter 1997, 62).

[11] The Stasi Commission recommended the addition of Islam in the curriculum in these schools.

[12] This leads one commentator to cleverly label it a Catholaïcité (quoted in Balibar 2004, 363, n.5).

distinctions and less well suited to religions that encourage public manifestations of beliefs, such as Islam, which often "is an all-embracing communal identity" (Laborde 2005, 320).[13] Under the pretenses of equality, an original inequality or violence is reinforced. Such "equal" treatment "create(s) a utopia of empty universality that no France ever possessed. Under the cover of individual detachment, *one grants the privilege to define France only to the oldest immigrants*" (Latour 2004, emphasis added).[14]

Further, the French public, those granted "the privilege to define France" or, following Arendt's views on judgment, those granted the privilege to define who could appear in the public sphere, did not themselves enter the public sphere with neutral views on laïcité. Adrien K. Wing and Monica Nigh Smith report that "for some French, the erection of mosques and loud Islamic calls to prayer represent 'clashes of civilizations',," and they further describe the effects of "France's Islamophobic tendencies" (2006, 753). The Stasi Commission did not interrogate its finding that singled out religious clothing, especially the Islamic headscarf, as aggressive proselytism, especially whether this decision was clouded by anti-immigrant or anti-Muslim feelings.[15]

Without serious interrogation of this original violence lurking behind the headscarf debates, there was no serious attempt to provide evidence of the extent of the "problem" or to question whether the 1989 decision was truly unworkable. According to Elaine Thomas, only "1256 foulards were reported in France's public schools at the start of the 2003–04 school years," and "only twenty of these cases were judged 'difficult' by school officials themselves" (2006, 239).

The "problem," though, may not have been the wearing of the headscarves itself, but what the headscarf came to symbolize in the French public sphere. Because the nuances of the young women's clothing were not seriously examined, the wearing of the headscarf became conflated with the Iranian chador or the burqa from Afghanistan, types of clothing that had assumed strong

---

[13] As I write this, a controversy has erupted in Phoenix over six imams who were pulled off an airplane as possible terrorists after three of them performed their evening prayers in the airport terminal. The ensuing controversy was often seen from the perspective of the hegemonic religion. Several letters to the editor of the local newspaper basically asked: Why can't they pray like us Christians, meaning in private.

[14] My translation: « C'est créer l'utopie d'une universalité aucun Français n'a jamais habité. Sous le couvert d'un respect des individus détachés, on n'accorde le privilège de définir la France qu'aux immigrés les plus anciens. »

[15] Discrimination *is* mentioned as an effect of the crisis of laïcité in part III. Part IV includes several recommendations for combating discrimination, but it is not self-critical about the role that discrimination may have played in framing the debate itself or the conclusions of the Commission.

negative connotations in France.[16] Aided by such conflation, the headscarf increasingly solely symbolized oppression of girls by a patriarchal religion and culture. Stasi himself concluded, "Objectively, the veil stands for the alienation of women" (Ruchet 2006, 19). Elizabeth Badinter, a leading French feminist, said, "Putting a veil on the head, this is an act of submission. It burdens a woman's whole life" (Moruzzi 1994, 662). In this context, it should not be too surprising that sixty leading French women signed a letter in the magazine *Elle* in support of a headscarf ban.

Against this hegemonic narrative, some commentators have stressed the multiple meanings that the headscarf represents. The testimonies of a range of young women reveal complex and thoughtful deliberations that touch on a range of personal, familial, and social issues:

> I will soon turn 20 years old and recently I decided to wear the headscarf. That has changed a lot of things in my life and above all, the way I view religion. Personally, I feel more feminine and freer than before, despite what some people may think. I am happy like this and I want to say never be ashamed to want to live your beliefs.

> Once you bear something for all to see, the second you display something for its beauty, you objectify it and diminish its value. Because its worth is built on its ability to attract, when it no longer elicits awe from onlookers it becomes worthless. (Wing and Smith 2006, 761)

> I [have] accepted hijab so that I can be appreciated for my intellect and personality rather than my figure or fashion sense. When I face a classmate or colleague I can be confident that my body is not being scrutinized, my brastrap or pantyline visible. I have repudiated the perverted values of our society by choosing to assert myself only through my mind. (Wing and Smith 2006, 764)

Based on numerous testimonies such as this, Wing and Smith (2006) conclude:

> There are a wide range of intersecting reasons why Muslim females may want to be able to wear the headscarf in schools and elsewhere. These may include the following: personal religious conviction, freedom of religion, acceptance as a good Muslim female, compliance with family values, neutralization of sexuality and protection from harassment from Muslim males, and individual choice and religious/cultural identity. Any individual may have more than one reason as a justification to wear the hijab, and her reasons may change over time. (758)

---

[16] Some rightly objected to equating the foulard with Islam as it is often more correlated with cultural background than religious background (Poulter 1997, 45).

At the same time, and not surprisingly, "There are a variety of intersecting reasons why such women may be against the headscarf, including the following: it is a symbol of oppression and not a free choice; it is sexist; it fosters extremism; and it separates Muslim women" (Wing and Smith 2006, 767).

As with any contested polysemy, hegemonic and anti-hegemonic groups attempted to affix their own meanings, but the hegemonic meaning will almost always take precedence. For the hegemonic group, the meaning was fixed as oppression or a manifestation of Islamic fundamentalism; the Stasi report barely mentioned any other possible meaning. The anti-hegemonic group unsuccessfully attempted to counter this meaning in a January 2004 protest in which 20,000 women wearing headscarves "carried French flags, marched with banners evoking 'Liberty, Equality, Fraternity, Secularism', and even wore headscarves emblazoned with the French tricolor" (Pantea n.d., 6).

Nonetheless, the hegemonic meaning of the headscarf was further reinforced by attaching it to much publicized accounts of abuses suffered by Muslim girls in the *banlieues*, including reports of a girl burned alive, and the publication of Samita Bellil's autobiography *Dans l'Enfer des Tournantes* (*In the Inferno of Gang-Rapes*).[17] In the context of such framing, it was not only considered anti-laïcité/anti-French but also misogynist to support the wearing of the headscarf. Thomas (2006) paraphrases one member of the Stasi Commission that "an atmosphere developed within which it became almost impossible to defend the right to wear headscarves without casting oneself as sexist and reactionary" (249).

L'Affaire and the Voice of the Other

L'affaire du foulard shows that voluminous discourse does not always lead to self-interrogation. This lack of serious reflection was made possible by the triumphalism of a hegemonic discourse and the simultaneous silencing of the Other. The young women whose fundamental rights were at stake were effectively silenced throughout much of the debate. This silencing began with the three young women in Creil in 1989 who were rarely asked their motivation for wearing the headscarves.[18] Women in general, and Muslim women

[17] For a more nuanced presentation of Muslim girls in the banlieues, see Keaton 2006. Scott (2005), Badiou (2004), and Balibar (2004) each discuss how the headscarf opposes the French view of sexuality where women are expected to be publicly on display. See also Fanon (1965) for eerily similar debates about the Algerian veil in the 1950s.

[18] See Gaspard and Khosrokhavar (1995) and Lévy and Lévy (2004) for some of the few extensive interviews with young women who wear headscarves. Moruzzi writes: "The national

specifically, were silenced in the ensuing debates. For example, one scholar conducted a content analysis of three major French newspapers and found:

> The voices heard in the articles are exclusively those of men – politicians, school principals, editorialists, and religious leaders. The only female voice acknowledged is Daniele Mitterand, wife of the former President of France. As for the young Muslim women, they are quoted only once and very briefly. (Ardizzoni 2004, 634)

The silencing continued during the extensive testimony taken by the Stasi Commission, which "only invited one French Muslim woman who wears a headscarf to give testimony out of 150 witnesses" (Wing and Smith 2006, 784). Men, of various stripes, assumed that they could speak for the young women. Etienne Balibar writes that young women "become the stake of a merciless struggle for prestige between two male powers which try to control them, one on behalf of patriarchal authority wrapped up in religion, the other on behalf of national authority wrapped up in secularism" (2004, 359, cf. Wing and Smith 2006, 758).

Such silencing of the Other is not as remarkable as it may seem at first glance. Once the Stasi Commission framed the debate in terms of the meaning of laïcité, past and present, young Muslim women, often immigrants, would no longer be considered experts in the matter. Moreover, once the young women were branded as oppressed, they were seen as defenseless and needed someone to defend them and speak for them. One is reminded of Arendt's unfortunate response to the criticisms of her essay on the desegregation of Little Rock Central High School when she wrote: "Oppressed minorities were never the best judges on the order of priorities in such matters" (Arendt 1959a, 46). Because their oppression made them unfit to speak in the polis, French leaders were willing to fight for them, or to paraphrase Gayatri Spivak's famous formulation: White men (and women) were willing to save brown women from brown men.

As with Arendt's theory of judgment and her analysis of the Little Rock crisis, a lack of voice and agency of the Other reinforced the hegemonic discourse. The multiple meanings of the scarf from the perspective of the Other were not able to call into question the meaning affixed by the hegemonic order. As the headscarf assumed greater symbolic meaning in the public discourse and this meaning became fixed, the young women themselves became

press referred to the girls only by their first names. Although Samira was identified as being of Tunisian origin, and the sisters Leila and Fatima as being from a Moroccan family, they were never dignified by being fully named, and I never saw them quoted. Although they caused an uproar, they were treated as though silent and without voice" (1994, 668 n. 14).

reduced – they became defined by whether they wore the scarf, when in fact this decision and the meanings of such adornment are often idiosyncratic and vary over time. One young woman remarked that she "felt pressured to go on stage by these men, and to demand her right to wear the headscarf at all times, even though she only wears it based on her 'spiritual meter' for the day" (Wing and Smith 2006, 749). The growing Muslim population in France was further marginalized by this hegemonic discourse, and a golden opportunity for dialogue with an oft-marginalized group was missed.

Several scholars such as Seyla Benhabib held out hope that a supranational institution, in particular the European Court of Human Rights, would step in and overturn the French ban, but these hopes were effectively dashed with the ECHR's rulings in *Sahin v. Turkey* that upheld a ban on headscarves in universities.[19]

LEYLA SAHIN V. TURKEY

Whereas l'affaire du foulard shows the limits of democratic discourse in ensuring human rights, especially of minorities, the *Sahin* case shows the limits of human rights institutions in upholding minority rights, especially when the institutions are explicitly founded on the principle of democracy and therefore give priority to democracy over rights. The Turkish situation was not a failure of a discursive democracy per se because genuine discourse was consistently thwarted, especially with several high-profile arrests for opposing the Turkish headscarf ban. The only member of Parliament who wore a headscarf was jeered mercilessly on the floor of the legislature and lost her Turkish citizenship only days after taking office (Kavakci 2004). Genuine debate was stifled even though most Turks[20] and their democratically elected bodies consistently opposed the ban on headscarves.

Despite this lack of democratic support for the ban, the ECtHR used Turkey's democratic status as a basis for upholding the ban. Such a counterintuitive decision can be traced to similar root causes as in the French l'affaire, a hegemonic discourse overriding the rights of the marginalized Other. For the ECtHR, the hegemonic discourse was rooted in the ECHR and the artificial typologies that had been developed in the ECtHR's jurisprudence. So, instead of the ECHR serving as a check on democracies infringing on minority rights,

---

[19] Even as late as 2005, after the unanimous 2004 decision in the *Sahin* case, Benhabib held out hope that the ECtHR would overturn the French law (Benhabib 2006, 160).

[20] A recent survey found that 71 percent of Turks believe that the "headscarf should be permitted in universities, and 64 percent say female parliamentarians should be allowed to wear it while in office" (Kavakci 2004, 66).

the ECtHR's decision will serve as a catalyst for future infringements of minority rights. Indeed, several European countries have already taken steps to ban headscarves in various public spaces since the *Sahin* ruling. Such a result should have been anticipated as the past decade has also seen an overt mutually reinforcing relationship between the French l'affaire and the decisions of the ECtHR. For example, the Stasi Commission and members of the French National Assembly approvingly quoted ECtHR jurisprudence on minority rights, especially the highly controversial 2003 *Refah Partisi* case that upheld the banning of a Turkish Islamist party. In the aftermath of the final *Sahin* ruling in 2005 there should be little doubt that the ECtHR would uphold the French ban.[21] This begs the question: If a human rights court refuses to uphold minority rights, who will?

Turkish Secularism

Turkey has struggled for decades with a tension between the secular state founded by Mustafa Kemal Atatürk and its overwhelmingly Muslim population, including many political parties and popular leaders that desire a larger role for Islam in Turkish politics and society. Many of Atatürk's secular reforms, now often referred to as Kemalism, were institutionalized in the 1921 Constitution and a series of amendments to the Constitution. These were followed by a series of legislative steps that closed religious schools, banned religious study from public education, and mandated government funding of schools for training imams and other religious leaders. A series of reforms in the 1920s and 1930s, such as the 1925 hat law that prohibited the wearing of the fez by men, banned various types of religious clothing, but it appears that Atatürk himself never supported an explicit ban on the headscarf. Electoral politics and changing economic and political realities led to a tempering of the meaning of secularism in Turkey from the 1940s to 1960s. Unlike the French Republic, the Turkish government could not attempt to cleanse the public sphere of religion as approximately 99 percent of Turks are Muslim and approximately three-fourths of Turkish women wear some type of headscarf (Secor 2005, 207). Instead, the government's actions can be seen as an attempt to contain or temper Islam, that is, to embrace a specific non-fundamentalist version of Islam, where the "true religion" has even been described as "the control of Islam through the state" (Belelieu 2006, 580).

---

[21] Cf. McGoldrick 2006, 104. But see Lovejoy (2006), arguing that *Sahin* may not be controlling in a potential French case.

Kemalist reforms also included a number of important measures aimed at ensuring the equality of women, including the banning of polygamy, the lifting of restrictions on inheritance rights for women, and granting women "the right to choose their spouses, initiate divorce, and maintain their maternal rights after divorce" (Arat 1998, 15). Women were granted the right to vote in 1934 (Arat 2005, 17). Large numbers of Turkish women attended professional schools and made important strides in the public sphere while inequality and patriarchy often continued to mark the private sphere.

An increasing rise in internal terrorism and political fighting led the military to be taken over by a bloodless coup in 1980. The 1982 Constitution reflected the new government's tougher stance on religion. It begins by reaffirming the principles of secularism and Kemalism:

> In line with the concept of nationalism outlined and the reforms and principles introduced by the founder of the Republic of Turkey, *Atatürk*, the immortal leader and the unrivaled hero, this Constitution, which affirms the eternal existence of the Turkish nation and motherland and the indivisible unity of the Turkish State, embodies....

Article 2 states:

> The Republic of Turkey is a democratic, secular and social State governed by the rule of law; bearing in mind the concepts of public peace, national solidarity and justice; respecting human rights; loyal to the nationalism of Atatürk, and based on the fundamental tenets set forth in the Preamble.

Although Article 24 provides "the right to freedom of conscience, religious belief and conviction"[22] it, like all guaranteed rights, is tempered by Article 14, which limits individual rights when they are determined to be endangering the state, infringing on the rights of others, or "establishing the hegemony of one social class over others, or creating discrimination on the basis of language, race, religion or sect, or of establishing by any other means a system of government based on these concepts and ideas." However, this clawback clause itself is, or at least should be, tempered by Section 3 of Article 14, which states, "No provision of this Constitution shall be interpreted in a manner that would grant the right of destroying the rights and freedoms embodied in the Constitution." Although the general thrust of these articles is clear, they are "vague and susceptible to politicized interpretation" (Bleiberg 2005, 139) and the vicissitudes of partisan politics.

---

[22] Article 42 also provides for the right to education, and article 10 protects against discrimination based on religion or sex (cf. Arat 2005, 25–26).

The 1980s saw an increasing divergence in women's attitudes toward secularism as many educated Islamist women began to critique what they saw
as an ambiguous place for women in a modernist, Kemalist society. Many
of these women were attracted to the Islamist Refah (Welfare) party[23] and
expressed their resistance to Kemalism by wearing the Islamic headscarf
(the turban as distinguished from the more traditional headscarf) (Arat 2005,
21–23). One of the rallying points for these women was the "discrimina-
tory" regulations preventing veiled women from higher education and from
employment (Secor 2005, 213). "Kemalist feminists," on the other hand, saw
the headscarf issue as a cover for a movement that "struggles to return our
society to the darkness of the Middle Ages" (Arat 2005, 28). As in the French
case, the headscarf issue intersected with attitudes toward national identity,
gender equality, modernization, and human rights; and a battle ensued over
dress codes, especially for women in schools and universities. The president's
party encouraged these regulations, but several contrary laws were passed by
the parliament, only to have the Constitutional Court declare them uncon-
stitutional because they infringed on secularism, liberalism, and equality.[24]
These regulations appeared to lead to a "radicalization of the Islamist movement" as university women and their supporters staged protests and sit-ins
against them (Göle 1996, 2).

Women's personal decisions to wear the headscarf in Turkey as in France
are multi-faceted and vary across space and time. They can manifest women's
agency by declaring oneself an "enlightened Muslim woman" (İlyasoğlu 1998,
258) or by expressing an allegiance to an Islamist political movement, but it
can be argued they can also manifest women's submission to Islamic fundamentalism (Göle 1996, 5–6 and chapter 4). Not surprisingly, the personal
deliberations of the young women often centered on the meaning of modernity as it intersects with women's rights.

> Young veiled lawyer: "Once at the university, I was (due to the headscarf)
> classified as someone who is not able to keep up with the times. By putting
> up obstacles in front of me and trying to check my prospects for a university
> education they [people with responsibility] wanted to push me even further
> behind. This was done to me, who had been struggling so hard in order to

---

[23] Refah Partisi was outlawed by the Constitutional Court, and the European Court upheld the
ban in a decision notable for its overt fear of a resurgence of Islamic fundamentalism (See
Refah Partisi v. Turkey 2001).

[24] This has been basically a battle between what Kuru (2005) has called passive and assertive
secularism; although such a dichotomy is a helpful heuristic, it may not reflect the wide variation along a continuum of positions.

advance not only myself, but my family as well, in line with the requirements of a modern society." (Özdalga 1998, 55)

30-year old shop owner: "The headscarf is forbidden at the university, fine; why isn't the miniskirt forbidden? I mean, when we talk about human rights, one is below and another is above. . . . What you did is wrong according to me, what is right to me is wrong to you. Politics is found in the center of this, but we can't find the center. We have no politics." (Secor 2005, 216)

The wearing of the headscarf was also often framed in terms of autonomy and performativity, and this freedom is often compared to the lack of women's freedom in a westernized/secularized society (Secor 2005).

Teacher in her thirties (PhD student in political science) who decided to wear the headscarf after approximately two years of study and having extensively contemplated the decision: "It was as if my feet were not touching the ground any more I was feeling so relieved and so happy. Here I had been, reading all those books, and then, suddenly, putting the headscarf on, it was as if I merged into the things I had read about. Really, it was as if I was floating through the air." (Özdalga 1998, 66)

As in the French case, the eventual decision of the European Court of Human Rights ignored this polysemy. Instead, based on pre-existing typologies, the ECtHR settled on the Turkish government's meaning of the headscarf and cauterized all the rest. The voices of the young women and their soul-searching deliberations ultimately played a very small role in shaping their own rights.

THE *SAHIN* CASE

In 1998, the Vice Chancellor of Istanbul University issued a circular, in the spirit of the rulings of the Constitutional Court, that called for the expulsion of students "whose 'heads are covered' (who wear the Islamic headscarf) and students (including overseas students) with beards" (Sahin 2005, § 16). Leyla Sahin, a fifth-year medical student, who had been wearing a headscarf for several years of her university career, was soon prohibited from sitting for her exams because she refused to remove her headscarf. After several months and several internal rulings against her, Sahin appealed to the Turkish courts and finally filed a complaint with the ECtHR alleging violations of the European Convention of Human Rights including the freedom of religion (Article 9), the right to respect for private and family life (Article 8), the freedom of expression (Article 10), the freedom from discrimination (Article 14), and the right to education (Article 2 of Protocol 1). While her case was working its way through the ECtHR, Sahin emigrated and enrolled at the University of Vienna. A chamber of the ECtHR made a ruling on June 29, 2004, unanimously uphold-ing the Turkish ban. The Grand Chamber issued its final ruling on November 10, 2005, upholding the ban by a vote of 16 to 1. As I will show in this chapter, the ECtHR's decision rested on artificial typologies from its jurisprudence that effectively served to silence the voice of the Other.

Both chambers of the ECtHR confined their analysis to the right-to-religion claim under Article 9. Section 1 of Article 9 reads:

1.   Everyone has the right to freedom of thought, conscience and religion; this right includes freedom to change his religion or belief, and free-dom, either alone or in community with others and in public or pri-vate, to manifest his religion or belief, in worship, teaching, practice and observance.

It is followed by a clawback clause, which limits the rights guaranteed in section 1:

2.   Freedom to manifest one's religion or beliefs shall be subject only to such limitations as are prescribed by law and are necessary in a demo-cratic society in the interests of public safety, for the protection of public order, health or morals, or the protection of the rights and freedoms of others.

It should be noted that the Court and the now defunct European Commission had both previously upheld bans on wearing the Islamic head-scarf. The Court upheld a ban in *Dahlab v. Switzerland* for teachers of small children who wear the headscarf. The Commission upheld a Turkish ban on headscarves in a 1993 case involving photos for a university graduation document.

In the *Sahin* case, the Grand Chamber laid out the key principles for deciding such a case, and in following the functionalism of the European Convention, each is framed in reference (and deference) to democracy. The religious freedom of Article 9 "is one of the foundations of a 'democratic soci-ety' within the meaning of the Convention" (§ 104). Additionally, "In demo-cratic societies, in which several religions coexist within one and the same population, it may be necessary to place restrictions on freedom to manifest one's religion or belief in order to reconcile the interests of the various groups and ensure that everyone's beliefs are respected" (§ 106). Thus, in order to ensure tolerance and pluralism "in a democratic society," it may be necessary for the state "to ensure that the competing groups tolerate each other" (§ 107). Although these principles are derived from the ideals of a democratic society, the majority's views in a given society do not necessarily "prevail" on these issues: "A balance must be achieved which ensures the fair and proper treatment of people from minorities and avoids any abuse of a dominant position" (§ 108). In other words, the rights of majorities may need to be infringed in order to guarantee democracy:

> Pluralism and democracy must also be based on dialogue and a spirit of compromise necessarily entailing various concessions on the part of individuals or groups of individuals which are justified in order to maintain and promote the ideals and values of a democratic society. (§ 108)

So, from the foregoing analysis it can be concluded that the rights of the ECHR are to serve the goal of democracy, but democracy is not the final arbiter of which rights need to be infringed in order to guarantee democracy.[25] As for what steps will need to be taken to ensure such tolerance, pluralism, and democracy, the Court relied on two cornerstones of its jurisprudence, the margin of appreciation doctrine and the consensus doctrine.

The Margin of Appreciation and Consensus Doctrines

International human rights institutions often employ some type of "interpretational tool" for dealing with the tension between the local and the universal (Mahoney 1998, 1). The ECtHR has developed the margin of appreciation doctrine to give democratic states "a certain measure of discretion in assessing the extent strictly required by the exigencies of the situation" (*Cyprus Case* 1958). The doctrine originated initially in several decisions involving national security, especially internal terrorism cases in the United Kingdom. At a time when the Court's legitimacy was still in question, there may have been a fear that if a country, especially such a prominent member of the Council of Europe (COE) as the United Kingdom, would ignore the Court's rulings on such important matters, it would undermine any credibility of the Court. Since that time, the margin of appreciation has become a standard interpretative tool in deciding a wide range of cases, but the amount of discretion to grant and when to grant it has raised a great deal of controversy. The Court has repeatedly stated that the margin of appreciation doctrine does not give "carte blanche" to states (e.g., *Klass v. Germany* 1979–1980, § 49). The ECtHR has consistently ruled that because human rights are a means to the democratic end, the Court will be more open to granting a margin of appreciation to democratic nations. Such countries are viewed as having deserved

---

[25] As Clinton Rossiter wrote in a different context, "No sacrifice is too great for our democracy, least of all the temporary sacrifice of democracy itself" (1948, 314).

good-faith latitude to deal with intractable human rights problems. This doctrine allows countries to experiment with various local solutions of rights problems in a way similar to arguments for dual federalism in the United States.[26] This discretion will allow a democratic nation to openly debate and choose among policy alternatives.

The Court has also relied on a consensus test when determining whether or not to grant a margin of appreciation.[27] In the European context, consensus refers to the number of other Council of Europe countries that have maintained a specific law. For example, in the Irish anti-sodomy case *Dudgeon v. United Kingdom* (1981), the Court was struck by the fact that Ireland was one of the few COE countries that had not repealed such a law. In such cases, the Court has been less likely to grant deference to the State.

However, as legal scholar Eyal Benvenisti argues, the deference allowed to democratic states under the margin of appreciation and consensus doctrines can undermine the very rights guaranteed in the Convention, especially as they pertain to minorities. In situations "which typically result in restrictions exclusively or predominantly on the rights of the minorities, no deference to national institutions is called for; rather, the international human rights bodies serve an important role in correcting some of the systemic deficiencies of democracy" (Benvenisti 1999, 847). In such cases, the margin of appreciation actually "assists the majorities in burdening politically powerless minorities" (Benvenisti 1999, 847). Benvenisti calls for a strict scrutiny type of analysis for discrete and insular minorities that tracks U.S. Supreme Court jurisprudence where the burden is on the state to show that it has a compelling interest and its remedies are narrowly tailored to address the problem at hand.[28] Although the Court has often been at the forefront of the progressive development of human rights law, and despite numerous pleas from scholars and attorneys, the ECtHR continues to use these doctrines in cases involving minority rights, including freedom of religion cases.

---

[26] Cf. "It is one of the happy incidents of the federal system that a single courageous state may, if its citizens choose, serve as a laboratory; and try novel social and economic experiments without risk to the rest of the country" (Justice Brandeis in *New York State Ice Co. v. Liebmann* 1932, Dissenting).

[27] This is similar to the "evolving public standards" doctrine that has been recently used in capital punishment and sodomy cases in the United States.

[28] As for narrow tailoring, Judge Tulkens' dissent in *Sahin* points out that "the authorities should have used other means either to encourage her (through mediation, for example) to remove her headscarf and pursue her studies, or to ensure that public order was maintained on the university premises if it was genuinely at risk. The fact of the matter is that no attempt was made to try measures that would have had a less drastic effect on the applicant's right to education in the instant case."

The ECtHR's Judgment

In the *Sahin* case, the Grand Chamber following the margin of appreciation doctrine concluded, "The role of the national decision-making body must be given special importance" (§ 109). This deference is magnified by the consensus doctrine as the Court failed, in its examination of religious clothing policies for public schools and universities in COE states, to find a widespread consensus of policies on religious clothing. The amount of margin of appreciation to grant Turkey also is based on the magnitude of the issues at stake (which are quite impressive), "the need to protect the rights and freedoms of others, to preserve public order and to secure civil peace and true religious pluralism, which is vital to the survival of a democratic society" (§ 110). The Court praised secularism as "undoubtedly one of the fundamental principles of the Turkish State which are in harmony with the rule of law and respect for human rights, may be considered necessary to protect the democratic system in Turkey" (§ 114).[29] Secularism also serves the fundamental principle of gender equality and "the protection of the 'rights and freedoms of others'," meaning those who do not wear the scarf will not feel coerced. Finally without elaborating, "The Court does not lose sight of the fact that there are extremist political movements in Turkey which seek to impose on society as a whole their religious symbols and conception of a society founded on religious precepts" (§ 115).

Faced with such deference and such compelling interests, the only remaining question was whether the Turkish ban met the Court's proportionality analysis. The Court notes favorably that Muslim students are still allowed to manifest their religion in other settings, that the ban did not only apply to Muslim dress, and the fact that the Chancellor went out of his way to explain his justifications for the ban. Most importantly, the Court noted "the process whereby the regulations that led to the decision of 9 July 1998 were implemented took several years and was accompanied by a wide debate within Turkish society and the teaching profession" (§ 120). According to the Court, this debate was not rigid:

> It is quite clear that throughout that decision-making process the university authorities sought to adapt to the evolving situation in a way that would not bar access to the university to students wearing the veil, through continued

---

[29] As Bleiberg argues, "The court then essentially assumed that any action Turkey takes to limit religious freedom in the name of secularism must be in harmony with human rights, since secularism – as an element of democracy – is itself in harmony with human rights" (2005, 152).

dialogue with those concerned, while at the same time ensuring that order was maintained and in particular that the requirements imposed by the nature of the course in question were complied with. (§ 120)

Finally, the court following precedence gave deference to local educational authorities: "The university authorities are in principle better placed than an international court to evaluate local needs and conditions or the requirements of a particular course" (§ 121).

To summarize: The rights of the European Convention are in the service of democracy, and the Turkish Constitution based on secularism is intended to protect democracy as well as fundamental human rights such as those in the Convention. Moreover, the Court gives a wide margin of appreciation to national and local school authorities in such a case. These authorities formulated a policy that sought to advance public order, protect the rights of others, and enhance gender equity. The Turkish government also developed these policies through a supposed democratic process with wide-ranging debate that attempted to accommodate the rights of the affected group. Moreover, Court (and Commission) precedence also supported such a ban. Framed this way, the Court's upholding of the Turkish ban should not be too surprising nor should its overwhelming vote (16–1).

Judge Tulkens' Dissent

Judge Tulkens' dissenting opinion more extensively deconstructs the purported secularism of the Turkish government and the typologies put forward by the Court. She refused to prioritize democracy over rights but viewed them as complementary, and she struggled to provide some voice for the Other or at least refused the paternalistic gambit of speaking for the Other.

Judge Tulkens begins her dissent by questioning whether Turkey deserved such a wide margin of appreciation in this case. For example, she doubts the majority's conclusion that no consensus could be found in European countries on this issue. Although there may be a wide diversity of policies in the COE on the wearing of religious clothing in *public schools*, no other European country had such a ban on the wearing of religious clothing at the *university level*. With such strong consensus among member states, the Court should limit its margin of appreciation given to the Turkish government.

Judge Tulkens does not subordinate religious freedom to the purported interests of the state: "In a democratic society, I believe that it is necessary to seek to harmonize the principles of secularism, equality and liberty, not to weigh one against the other."³⁰ Without a clear hierarchy and without "indisputable facts and reasons whose legitimacy is beyond doubt – not mere worries or fears" (§ 5), then freedoms should not be interfered with. Whereas she notes the importance of secularism and equity, these principles do not outweigh religious liberty but must be considered together. Within such a framework, then the state must face something akin to strict scrutiny in U.S. law as Benvenisti urged. Judge Tulkens then considers the majority's analysis of secularism and gender equality in turn.

Against the majority's claim that Sahin failed to "respect the principle of secularism" (§ 7), Judge Tulkens pointed out that there is no evidence that Sahin intended to defy the principle of secularism or that any of her conduct "contravened that principle" (§7). The factual record simply does not fit the Court's interpretation. No evidence had been submitted that Sahin's head-scarf was "ostentatious or aggressive or was used to exert pressure, to provoke a reaction, to proselytise or to spread propaganda and undermined – or was liable to undermine – the convictions of others" and "it has been neither suggested nor demonstrated that there was any disruption in teaching or in every-day life at the University" (§8). If the Turkish government and the Court had the goal of curbing Islamic fundamentalism, "merely wearing the headscarf cannot be associated with fundamentalism and...there is nothing to suggest that the applicant held fundamentalist views" (§10).

Judge Tulkens emphasized that the headscarf can symbolize a plethora of meanings, not merely the oppression of women. Moreover, "what is lacking in this debate is the opinion of women, both those who wear the headscarf and those who choose not to" (§11). Without considering the opinion of women, the Court in the present case and in the previous *Dahlab* decision affixed the hegemonic meaning to the headscarf. According to Judge Tulkens, this was an improper role for the Court, which should instead give deference to the views of the applicant. She wrote, "It is not the Court's role...to determine in a general and abstract way the signification of wearing the headscarf or to impose its viewpoint on the applicant. The applicant, a young adult university student, said – and there is nothing to suggest that she was not telling the truth – that she wore the headscarf of her own free will" (§12). Judge Tulkens calls such supplanting of Ms. Sahin's voice "paternalism" and states forcefully that "equality and non-discrimination are subjective rights which must remain under the control of those who are entitled to benefit from them" (§12).³¹ Ms. Sahin's views were silenced in the majority opinion, and its decision will lead the further

---

³⁰ A similar attempt at harmonizing secularism and the freedom of religion can be seen in the 1989 Conseil d'Etat decision in l'affaire du foulard.
³¹ That rights "must remain under the control" of the Marginalized Other is a central theme of this book and is elaborated in great detail in Chapters 6 and 7.

silencing of thousands of women who will not be able to continue their education. As Judge Tulkens writes, "a tolerance-based dialogue between religions and cultures is an education in itself, so it is ironic that young women should be deprived of that education on account of the headscarf" (§19).

The Aftermath of Sahin

The Sahin case has drawn condemnation from many quarters. Human Rights Watch concluded, "One is struck by the judges' reluctance to really tease out the issues, their too ready willingness to accept the government's assertions, and the presence of some rather glaring internal contradictions" (Sudgeon 2004). The ruling appears to have given momentum to further banning of the headscarf from public spaces in Turkey. "Women who wear the headscarf for religious reasons continue to be excluded from higher education, the civil service, and political life. Female lawyers who wear the headscarf are not permitted to enter courtrooms, and...the Ankara Bar took disciplinary action against a lawyer who wore a headscarf while carrying out her duty to a client in a bailiff's office" (Human Rights Watch 2006). Even speaking out against the ban can lead to harsh consequences: It was reported that "the High Court of Appeals upheld the conviction and 20-month prison sentence of Mehmet Sevket Eygi for writing against the official ban on headscarves at universities and among civil servants" (U.S. State Department 2005). In May 2006, one of the judges who supported the Turkish ban was shot and killed and four other judges were wounded in an attack motivated by the court's decision on the wearing of headscarves while not working.

Many commentators hold out hope that Judge Tulkens' dissent will ultimately prevail, but considering the lopsidedness of the decision, the firm basis in court precedent, and the fact that both chambers supported the decision, such an abrupt change appears unlikely for many years to come. In the meantime, the French ban will surely be appealed to the ECtHR and will almost certainly be upheld. Other nations such as Germany have also considered similar bans and others will be more likely to consider them as anti-immigrant feelings and anti-Muslim sentiments swell. Holding firmly to the consensus doctrine, the ECtHR has given its imprimatur to a possible tidal wave of anti-Muslim feelings, and it could lead to further marginalization of all immigrant groups. This situation begs another question: If citizens are treated this way by the ECtHR and the French government, should one be surprised that national governments and the ECtHR have responded poorly if at all to the needs of asylum seekers, refugees, and undocumented immigrants (cf. Urbinati 2005, 103–104)?

BENHABIB'S DEMOCRATIC ITERATIONS
AND L'AFFAIRE DU FOULARD

In a series of works, Seyla Benhabib has examined the dilemmas of minority rights in contemporary democracies often focusing on how issues of exclusion challenge discursive democratic theories. In *The Rights of Others: Aliens, Residents, and Citizens* she worked through the challenges facing theories of political membership posed by regional integration of Europe and the latest waves of immigration including the headscarf affairs. In the face of these radical socio-political changes, Benhabib correctly claims that "our normative map has not changed" (2004, 6). Instead of offering a new normative map, Benhabib attempts to shape theories of discursive democracy to be more sensitive to current practical, theoretical, and legal problems of the marginalized Other.

Discursive democracy has not always adequately addressed questions of the Other. Instead, it has most often focused on procedural rules that have been predicated on a priori rules of exclusion. Benhabib rightly notes that discursive democratic theory's "exclusion problem" is exacerbated by the simultaneous regional integration and increasing heterogeneity of Europe. In the new Europe, the discursive community is even more out of synch with traditional paradigms of political membership such as state citizenship. In response, Benhabib argues for a theory of "just membership" in which refugees and asylum seekers are admitted through "porous borders" but then must meet certain qualifications to be admitted as a citizen in the democratic community. Although such a theory addresses the evolving problems of political membership, it is not sufficient for tackling other crucial challenges that the conflict between exclusion and minority rights poses to discursive democracy.

To further address these issues, Benhabib develops a theory of democratic iterations, which she defines as:

> Complex processes of public argument, deliberation, and exchange through which universalist rights claims and principles are contested and contextualized, invoked and revoked, posted and positioned, throughout legal and political institutions, as well as in the associations of civil society. These can take place in the "strong" public bodies of legislatures, the judiciary, and the executive, as well as in the informal and "weak" publics of civil society associations and the media. (2004, 179)

She likens her theory of democratic iterations to Robert Cover's theory of jurisgenerative politics, in which the people are the authors of continuously developing norms and laws. These norms and laws, what Cover calls *nomoi*, are developed in "autonomous interpretive communities" (Cover 1983, 14) that can be found in both formal institutions and informal associations. Democratic iterations then involve overlapping sets of norms and laws where any demos is always in relation to other *demoi*. Benhabib supplements Cover's theory by arguing that in the new Europe these overlapping norms and laws are also embedded within a framework of international norms found in human rights treaties and courts, especially the ECtHR. Cosmopolitan norms will thus, in her theory, increasingly seep into national democratic deliberations, causing the demos to "critically examine[s] and alters its own practice of exclusion" and therefore lessen any potential assault on minority rights. The state, however, would continue to exercise its discretion based on its own deliberative process. For example, the international norms found in the 1951 Convention Relating to the Status of Refugees would mandate protection for asylum seekers and refugees, but the democratic legislature would still have deference to set the rules of political membership. The actions of the state will be done, hopefully, through a process of self-critical deliberation to minimize exclusion and make "distinctions fluid and negotiable through processes of continuous and multiple democratic iterations" (Benhabib 2004, 177). However, Benhabib concedes that "the lines separating we and you, us and them, more often than not rest on unexamined prejudices, ancient battles, historical injustices, and sheer administrative fiat" (2004, 178). Benhabib imagines, though, that international norms or some type of self-criticism will ameliorate these "unexamined prejudices."[32]

Benhabib and L'Affaire du Foulard

In the final part of her work, Benhabib applies her theory of democratic iterations to three "complex legal, political, and cultural phenomena," including l'affaire du foulard in France, which she describes as one of the "spectacular examples of multicultural conflict" (2004, 184). She claims that l'affaire is an exemplar of discursive democracy in which "democratic iterations have occurred and collective resignifications have emerged" (2004, 181).

What is striking is how, in crucial ways, Benhabib's analysis of l'affaire adopts the stances of the Stasi Commission and the *Sahin* court. She is overtly aware of the polysemy of the headscarf, what she calls the "complex semiotics

[32] As I discuss in this chapter, Cover is much less optimistic about the openness of the state, especially judges, to competing *nomoi*. He famously writes, "The commitment to a jurisgenerative process that does not defer to the violence of administration is the judge's only hope of partially extricating himself from the violence of the state" (1983, 59).

of dress code" (Benhabib 2002, 95), and argues for a prominent place for the voice of the Other. Nevertheless, her implicit acceptance of the hegemonic discourse derived from her embrace of discursive democracy colors her views on several other aspects of l'affaire so that although she wishes to take the side of the young women, she is not able to do so convincingly and she under-appreciates the growing resistance of the French people to the headscarf.

In her discussion of the three girls from Creil who were ordered to take off their headscarves in 1989, Benhabib argues "that wearing the scarf was a conscious political gesture on their part, a complex act of identification and defiance" (2004, 187). From this reaction to the previous action of the state, she concludes that the girls "and their followers and supporters forced what the French state wanted to view as a private symbol – an individual item of cloth-ing – into the shared public sphere, thus challenging the boundaries between the public and the private" (2004, 187). Whether Benhabib sees this as a per-formative act challenging a hegemonic discourse or frowns on their political move is not clear, but it is questionable whether the French state saw this as a private act or merely "an individual item of clothing." Further, Benhabib emphasizes that the three young women "no longer treated the school as a neutral space of French acculturation, but brought their cultural and reli-gious differences into open manifestation" (2004, 187). Again, it appears that Benhabib is arguing that it was the young women who elevated this issue to a political issue, and she appears to accept the claim that the French school is a "neutral space" that was disturbed by the actions of the three young women.

Although Benhabib argues convincingly for a place for the voices of the young women, with her ideological view of the French "speech community" their voices will not serve to interrogate the *nomoi* of the French state or the French majority, but rather to give an account of their actions to the heg-emonic system. The onus is on the young women who should be held "to account for their actions and doings at least to their school communities, and to encourage discourses among the youth about what it means to be a Muslim citizen in a laic French Republic" (2004, 191). This view results in an asymmetry in which the minority group is required to justify itself and edu-cate the French public, whereas the French public is not required to question its own assumptions of Islam or recent immigrants. Although the "French society would have to learn not to stigmatize and stereotype as 'backward and oppressed creatures' all those who accept the wearing of what appears at first glance to be a religiously mandated piece of clothing," it is "the girls them-selves and their supporters... [who] have to learn to give a justification of their actions with 'good reasons in the public sphere'" (2004, 192). One could argue that if the French society continues to hold such stigmas and stereotypes, it should address those first before asking someone to change the manifestations of their religious beliefs or be called to justify them to the French public. After all, the French beliefs may be coloring the entire issue including their interpretation of the accounts provided by the young women, especially as to whether they are reasonable. As long as the French beliefs about Islam and young Muslim women remain un-interrogated, the views of the young women will most likely not be taken seriously.

This asymmetry is even more apparent as the burden is on the young women to educate the French. "They have to clarify how they intend to treat the beliefs of others from different religions, and how, in effect, they would institutionalize the separation of religion and the state within Islamic tradition" (Benhabib 2004, 192–193). Of course, this turns strict scrutiny analysis on its head. Those whose fundamental rights are being infringed must justify why they wish to do something different from the majority and must provide an alternative means to meet the state's compelling interest. An imperfect analogy might be a search and seizure case in the United States where the one searched in violation of the Fourth Amendment would have the onus to show a less intrusive way of fighting crime.

The failure to question the predominant discourse is also apparent in her subtle and not so subtle judgments about l'affaire. Benhabib praises the French debates as "a series of democratic iterations" (2004, 197), as "a soul-searching on the questions of democracy and difference in a multicultural society" (2004, 191), which she claims included "the intense debate among the French public about the meaning of wearing the veil, to the self-defense of the girls involved and the rearticulation of the meaning of their actions" (2004, 197). The French society is even praised by Benhabib for wanting "more autonomy and egalitarianism in the public sphere than the girls themselves wearing headscarves seem to wish for" (2004, 190).

Benhabib, Multiculturalism, and the Other

The shortcomings of Benhabib's analysis are quite surprising. After all, she has done more than any other theorist to infuse the concerns of a highly nuanced version of multiculturalism into discussions of discursive democracy. Her work *Claims of Culture* convincingly argued that cultures are not monolithic but performative; that is, they are always in flux and being contested just as the *nomoi* in Cover's jurisgenerative politics. So, her recently developed theory of democratic iterations seems to have grown out of her performative view of cultural identity, a view that is quite sensitive to the voice of the concrete Other. As she writes, "Neither the concreteness nor the otherness of the 'concrete other' can be known in the absence of the voice of the other. The viewpoint of the concrete other emerges as a distinct one only as a result of self-definition. It is the other who makes us aware of both her concreteness and her otherness" (Benhabib 1992, 168).

So, how does Benhabib go astray in l'affaire du foulard? Her failure to appreciate the voice of the Other and her consonance with the Stasi Commission and the Sahin case can be traced to the vestiges of Habermas' discursive democracy and Arendtian judgment in her thought.

Benhabib's democratic iterations are closely tied to the main principle of discourse ethics: "Only those norms and normative arrangements are valid which can be agreed to by all concerned under special argumentation situations named discourse" (Benhabib 2002, 107; see also Mendieta 2005). By confining normative and democratic validity to those situations that fit a preconceived definition of discourse, procedural rights, however minimal, trump substantive rights. Though Benhabib ultimately waters down Habermas' emphasis on the procedures of democratic deliberations, she insists that democracy requires a fair and impartial "empty space" in Lefort's sense of the term, where discourse is possible. This requires "impartial institutions in the public sphere and civil society where this struggle for the recognition of cultural differences and the contestation of cultural narratives can take place without domination" (Benhabib 2002, 8). The establishment of impartial institutions will require procedural safeguards founded in a priori rules or "nonnegotiable constitutional essentials" (Bohman 2005, 720) where "the content of such essentials would also be removed from deliberation" (720). This embrace of constitutional essentials recalls Arendt's and Aristotle's insistence that judges agree or have like-mindedness (*homonoia*) about "the realm of great matters," and this will only be possible among those who have shed self-interest. Benhabib, following Arendt and Aristotle, privileged non-interested speech; that is, she sought to "filter out 'strategic reasons'" (2002, 144), to de-legitimize personal motives. Of course, this exclusion will be subject to the pre-existing biases of the judges.

This modicum privileging of procedural rights based on constitutional essentials cauterizes the Other and her substantive rights. The constitutional essentials, as we saw in l'affaire du foulard, most likely contain an original violence, especially as to who can bring forward claims and which claims will be heard. Some groups will always maintain a form of "epistemological authority." As Sanders (1997) writes, "taking deliberation as a signal of democratic practice paradoxically works undemocratically discrediting on seemingly democratic grounds the views of those who are less likely to present their arguments in ways that we recognize as characteristically deliberative" (349). Recall that one commentator remarked in the context of l'affaire du foulard that "under the cover of individual detachment, *one grants the privilege to define France only to the oldest immigrants*" (Latour 2004, emphasis added). This view imbricates the "primary" problem of discursive democracy: "how more of the people who routinely speak less…might take part and be heard and how those who typically dominate might be made to attend to the views of others" (Sanders 1997, 352). Moreover, whereas a theory of democratic iterations is more willing to challenge some constitutional essentials, the cauterization of the Other will continue as the original violence remains un-interrogated. The Marginalized Other will remain *aneu logou*.

THE NEED FOR A CONTINUOUS DECONSTRUCTION OF LAW

As with Arendt, the shortcomings of Benhabib's concrete universalism are not idiosyncratic to an occasional essay but flow from her theoretical stance. In this case, Benhabib's version of a discursive community, like that of many theorists, rests on a tautology. She claims that rights "need to be periodically challenged and rearticulated in the public sphere in order to enrich their original meaning" (2004, 196), but this rearticulation will occur in a context where a priori it has already been determined who will be excluded from the discourse. Put simply, the voiceless will not be in a position to push for their rights, and they most likely will not be given a voice. If they are given a voice, it will be on the terms already determined by the hegemonic discourse and within a constitutional framework that sets the boundaries for proper or reasonable dialogue.

Benhabib holds out hope that law as found in treaties and tribunals will, when needed, outpace the public and be the driver of change, whereas other times the public will push the law. Nonetheless, to the extent that public opinion and law, even cosmopolitan law, arise from a common set of structural or hegemonic factors, they will be mutually reinforcing. This cross-fertilization will be especially likely in the case of a human rights institution such as the ECHR that gives great deference to democracy. As jurisgenerative, law is constantly refreshed, there is no fixed original sense of law, but (and Benhabib does not stress this point enough) the law can also be constantly reinforced through these iterations. I think it is safe to say that the "self-reflexive transformations" in l'affaire du foulard did not end in a progressive development of rights that challenged the discursive community. Instead, the headscarf affairs, especially the *Sahin* decision, seem to exemplify Cover's view that courts are often jurispathic; that is, they can serve to silence discourse. Cover writes, "By exercising its superior brute force...the agency of state law shuts down the creative hermeneutic of principle that is spread throughout our communities" (1983, 44).

Benhabib is correct, democracy must be constantly vigilant, subject to an internal critique and an external critique by international norms, but deconstructionists such as Jacques Derrida would insist that these norms themselves contain an original violence. Human rights of the Other would require an interrogation of all typologies such as the margin of appreciation and consensus doctrines. It requires an interrogation of all hegemonic terms that appear to trump debate such as laïcité, gender equality, and Kemalism. It even requires an interrogation of all procedural rights, including pleas for an "open space" for discursive democracy. Derrida will insist on a more radical critique of democracy and international human rights norms – not to dismiss such norms, but to reinvigorate them. As Derrida says, "one has to constantly re-examine the axiomatics of human rights and transform them, one has to deconstruct them to improve them" (1997, 26).

Is it possible to retain the exalted status of democracy, judgment, human rights law, and constitutional essentials and yet theorize a type of justice that calls the system and its hegemonic terms into question? For Derrida (and Levinas), deconstruction must begin from a transcendent justice that is undeconstructable and thus prior to democracy and all typologies, and yet any reformulation of transcendent justice requires democracy and typologies in order to do justice to justice.

Derrida and the Force of Law

Derrida, like Benhabib, offers extensive meditations on the intersections of the recent disaggregations of citizenship, international law, the potential for democracy to be self-critical, and the rights of the Other, especially in a series of essays and talks after his so-called ethical turn. Here I will focus on his influential essay "Force of Law: The 'Mystical Foundation of Authority,'" what Gayatri Spivak called "the central statement of Derrida's ethical turn" (1999, 426). This essay was originally presented at a symposium at Cardozo School of Law, where Derrida was called to give an account of the relationship between justice and deconstruction. Derrida cryptically concludes, albeit with some reservation, that "deconstruction *is* justice" (1992, 14–15, emphasis added). Derrida reaches this surprising conclusion by making a sharp distinction between justice and law. Law, for Derrida, seems to have two distinguishing features: First, it is enforceable, not that it necessarily is enforced, but that force could be used legitimately on behalf of law; and secondly, it is a human creation so it is deconstructable, it can be critiqued, and it can be improved.

Justice on the other hand, "if there is such a thing,"[33] like one of Plato's forms, is transcendent and thus undeconstructable. It is beyond the reach of human activity and *knowledge*. We can never know the "x of justice" – if we did, then it is deconstructable and then it is not justice. "Wherever one can replace, translate, determine the x of justice, one should say: deconstruction is possible, as impossible, to the extent where there is (undeconstructable) x, thus to the extent (there) where there is (the undeconstructable)" (Derrida 1992, 15).

Derrida's overall framework that will situate deconstruction between law and justice comes into focus. Justice is "outside or beyond law" (1992, 14), and between justice and law is deconstruction. Deconstruction resembles a bridge that attempts to bridge the gap between transcendent justice and human-created law. Derrida writes, "Deconstruction takes place in the interval that separates the undeconstructability of justice from the deconstructability of droit [law]" (1992, 15). Deconstruction is only possible because justice is undeconstructable *and* law is deconstructable. Without the sharp distinction between the two, deconstructionists would have no task,[34] as deconstruction is the tackling in good faith of the aporiai or questions between deconstructable law and transcendent justice. Derrida insists on the etymological meaning of aporiai as "non-roads"; thus, they are questions that must be thought, but they will defy permanent and satisfactory answers. The main aporia is the tension between the undeconstructability of justice and the deconstructability of law: justice should inspire law, but its transcendent nature will resist any (uncomplicated?) application to law. From this aporia, Derrida derives three more specific aporiai that will need to be considered for any deconstruction of law:

> Aporia 1. A judge issuing a decision in order to be fair must follow a rule, but the judge also must consider the singularity of each case so the law must be constantly invented. Since the lawmaker must have freedom to develop the law, the rules must be suspend-able. So, justice involves following rules but at the same time suspending rules. "It must conserve the law and also destroy it or suspend it enough to have to reinvent it in each case" because "each case is other, each decision is different and requires an absolutely unique interpretation." (1992, 23)

[33] Derrida almost always qualified his use of the term justice and other transcendentals with the phrase "if there is such a thing" (*s'il y en a*). He explains, in the context of transcendental forgiveness: "When I say 'if there is such a thing,' I do not mean that I doubt the possible occurrence of such a thing. I mean that if forgiveness happens, this experience should not become the object of a sentence of the kind 'S is p', 'this is, presents itself as forgiveness', because forgiveness should not present itself. If it happens, it should not be in the form of something present" (2001b, 52–53).

[34] John Caputo writes, hopefully with a bit of irony, that justice "is what deconstructors do for a living, how they fill their days, for justice is what deconstruction is" (1997, 133).

Aporia 2. Decisions must be made for justice to be served but decisions are rooted in undecidability and once they are made they become non-decisions. In order for a decision to be a decision, it cannot be based on a legal recipe where the judge applies the law mechanically. "The just decision must be made decisively and is only possible in the consciousness of undecidability." And, as soon as a decision is made it becomes a rule so "it is no longer presently just, fully just" (1992, 24) but even as a rule it still contains "the ghost of the undecidable." This undecidability should call into question any certitude of the justness of the decision. "Its ghostliness deconstructs from within any assurance of presence, any certitude or any supposed criteriology that would assure us of the justice of a decision" (1992, 24–25).

Aporia 3. Justice requires infinite knowledge, but justice demands a speedy trial, it cannot be delayed. As Gladstone said, "Justice delayed, is justice denied." "The just decision is required right away, immediately and always remains to-come" (1992, 26) because it always requires more information and more reflection. Without adequate knowledge and reflection the moment of the decision is madness.

Law requires decisions, rules, and promptness, but justice requires an attention to the singular nature of each case, undecidability, and complete knowledge. At the same time, transcendent justice requires law in order to be realized concretely. It must be universalized into law, and yet this law must continuously be deconstructed by justice in order to make it more just. Justice unsettles all laws, all decisions, all theories, and all typologies. Further, because justice requires law, and law requires and sanctions force, then justice requires force or violence on its behalf. Justice thus can never be attained, or in Levinas' succinct formulation, "justice is always a justice which desires a better justice" (Levinas et al. 1988, 178). Justice must always remain to-come (*a-venir*), and so it cannot be a constative; it cannot be reified as a decision, as a rule, as a formula, or a typology. So, deconstruction is justice in a way; it is the continuous critique of the violence of law in the name of justice. To do justice to justice we must, in the name of justice, deconstruct all pretensions of justice.

A Deconstruction of Founding Violence

In the second section of the essay, Derrida engaged in a sustained reading of Walter Benjamin's influential essay "Critique of Violence." Whereas Derrida overtly analyzes such Benjaminian themes as the general strike and the abolition of the death penalty, he is ultimately engaged in a second reading that further explores the aporiai between deconstruction and justice. Here, though, the main focus has shifted to an analysis of the two types of violence inherent to law: founding violence and conserving violence.

Founding violence is apparent when law is successfully challenged in "terrifying moments" as through general strikes or a revolution. The "successful revolution" will create its own legitimating narrative that justifies its founding violence, but the ghosts of that violence will linger within subsequent law. Violence is then reproduced or conserved through a series of iterations. Derrida writes, "It belongs to the structure of fundamental violence that it calls for the repetition of itself and founds what ought to be conserved" (Derrida 1992, 38). Indeed, founding and conserving violence bleed into one another. The founding violence contaminates the conserving violence, and the conserving violence constantly re-imagines the founding violence at the same time it reinforces it. Derrida labels this "the paradox of iterability" (1992, 43), where "iterability requires the origin to repeat itself originarily, to alter itself so as to have the value of origin, that is, to conserve itself" (1992, 43). Such conserving violence will necessarily seep into new spheres of society – spheres never implicated during the founding moments.

Law seeks to conserve itself. "Law's interest" then is not "just and legal ends (*Rechtszwecke*) but law itself" (Derrida 1992, 33). Law preserves itself through a monopoly of violence. Thus, anyone or anything that threatens the law is deemed to be violent, and anyone who disrupts law's monopoly of violence is literally an outlaw. Law's greatest fear then is not the criminal enterprise, which law is equipped to handle, but the disruption of the rule of law itself. Such a disruption is epitomized for Benjamin by the "general strike," which as opposed to the lawful strike threatens "to create a revolutionary situation in which the task will be to found a new droit [law]" (Derrida 1992, 35). By operating outside of the established rule of law, the new state is always founded in violence.

Alongside law's incessant violence, Derrida finds an incessant interruption of law. Law's disruption occurs more often than the infrequent general strike or successful revolution. Even though law seeks to exclude all outlaws, it is filled with gaps or moments of discretion during which law is suspended and thus must be created. As we saw earlier in this chapter, any true decision qua decision must be rooted in undecidability, it must involve the suspension of the law. In the moment of law's suspension, law relies totally on the performative act of the individual judge (Derrida 1992, 36). Thus, Derrida discovers an "extraordinary paradox": that law can only be transcendent to the extent that it relies on the individual immanent judge who must found law. Derrida writes: "The law is transcendent and theological, and so always to come always promised, because it is immanent, finite and so already past. Every 'subject' is caught up in this aporetic structure in advance" (Derrida 1992, 36). This suspension of law: "This moment always takes place and never takes place in a presence. It is the moment in which the foundation of law remains suspended in the void or over the abyss, suspended by a pure performative act that would not have to answer to or before anyone."

Such a suspension of the law in the name of justice by an immanent judge can be seen in the famous response of Judge Stern in the extraordinary *Tiede* case. This case stemmed from the prosecution of two East Germans who in 1978 attempted to flee to the West by hijacking a plane to a U.S. military base in West Germany using a toy pistol. When the West German government refused to prosecute the two, U.S. District Judge Herbert Stern was appointed to hear the case in Berlin. After countless battles with the U.S. government, including Stern's insistence that the trial proceed as a jury trial with due process guarantees, Stern was faced with handing down a sentence for one of the defendants on the charge of hostage taking. Stern announces his sentence aiming it directly at the U.S. authorities:

> Gentlemen [addressing the State Department and Justice Department lawyers], I will not give you this defendant....I have kept him in your custody now for nine months, nearly....You have persuaded me. I believe, now, that you recognize no limitations of due process....Under those circumstances, who will be here to protect Tiede if I give him to you for four years? Viewing the Constitution as non-existent, considering yourselves not restrained in any way, who will stand between you and him? What judge? What independent magistrate do you have here? What independent magistrate will you permit here?
>
> When a judge sentences, he commits a defendant to the custody – in the United States he says, "I commit to the custody of the Attorney General of the United States" – et cetera. Here I suppose he says, I commit to the custody of the Commandant, or the Secretary of State, or whatever....**I will not do it**. Not under these circumstances....I sentence this defendant to time served. You...are a free man right now. (Stern 1984, 370, quoted in Cover 1986, 824–825, emphasis added)

Judge Stern with his simple but forceful "I will not do it" suspends the law, creates a space of undecidability and inserts what most would agree to be a just sentence. More ominously though, the interstices of law can also be filled by those seeking to preserve and extend the original violence of the law. Benjamin provides the example of the police who, akin to Giorgio Agamben's (2005) recent formulations, negotiate the interstices or states of exception within the law. The police as lawmakers "are no longer content to enforce the law, and thus to conserve it; they invent it, they publish ordinances, they inter-vene whenever the legal situation isn't clear to guarantee security" (Derrida 1992, 42). Derrida goes further and sees Benjamin's police as a metaphor, representing all institutions and customs that support the force or violence of law. The police "become hallucinatory and spectral because they haunt everything; they are everywhere, even there where they are not" (1992, 45). "They are present...wherever there is preservation of the social order" (44). So, the distinction between founding and conserving violence is not clear cut. Those whose task is to conserve the original violence are also engaged in creating law, and it follows that even those who are the greatest lawmakers (Solon, Washington, Nkrumah, etc.) are conserving a pre-original violence. These interstices within law point to the iterability of law but also point to the interruptions within law, where law can be supplemented with transcendent justice by the singular judge such as Judge Stern.

Then, in a difficult passage, Benjamin claims that the police in democra-cies commit more violence than those under authoritarian regimes. In the latter regimes, violence from the police is expected, "in democracy, on the other hand, violence is no longer accorded to the spirit of the police....It is exercised illegitimately, especially when instead of enforcing the law, the police make the law" (Derrida 1992, 46). In a democracy, the violence of the law is surreptitious and thus more violent because it is not sanctioned by law itself. It is a non-sanctioned founding violence that masquerades as a conserving violence. This may be best understood through Benjamin's critique of parliamentarian democracies in which the original violence is concealed by "the supplement of a substitute" and the "original violence is consigned to oblivion" (1992, 47). Thus, it appears to be in the nature of parliaments to "live in forgetfulness of the violence from which they are born....[I]nstead of coming to decisions commensurable or proportional to their violence and worthy of it, they practice the hypocritical politics of compromise" (1992, 47). It seems that democracies, like law itself, resist ethi-cal critiques, because they "claim(s) to recognize and defend said humanity as end, in the person of each individual" (1992, 41). So, Derrida concludes that no democracy will be "worthy of the name" (1992, 46) but can only be a democracy *a-venir* (to-come). It is up to the deconstructionist or the indi-vidual immanent judge such as Judge Stern, or even Judge Tulkens in the *Sahin* case, to constantly call into question or deconstruct the violence of the law even when it is concealed by the good conscience of democracy. Moreover, for Derrida, law is only deconstructable to the extent that it is exposed to undeconstructable justice.

TRANSCENDENTAL JUSTICE, DEMOCRATIC ITERATIONS, AND L'AFFAIRE DU FOULARD

The philosophies of Benhabib and Derrida share many commonalities. With their emphases on the authorship of law, they both hold out hope for a democracy *a-venir*, that is, a perfectibility of democracy that will never be perfect. Each applies the structure of iterability, which is akin to Robert Cover's jurisgenerative politics, to show how democracies evolve over time but remain, in Derrida's terms, haunted by their origins. For each, how democracies address human rights, especially of the Other, is crucial for determining progress toward this perfectibility.

Whereas each would agree that law's deconstructibility signals that laws can be improved, Benhabib is more optimistic that this evolution will lead to a progressive development of human rights. Derrida is more concerned about democracies conserving their original violence, and thus he, like Benjamin, remains especially skeptical of democracy's claims to serve humanity. These claims, themselves, (of necessity perhaps) are forms of conserving violence that are concealing and reinforcing founding violence. In the headscarf affairs, democracy's founding violence was not seriously interrogated. In the French case, the founding violence could likely be traced to the excesses of the nineteenth-century battles between royalists and republicans and the original compromises with the Church. France created a secular/neutral state that is not truly secular/neutral despite extraordinary claims of neutrality (such as its claim that it contains no minorities). Concomitantly, the founding violence of the European Court of Human Rights can most likely be traced to its founding at the onset of the Cold War in a time when extra-national judicial legitimacy appeared anachronistic. This led to an undue emphasis on democracy and deference to member states through the margin of appreciation and consensus doctrines.

To call into question such violence in the guise of serving the people, it is necessary to make "decisions commensurable or proportional to their violence and worthy of it" (Derrida 1992, 47). Recall that according to Derrida's first aporia, judicial decisions, when they are truly decisions, by their very nature must be madness. Here were have yet a higher type of madness, calling into question the conserving violence of a democratically enacted edict. For Derrida, the only justification for such deconstruction of democratically enacted law is a type of transcendent justice. The headscarf affairs and Benhabib's analysis suggest that Derrida is correct; democracy and even human rights need to be called into question by an a priori, by the transcendent, that is by the Other, or in Derrida's phrase, *le tout autre*, the wholly other.

Not surprisingly, many scholars have criticized Derrida's transcendental view of justice for not being applicable to the real world of politics. For instance, Nancy Fraser has written "so long as deconstruction remains committed to privileging even negative transcendental reflection, so long as it continues to concentrate its efforts on disclosing the prior, enabling *Abgrund* behind every merely critical normative judgment about every merely ontic state of affairs, it will never get to ethics or politics" (1997, 159). Can transcendental justice provide enough of a ground for making complex political decisions as in the l'affaire du foulard? When law is suspended, be it by the immanent judge or by the police, what will guide the decision? Will that decision be grounded in justice or will it conserve original violence? Must the distrust of politics and law that motivates Derrida's search for a transcendental justice ultimately undermine any attempts to extend his philosophy to the political sphere as Fraser suggests? Can a type of transcendence be described that will adequately deconstruct *and* reinvigorate human rights law?

I contend that the answers to these questions hinge on the extent to which the transcendent Other can be equated with the Marginalized Other whose voice is so starkly absent from the Little Rock crisis and the headscarf debates. For Levinas, transcendence manifests itself through an ethical response to the face of the marginalized human Other, that is, the widow, orphan, and stranger; and thus his formulation lends itself to at least a modicum of normativity. Because Derridean justice shares so many Levinasian themes and was often developed in the context of a homage to Levinas, it is easy to conflate Derridean justice with Levinasian ethics, but they may not be equivalent.[35] After all, Derrida never strictly equates them, and when he draws analogies between his justice and Levinas' ethics, it is always with great hesitancy and serious reservations. As we shall see, the Derridean *tout autre* is not the marginalized Other. Indeed, in the next chapter I will argue that it risks, like the banisters of Arendt and Benhabib, calling the marginalized Other to its tribunal and thus, further cauterizing the Other.

---

[35] For example, Plant concludes: "All the conceptual building blocks of Derrida's analyses are nevertheless already present in Levinas' thinking...the real value of Derrida's recent work lies in his development, refinement, and cautious re-articulation of the Levinasian themes examined above" (2003a, 443). Interestingly, in "Force of Law" Derrida is tempted to compare his indeconstructible justice to Levinas' formulation but gives up after briefly quoting a few Levinasian texts.

Phenomenology of the Saturated Other

3

Derrida, Levinas, and the Rights of the Other

The previous two chapters outlined the concrete universalisms found in Hannah Arendt's and Seyla Benhabib's writings. Whereas they offer important theoretical frameworks for understanding judgment and democracy, the examples of the Little Rock crisis and l'affaire du foulard illustrate that such concrete universalisms with their reliance on un-interrogated typologies have a tendency to cauterize the Other and thus must be subject to a continuous deconstruction. The two chapters of Part II will use the writings of Derrida, Emmanuel Levinas, Jean-Luc Marion, and Enrique Dussel to develop a concrete universalism founded in the encounter with the Marginalized Other. Their philosophies of the Other share the same basic structure; the Other is transcendent to politics, ontology, and law, and thus is in a position to question all typologies as well as democracy, human rights, and even the pronouncements of the Arendtian judge. Nevertheless, their ultimate conceptions of the Other vary widely. Derrida's phenomenology relies much more on a "pure" transcendence, whereas Levinas' and especially Dussel's works seek transcendence in the concrete marginalized Other human person.

This chapter begins by exploring Derrida's and Levinas' conceptions of the Other. I argue that Derrida's conception of the *tout autre* relies too much on an abstract or "desertified" (Kearney 1999) account of the Other and thus has an asymptotic relationship with immanence; that is, transcendence approaches but never quite intersects with immanence. Levinas' conception of the Other much more clearly refers to the concrete marginalized human Other, but, as we shall see, his writings provide only a modicum of normativity. This becomes clear in the concluding section of the chapter that compares the writings of Levinas and Arendt on human rights and crimes against humanity, including Levinas' infamous interview discussing the massacre of Palestinians at the Sabra and Chatila refugee camps in 1982.

DERRIDA AND LE TOUT AUTRE

For Derrida, transcendence must mean transcendence. Derrida attempts to remove all vestiges of presence from his conception of transcendence, what he labels the *tout autre*. All we can know about the totally other is that it is wholly other (*le tout autre est tout autre* – "the wholly other is totally other"). The *tout autre* must be totally unknowable and un-nameable. It is beyond totality, beyond presence, beyond intentionality. If all we can say about the *tout autre* is that it is *tout autre*, it cannot be located; it cannot be constrained by thought. To say that God comes to mind in the experience of the face-to-face relationship as Levinas does in his later writings would impermissibly constrain the *tout autre*. So, despite many affinities, Derrida's *tout autre* is not the human Other. It cannot even privilege the human Other, especially any Other imbued with ontological categories such as the marginalized Other.

Without a location for transcendence, at most Derrida can develop a framework that highlights the gap between the *tout autre* and the world of immanence. This framework or typology most likely encompasses all "horizons of the same type," one that could be applied without a concern or at least a special concern for the marginalized Other of Levinas (or of Little Rock or France).

In his later writings, Derrida applies his typology of transcendence to a range of other quasi-transcendentals. As "justice" in "The Force of Law" essay was undeconstructable, Derrida writes of analogous transcendent conceptions of hospitality, the gift, forgiveness, cosmopolitanism, and democracy. The task of deconstruction then is to negotiate the aporiai or non-roads between the non-deconstructable or purified conception of each of these terms and its immanent manifestation or everyday meaning. It is deconstruction's job to make the transcendent version of each of the quasi-transcendentals immanent, or at least to call forth the transcendent version to unsettle the more immanent version. One wonders, though, if the absolute transcendence of Derrida's quasi-transcendentals makes this task impossible.

It seems that all that can be known of the figures of the impossible, *if they exist*, is the structure of transcendence, a structure that appears to be knowable and thereby reducible despite some recurrent aporiai. Derrida's aporia of impossibility can become reified into a typology that can be applied to all quasi-transcendentals. After all, how else could such disparate terms as cosmopolitanism, justice, democracy, forgiveness, and so forth, share the same structure? Thus, instead of the gift or forgiveness being called into question by the Other, the concrete Other along with much of reality is called to account by Derrida's typology of transcendence.

If the Other is the totally Other, as a transcendental always seeking to be more transcendental, then one also wonders whether it will ever affect immanence with anything more than a frisson or what Levinas has called a "moment of negation" (Levinas 1981, 194), and thus, it most likely will be ill-suited for developing a politics or even an ethics. This moment of negation may suspend, for a moment, the certainty of any decision, but most likely will not even be capable of providing a modicum of normativity or substance to any decision. Although it may introduce a certain madness to any decision, I seriously question whether the *tout autre* has the power to call into question the ego, democracy, or human rights let alone provide any means for their reinvigoration. The hegemonic system, the violence of democracy and human rights, is so proficient at reproducing itself, at conserving its violence, that more than moments of negation are needed to "get to ethics or politics" (Fraser 1997, 159).

This is perhaps most apparent in Derrida's well-known discussion of forgiveness. As expected, Derrida finds that forgiveness shares an identical structure with all the other figures of the impossible. Absolute forgiveness as undeconstructable would be to forgive the unforgivable with no expectation of reward, whereas our everyday or deconstructable sense of forgiveness is to forgive the forgivable. "These two poles, the unconditional and the conditional are absolutely heterogeneous and must remain irreducible to one another. They are nonetheless indissociable" (Derrida 2001, 44–45). So, forgiveness does not accurately describe our everyday sense of the term, and the only forgiveness worthy of the name must be absolutely heterogeneous to immanence and politics. Indeed, forgiveness as a transcendental "is not, it should not be, normal, normative, normalizing" (32).

Derrida imagines that unconditional forgiveness may be approached in the most harrowing of circumstances. "We can imagine that someone, a victim of the worst, himself, a member of his family, in his generation or preceding, demands that justice be done, that the criminals appear before a court, be judges and condemned by a court – and **yet in his heart forgives**" (2001, 54, emphasis added). This exceptional and highly rare type of forgiveness must remain private. For if it was brought into the world of politics, it would become tainted by a series of conditionalities and would no longer be pure forgiveness. Here, Derrida agrees with Arendt that such a private act of forgiveness (just as Christian goodness as exemplified by the Melville character Billy Budd) must remain private; it must remain in the realm of saints. Indeed, one of Derrida's few political principles is to call for sealing the political realm from such a secret.

> The secret of this experience remains. It must remain intact, inaccessible to law, to politics, even to morals: absolute. But I would make of this transpolitical principle a political principle, a political rule or position taking; it is necessary also in politics to respect the secret, that which exceeds the political or that which is no longer in the juridical domain. . . . [T]his zone of experience remains inaccessible, and I must respect its secret. What remains to be done, then, publicly, politically, juridically, also remains difficult. (Derrida 2001, 54–55)

Not surprisingly, then, when Derrida in the same essay ponders the possibility of forgiveness for the series of crimes against humanity in Algeria, he does not rely on this secret forgiveness but instead argues that these are very political decisions that must be done in madness: "One is never sure of making the just choice; one never knows, one will never know with what is called knowledge" (Derrida 2001, 56). He poignantly describes this madness as "infinitely distressing. It is night" (56). This is not to say that quasi-transcendental forgiveness does not have some political import. Just as Arendt insisted that private emotions be filtered through the practical reason of the judge, Derrida will insist that the private act of forgiveness be filtered through the responsible acts of the judge-deconstructionist.

Arendt and Derrida, from diametrically different motives, insist on the exclusion of the transcendent from the political sphere. Arendt argued that transcendence as shown in unconditional forgiveness, just as Christian goodness as exemplified by Melville's character Billy Budd, and other private emotions would be inappropriate for the political realm with its emphasis on action, speech, and judgment. Derrida, too, wishes to remove the transcendental from the political sphere, not necessarily to purify politics, but to purify the transcendent. Two metaphors come to mind. Arendt's hero appears to be Judge Atlas (not Dworkin's Hercules) who is tasked with keeping the heavens (the transcendent) from reaching the agonistic debates on earth. Derrida's hero would be the deconstructionist who, like a mad scientist trying to capture lightning in a bottle, continuously reaches to the skies hoping to grasp the asymptote and pull it to the immanent, at least for a split second.

So, forgiveness as a quasi-transcendental opens the deconstructionist to the madness of a decision, or a state of exception. It breaks down any recipe for forgiveness, or any forgiveness done in good conscience, but it provides little guidance as to when or how to forgive. The deconstructionist judge will have precious little guidance from the (quasi-) transcendental in making decisions as any guidance will remove the madness of the decision and, thus, fail to do justice to the (quasi-) transcendental.

LEVINAS AND THE OTHER

Levinas, in his groundbreaking ethical writings, also relies on the same general structure of transcendence laid out by Derrida in "The Force of Law" and other writings. The Other is transcendent to politics, law, rights, and typologies and thus can call these into question. However, instead of Derrida's "desertified" account of the Other that offers little normative guidance, Levinas finds the locus for transcendence in the face of the concrete human Other, what following the Torah, he often refers to as the widow, orphan, and stranger. Despite this emphasis on the face of the concrete Other, a tension remains in Levinas' writings between a more formal or abstract account of the Other and a more concrete account of the Other, which would be more amenable to reinvigorating human rights law. The conflation between these two becomes most apparent in his infamous remarks on the Palestinian question in which Levinas is unable to equate the Palestinian victims with the Other who demands an infinite ethical responsibility. I will argue that to the extent that Levinas relies on the more formal account of the Other, his philosophy will be insufficient for a reinvigoration of human rights law. Before exploring these issues, I will first develop his ethics of the Other founded on transcendence and the crucial but secondary role that political institutions including human rights law play in his philosophy.

Transcendence and the Other

I argue, with admitted violence to his work, that transcendence plays two major interrelated roles in Levinas' "phenomenology" of the face-to-face relationship. These are often not analytically distinct, and in the course of his writings, depending on the context, Levinas will emphasize one more than the other.

First, the phenomenological structure of the ego's exposure to the face of the Other mirrors Descartes' "idea of the infinite" from the "Third Meditation" as "a thinking that finds itself thinking more than it can embrace, the blinding bedazzlement of the gaze by an excess of light and a bursting of knowledge in adoration" (Levinas 1999a, 4). Clearly Levinas refers here to what medieval scholastics labeled a hyper-presence that is paradoxically both present and cannot be reduced to presence. It is a "presence stronger and more venerable than the totality . . . that cannot . . . be peremptorily relegated to presence" (Levinas 1999a, 4).

The hyper-presence of the face sets Levinas' ethics in motion. This face that bedazzles the ego and overwhelms its categories and intentionality is pure expression. It paradoxically expresses both weaknesses and force. Indeed, the nakedness of the face is its force. What calls the ego into question is "not the knowledge of his character or his social position or his needs, but his nudity as the needy one; the destitution inscribed upon his face" (Levinas 1998b, 99). The face is so naked that it calls the ego to an infinite and un-substitutable responsibility: "In its mortality, the face before me summons me, calls for me, begs for me, as if the invisible death that must be faced by the Other, pure otherness, separated, in some way, from any whole, were my business" (Levinas 1989b, 83). Levinas often wrote that the first commandment of the face is "Thou Shall Not Kill." When confronted and bedazzled by the face of the Other, the ego is no longer concerned primarily with itself and its suffering but is overwhelmed by the suffering of the Other. The ego must not only refrain from killing the Other, the ego must consider whether its everyday existence isn't already causing the Other to suffer. Levinas writes, "My being-in-the-world or my 'place in the sun', my being at home, have these not also been the usurpation of spaces belonging to the other man whom I have already oppressed or starved, or driven out into a third world; are they not acts of repulsing, excluding, exiling, stripping, killing" (Levinas 1989b, 82)? To ameliorate this suffering, "the ego must respond concretely to the Other: 'to give, to be for the other, in spite of oneself, but while interrupting the for-oneself, is to take the bread out of one's mouth, to feed the hunger of the other with my own abstinence" (Levinas 1981, 56).

In addition to the hyper-presence that triggers an infinite responsibility, a feeding "with my own abstinence," transcendence in the form of a higher power also appears in the ego's response for the Other. In this response, in this disinterestedness, the ego testifies to that which is beyond Being or what Levinas increasingly labeled "the word of God." Without the strength derived from the divine, the ego could not answer the infinite command of the Other. Only "on the basis of this obedience" (Levinas 1999a) does God who "remains absolutely other or transcendent" (Levinas 1998a, 219) come to mind. Here, Levinas' God as "absolutely other" begins to resemble Derrida's *tout autre*. This second type of transcendence has opened Levinas' phenomenology to the critique of being a thinly disguised theology. Alain Badiou (2001) writes of Levinas' thought, "There can be no finite devotion to the non-identical if it is not sustained by the infinite devotion of the principle to that which subsists outside it. There can be no ethics without God the ineffable" (22). Badiou is well aware that Levinas' ethical thought does not begin from a proof of God's existence, but God appears through the ethical relationship with the human Other. God cannot be removed from the equation; it is God that sustains the original ethical relationship. As Levinas writes,

"The problem of transcendence and of God and the problem of subjectivity irreducible to essence – irreducible to essential immanence – go together" (Levinas 1981, 17). Through the hyper-presence of the Other and the ego's response, transcendence, God, and the irreducible Other "go together." However, Levinas also warns that "the passage from the Other to divinity is a second step, and one must be careful to avoid stumbling by taking too large a step" (Levinas 1989c, 246).[1]

By "founding" his ethics on the transcendence of the face-to-face relationship, Levinas, like Derrida, attempts to establish a form of transcendence that calls into question or deconstructs democracy, human rights, and all typologies and at the same time provides a rethinking and resuscitation of these terms. However, by founding it ultimately on theology, Badiou would argue that Levinas risks invoking the critique of deconstruction outlined by Nancy Fraser in Chapter 1, that it cannot provide any positive foundation for ethics, politics, or human rights. I will argue that to the extent that Levinas' conception of transcendence mirrors that of Derrida, it will not be able to answer Fraser's critique and will be mostly inapplicable to politics. Levinas sketches the structure of a politics based on this transcendence that originates in the face of the Other, but the success of this endeavor will hinge on the type of transcendence that Levinas relies on.

Law and Institutions

Whereas the original ethical relationship with the Other incessantly calls into question all institutions and all typologies, it also requires institutions and law in order to be realized. This is readily apparent from Levinas' phenomenology of the third person, the Third (*le tiers*).[2] When approached with one Other, Levinas' philosophy is clear: the ego is called to an infinite and concrete ethical responsibility. However, the ego is always already confronted with other Others – "in the very appearance of the other the third already regards me" (Levinas 1998b, 82). With the inevitable approach of the Third, the infinite and concrete ethical relationship becomes much more complex. Levinas poignantly asks, "Can that responsibility toward the other who

---

[1] Marion (2000) rightly connects the "anonymity" problem in Levinas' phenomenology with the "theology" problem: "Who (or what) calls – God and his word, or the Other and his or her face? As clarifying and magnificent as it is, does not the emergence of the theme of the à-Dieu [to God] nonetheless hypostatize this ambiguity to the point of rendering it exemplary and insurmountable?" (228).

[2] For extensive discussions of Levinas' phenomenology of the Third, see Simmons (1999) and Simmons (2003).

faces me, that response to the face of my fellow man ignore the third party who is also my other? Does he not also concern me?" (Levinas 1998d, 202). The ego is called to respond infinitely to each and every Other. The appearance of the Third calls the ego to make judgments, to make decisions as to who to respond to first. The ego must also take sides in conflicts between the Others. "The right of the unique, the original right of man, calls for judgment and, hence, objectivity, objectification, thematization, synthesis. It takes institutions to arbitrate and a political authority to support all this" (Levinas 1998c, 195). From the original ethical relationship, Levinas derives a need for political institutions, for law, and for the liberal state in order to respond to the Other and the Third.

Pace Hobbes and Locke, the raison d'être of the liberal state is not self-preservation or protection of the ego's property, but it stems from the original ethical relationship. As in Derrida's analysis from "The Force of Law," the undeconstructable ethical relationship requires law and institutions to do justice to justice. At the same time, the original undeconstructable ethics will also require that the same laws and institutions be suspendable to do justice to justice. As Derrida writes, justice "must conserve the law and also destroy it or suspend it enough to have to reinvent it in each case" (Derrida 1992, 23). So Levinas calls for a liberal state, but it is one "always concerned about its delay in meeting the requirement of the face of the Other" (1998d, 203). Similarly, Levinas will call for human rights, but human rights law and institutions must derive their sustenance from the original face-to-face relationship with the Other. As such, human rights law is needed, and yet it must be suspendable in order to do justice to the Other.

LEVINAS AND ARENDT ON HUMAN RIGHTS

Levinas never fully fleshed out the relationship between the original ethical relationship with the Other and political institutions such as human rights law beyond the preceding structure. In the remaining sections of this chapter, I will discuss his writings on human rights in the context of Arendt's famous discussion of rights from *The Origins of Totalitarianism*. I hope to make three points here: First, Levinas' (and Derrida's) emphasis on transcendence usefully supplements Arendt's (and Benhabib's) concerns about the need for a new guarantee for human rights; that is, Levinas' thought provides a modicum of normativity on which to reinvigorate human rights. Second, Arendt's (and Benhabib's) emphasis on restoring the political sphere, with its important role for active citizenship and political legitimacy, is a useful supplement to Levinas' (and Derrida's) under-developed political thought. Finally, Levinas' conception of transcendence, although it provides a modicum of normativity, is insufficient by itself for reinvigorating human rights law because it often emphasizes the formal structure of transcendence (as with Derrida's *tout autre*) instead of the hyper-presence of the Other. This will be most apparent through an analysis of his infamous remarks about the 1982 massacre of Palestinians at the refugee camps of Sabra and Chatila.

First, I will compare Arendt and Levinas on the rights of man, more specifically, their analyses of two apparent hendiades (plural of hendiadys; a coupling "in which the first term is actually always already contained in the second" [Agamben 1996, 161]): the "rights of man and citizen" in the French Declaration and Levinas' "rights of man and the Other."[3] The second terms "citizen" and the "Other" both already contain the first, the rights of man; that is, they are subsumed by the first and no longer have a separate existence. For Arendt, the rights of man should be primordial, but historically the rights of the citizen have taken precedence. For Levinas, the rights of the Other should be primordial, but historically the rights of man have prevailed. For both, the second terms must be strengthened to ensure that they serve as a check against the rights of the citizen and the rights of man, respectively. I will propose another hendiadys as a provisional synthesis: the right to have rights and the rights of the Other with the rights of the Other as a check on the right to have rights. This synthesis will serve as the broad theoretical framework for the remainder of this work, but both Levinas' rights of the Other and Arendt's right to have rights will need to be rethought based on the phenomenology of the Saturated Other that I develop in the next chapter.

The First Hendiadys: Arendt's The Rights of Man and the Citizen

Hannah Arendt takes seriously the hendiadys, mostly neglected since the early writings of Karl Marx, in the title of the French Declaration ("*The Rights of Man and the Citizen*"). She argues that by grounding the rights of man in sovereignty and therefore national citizenship, in the third article of the Declaration ("The principle of all sovereignty resides essentially in the nation. No body nor individual may exercise any authority which does not proceed directly from the nation."), citizenship became the sine qua non of human rights – "from then on human rights were protected and enforced only as national rights" (Arendt 1951, 230). So in the wake of World War I, as nation-states disintegrated, removing citizenship from millions, the only guarantee for rights collapsed. The inalienable rights of man were shown to be

[3]   An expanded version of this argument can be found in Simmons (2006).

	Normally Privileged Term that Tends to Subsume the Second	Term that Needs to Be Strengthened so it Retains an Independent Existence and is Not Subsumed
Arendt's Reading of the "Declaration of the Rights of Man and of the Citizen (Declaration des droits de 1'Homme et du citoyen)	Rights of the Citizen	Rights of Man (Arendt's "Right to Have Rights")
Levinas' "Rights of Man and the Rights of the Other"	Rights of Man (Arendt's "Right to Have Rights")	Rights of the Other
Note: The rights of man will continue to be subsumed into the rights of the citizen, unless there is a prior foundation for the rights of man, namely the rights of the Other.		
My Synthesis: A Third Hendiadys with the Rights of the Marginalized Other as Primordial	Rights of Man (The Right to Have Rights—the right for everyone to have a voice, define oneself, and define their rights)	Rights of the Marginalized Other (The Marginalized Other having a Privileged Place to have a voice, define oneself, and define their rights)
The rights of man in my hendiadys, are preceded by duties. Those within the political community have a duty to respond to the Marginalized others, that is, they have a duty to patiently listen to the Other, assist in the deconstruction of the system that marginalizes them, and to work with them to realize their *proyectos de la vida.*		

FIGURE 3.1. Competing hendiades. Hendiades are couplings "in which the first term is actually always already contained in the second" (Agamben 1996, 161). One term is always at risk of being subsumed in the second, but according to Arendt and Levinas, they must remain separate.

illusory when nation-states were faced with millions of stateless or denationalized people. From the perspective of nation-states, non-citizens could only be managed in terms of citizenship, that is, through asylum or assimilation. However, the sheer numbers of refugees precluded such responses; and without the guarantees of the state through citizenship, millions became rightless and human rights discourse became "hopeless idealism or fumbling feeble-minded hypocrisy":

> The incredible plight of an ever-growing group of innocent people was like a practical demonstration of the totalitarian movements' cynical claims that no such things as inalienable rights existed and that the affirmations of the democracies to the contrary were mere prejudice, hypocrisy, and cowardice in the face of the cruel majesty of the new world. The very phrase "human rights" became for all concerned – victims, persecutors, and onlookers alike – the evidence of hopeless idealism or fumbling feeble-minded hypocrisy. (Arendt 1951, 269)

The title of the 1789 Declaration would suggest that those who have lost their rights as citizens could, at minimum, claim their rights as men; but instead, "the world found nothing sacred in the abstract nakedness of being human." Indeed, "the abstract nakedness of being nothing but human was their greatest danger" (Arendt 1951, 299–300). Even the right of asylum with its "long and sacred history" (280) could not guarantee the rights of man from the onslaught of totalitarianism.

Arendt argues that this stripping of rights points to the need for "a right to have rights," (177) that is, a right to belong to a political community in the Aristotelian sense, "a place in the world which makes opinions significant and actions effective" (Arendt 1951, 296). This original right to participate in a political community would then lead to action and speech by which additional rights could be secured that would guarantee human dignity. Without a political community, on the other hand, without law, the refugees' freedom was "illusory because they have no place to go, and their freedom of opinion is a fool's freedom, for nothing they think matters anyhow.... They are deprived, not of the right to freedom, but of the right to action; not of the right to think whatever they please, but of the right to opinion" (Arendt 1951, 296). Deprived of citizenship and the "right to action," the stateless literally became *aneu logou*, that is, without speech. In short, they have no agency, they are pure naked humanity, and they merely exist in "a peculiar state of nature" (Arendt 1951, 300). They are cauterized in the three senses developed earlier in this work: They are branded as inferior, they are sealed off from the polis through forced emigration or placement in camps, and those in the polis deaden their feelings toward them; they can be disposed of in good conscience.

In the aftermath of millions of former citizens becoming *aneu logou*, Arendt pleads for a new foundation for the rights of man – based **not** on an extra-political solution as Levinas and Derrida suggest, but a reinvigoration of the political sphere to restore the right to have rights.

> Human dignity needs a **new guarantee** which can be found only in a new **political principle**, in a new law on earth, whose validity this time must comprehend the whole of humanity while its power must remain strictly limited, rooted in and controlled by newly defined territorial entities. (Arendt 1951, ix; cf. Isaac 1996, emphases added).

This quote reveals several important tensions in Arendt's thought – tensions that, in a positive light, evince her (stubborn) willingness to tackle political complexities. For example, from her understanding of interwar European history, Arendt seeks a universalism that applies to "the whole of humanity," but this universalism will be "strictly limited" by the realities of state sovereignty. Although Arendt is calling for a challenging or "perforation" (Agamben 1996, 164) of the nation-state, she is also well aware, as a practical matter, that such rights must remain tied to "newly defined territorial entities." She writes: "The restoration of human rights, as the recent example of the State of Israel proves, has been achieved so far only through the restoration or the establishment of national rights" (Arendt 1951, 299).

The alternative would be for any new extra-territorial rights (the "new law on earth") to be legitimized by a new transnational political community such as a new type of supranational government or citizenship. However, Arendt's paradigm for a political community is the Greek polis, a small community of like-minded elites who share a common world. The chances of instituting such a worldwide polis in her day or ours would be remote.

So, despite her initial concerns drawn from the interwar European experience, the rights of man will continue to be tied to the rights of the national citizen for the foreseeable future.

This is most apparent in her hesitance to embrace an international criminal court in the aftermath of the Eichmann trial. Arendt bemoaned the appearance of partisan judgment as the Israeli tribunal focused on crimes against Jews and failed to pay due respect to the wider crimes against humanity where the international order was attacked. This failure to see Eichmann's crimes as a crime against humanity, or more aptly the newly defined crime of genocide, prevented the court from breaking new legal ground by claiming that it was exercising universal jurisdiction under the Genocide Convention. Further, Arendt wished the Israelis were in a position to turn Eichmann over to an international criminal tribunal that could more properly try him for crimes against humanity as advocated by her mentor Karl Jaspers. Arendt critiques the court for such lapses because "the very monstrousness of the events is 'minimized' before a tribunal that represents one nation only" (Arendt 1963a, 270). Nevertheless, in keeping with her political pragmatism, she ultimately concludes that an Israeli tribunal and its decision to emphasize crimes against Jews was all that could be done politically in Israel at that time. In the 1960s, the global political sphere was not ready to embrace such an institution as the International Criminal Court that was ultimately established with the 1998 Rome Statute. Without discursive validity, such an institution would not provide a new guarantee for rights when citizenship is stripped away. The rightless, the Other, would once again have to "fall back upon their minimum rights" as they did between the wars when international agreements lacked political legitimacy and their rights had "no authority . . . left to protect them and no institution was willing to guarantee them" (Arendt 1951, 292).

The "new guarantee" for human dignity requires both the rights of man reformulated as the right to have rights *and* the rights of the citizen. The hendiadys cannot be broken; but we are left wondering what will prevent the rights of the citizen from subsuming the rights of man, especially for those without a voice in the political community. As we saw with Arendt's analysis of the Little Rock crisis, tying a new guarantee for human dignity to her ideal polis risks cauterizing the marginalized Others, just those who would be most in need of this new guarantee for human dignity. Without any foundation for rights outside of the polis, Arendt's normative justification remains unclear. Benhabib rightly asks:

> If we insist that we must treat all humans as beings entitled to the right to have rights, on the basis of which philosophical assumptions do we defend this insistence? Do we ground such respect for universal human rights in nature, in history, or in human rationality? One searches in vain for answers to these questions in Arendt's text.... Arendt also leaves us with a disquiet about the normative foundations of her own political philosophy. (Benhabib 1996, 82)

Such a "disquiet" about "normative foundations" for human rights points to Levinas' most significant contribution to human rights, his ethics as first philosophy; that is, ethics is prior to ontology, politics, and human rights.

The Second Hendiadys: Levinas' The Rights of Man and the Other

In several short essays, Levinas praises the "discovery" of the rights of man as a form of legalizing the ancient "Biblical imperatives" (1998e, 155) as "an obligation to spare man the constraints and humiliations of poverty, vagrancy, and even the sorrow and torture which are still inherent in the sequence of natural – physical and psychological – phenomena, and the violence and cruelty of the evil intentions of living beings" (156). Nevertheless, like Arendt, he questions whether the traditional philosophical foundations for the rights of man are a sufficient guarantee for human dignity in the modern world. He argues for a new normative guarantee for the right of man through an analysis of another hendiadys: the rights of man and the rights of the Other.

First, Levinas focuses on the a priori nature of the traditional rights of man, what he calls the "normative energy" of rights (Levinas 1999b, 146), which allows them to be the "measure of all law" (Levinas 1993, 116). They are "attached to every human person independently from any prior granting by any authority or tradition, and also independently from any act of taking upon oneself or of meriting those rights" (Levinas 1999b, 145). The rights of man have their own unique justification separate from the rights of the citizen even if they ultimately require the nation and citizenship rights.

Nonetheless, Levinas worries that traditional rights theories, such as those of Hobbes and Locke, are grounded in the autonomous ego claiming a priori rights based on its prior freedom and/or self-preservation. Paradoxically, rights that guarantee the ego's freedom also require a check on the ego's freedom as they encounter the freedom claims of all others. Moreover, as rights claims proliferate, so too does the tension between all egos and their conflicting rights claims.[4] Without another foundation, Levinas argues that this contentiousness inherent to traditional rights theories will devolve into a state of war. Somewhat counterintuitively, we can even derive "the war of each against all, based on the Rights of Man" (Levinas 1999b, 147). The burgeoning of fundamental rights claims as seen in the twentieth century will exacerbate the contentiousness and selfishness in society, and thus, without "a new guarantee," the rights of man are again at risk in a "precarious peace."

To shore up this precarious peace, Levinas finds a new guarantee for rights, a new authority on which to ground rights. This is an a priori that exists even before the a priori that founds traditional rights theories. It is founded on "a prior peace that is not purely and simply non-aggression, but has, so to speak, its own positivity" (Levinas 1993, 123–124). This positivity will be found in the disinterestedness of the loving response of the ego to the face of the concrete Other.

If the rights of man are founded on the a priori rights of the Other, the burgeoning of fundamental rights claims will not increase contentiousness but will increase fraternity as the ego is called to "an inexhaustible responsibility" (Levinas 1993, 125) for the Others that approach it. Levinas appears to respond directly to Arendt's call for a new guarantee for human rights:

> Should not the fraternity that is in the motto of the republic be discerned in the prior non-indifference of one for the other, in that original goodness in which freedom is embedded, and in which the justice of the rights of man takes on an immutable significance and stability, better than those guaranteed by the state? (Levinas 1993, 125)

Again, Levinas insists that these rights based on the "prior non-indifference of one for the other" are not founded on a proof of God but "are the rights of man constituting a juncture in which God comes to mind" (1998e, 158). In the ego's response to the rights of the Other, the ego testifies to that which is beyond being. "No doubt it is important in good philosophy not to think the rights of man in terms of an unknown god; it is permissible to approach the idea of God setting out from the absolute that manifests itself in the relation to the other" (158).

---

[4] The proliferation of rights claims is a common concern of communitarian scholars (see, e.g., Glendon 1991). Levinas also writes: "The right to oppose exploitation by capital (the right to unionize) and even the right to social advancement; the right (utopian or Messianic) to the refinement of the human condition, the right to ideology as well as the right to fight for the full rights of man, and the right to ensure the necessary political conditions for that struggle. The modern conception of the rights of man surely extends that far!" (Levinas 1993, 120).

The two apparent hendiades complement one another and point to a third hendiadys. Recall that Arendt reformulates the rights of man into the right to have rights. Without the right to have rights, the rights of the citizen will be in peril, and vice versa. Each requires the other to have an independent existence. For Levinas, without the a priori rights of the Other, the rights of man will be in danger, and vice versa. Combining Arendt's and Levinas' conclusions: To the extent that the rights of man do not subsume the rights of the Other, the rights of man will not be subsumed into the rights of the citizen and the state. So we are left with another hendiadys: the right to have rights and the rights of the Other.[5] In this fashion, Levinas' ethics as first philosophy will provide a much-needed a priori normative foundation to Arendt's thought, and Arendt's call for a deliberative political community with each guaranteed the right to have rights will provide a much-needed political supplement to Levinas' ethical thought. The key, though, is for the rights of the Other to take precedence. In order to guarantee the rights of the Other, those who have a voice in the polis have a prior duty to respond to those marginalized and without a voice. Their responsibility even pre-dates their rights.

Levinas on Sabra and Chatila

By finding an a priori peace in the transcendence of the face-to-face relationship with the concrete Other, Levinas' thought would seem to provide a means for creating an ethical politics and for reinvigorating human rights law. However, the normative limits of Levinas' ethical thought are apparent in the most infamous passage in Levinas' work, his comments concerning the crimes against humanity at the Palestinian refugee camps of Sabra and Chatila in 1982. This massacre occurred in the context of the Israeli invasion of Lebanon and the continuing civil war there between Christians and Palestinians. After the assassination of Lebanese President Bashir Gemayel in September 1982, the Israeli Defense Force (IDF) entered West Beirut and disarmed all Palestinian factions. The IDF then sealed off the refugee camps at Sabra and Chatila and allowed the Christian Phalangists to enter the camps to round up any remaining Palestinian fighters. Over the course of two days, the Phalangists engaged in a brutal massacre of between 800 and 3,000 refugees including several dozen women and children, all under the watchful eye of the IDF. The world was outraged. Israelis were outraged. A week after the massacre, approximately 300,000 Israelis took to the

---

5   To what extent the rights of the citizen drops out of this equation, especially in the context of human rights law, will be discussed in Chapter 8.

streets in the largest protest in Israeli history demanding accountability for
the massacre. Three days after the protest, Levinas and fellow philosopher
Alain Finkielkraut engaged in a radio discussion about the massacre with
the writer Shlomo Malka. Their discussion focused on the extent of Israeli
responsibility. All agreed that Israel must not invoke the temptation of innocence derived from the Jewish experience in the Shoah. Levinas sharply
said, "Evoking the Holocaust to say that God is with us in all circumstances
is as odious as words 'Gott mit uns' written on the belts of the executioners"
(Levinas 1989a, 291).

In the most commented on segment of the interview, Levinas considers
the relationship between ethics and politics. He argues that politics has its
own justification, but it too must be in the service of ethics; and even if it is
justified by ethics, politics has an ethical limit. He then applies this theoretical formulation to the Israeli-Palestinian situation. Levinas first highlights the
political justification of the overall Israeli offensive into Lebanon. He says that
President Begin's phrase that "Jewish blood must not flow with impunity" "is
quite invaluable" (Levinas 1989a, 293), but such a political justification must
be grounded in, and called into question by, an original ethical responsibility.
Levinas finds that the events at Sabra and Chatila disrupt any prior political
justification for the Israeli action. Indeed, those events disrupt "everything."
"The place where everything is interrupted, where everything is disrupted,
where everyone's moral responsibility comes into play, a responsibility that
concerns and engages even innocence, unbearably so, that place lies in the
events at Sabra and Chatila" (293). Malka, apparently sensing some vacillation
in Levinas' position, asks whether the Palestinian was the Other to whom the
Israeli owed responsibility. I quote Malka's question and Levinas' infamous
answer:

SM: Emmanuel Levinas, you are the philosopher of the "other." Isn't history,
     isn't politics the very site of the encounter with the "other," and for the
     Israeli, isn't the "other" above all the Palestinian?
EL: My definition of the other is completely different. The other is the neigh-
     bour, who is not necessarily kin, but who can be. And in that sense, if you're
     for the other, you're the neighbour. But if your neighbour attacks another
     neighbour or treats him unjustly, what can you do? Then alterity takes on
     another character, in alterity we can find an enemy. Or at least then we are
     faced with the problem of knowing who is right and who is wrong, who is
     just and who is unjust. There are people who are wrong. (294)

Levinas' reluctance to name the Palestinian as Other, to seemingly refuse
to implicate Jewish responsibility for the massacre within the context of his

ethical responsibility for the Other, has elicited numerous commentaries, many of which have wrongly dismissed it as some type of hypocrisy between Levinas' philosophical writings and his political partisanship.[6] These critiques ignore the entire context of the interview, in which Levinas shares in the condemnation of the massacres. In addition to disrupting "everything," he makes clear that, "what gripped us right away was the honour of responsibility" (290). Levinas goes much further: The events of Sabra and Chatila call into question any justification, political, historical, or ethical, for the state of Israel and even shake the conscience of Judaism itself. He says, "Not enough has been said about the shock that the human possibility of the events at Sabra and Chatila...signifies for our entire history as Jews and as human beings" (296). These events have called into question the Jewish soul "and that which upholds our souls: our books!" These books "carry us through history, and which, even more deeply than the earth are our support" (296). These books, for Levinas, represent the prophetic voice, the responsibility of the Jewish people as made real in history. So, Sabra and Chatila shake the good conscience of Judaism and Zionism. It is a rupture in what was considered an ethically necessary politics. Malka asks Levinas to elaborate on this point: "Why is it our books that are in question?" Levinas responds with a discussion of two Talmudic passages, the lessons of which are directed at those who confuse Zionism with merely a political claim to land. Levinas' brief Talmudic commentary concludes, "A person is more holy than a land, even a holy land, since, faced with an affront made to a person, this holy land appears in its nakedness to be but stone and wood" (297). The ethics of the Other calls into question all politics including the ethical politics of the "holy land."

Why then was Levinas unable to name the Palestinian as Other? In my reading, Malka's question shifted Levinas from a commentary on the Israeli action that he obviously found deplorable to an exposition of his more formal philosophical formulations. Levinas responded by giving a brief account of his philosophy of the Other and how only in a second step with the appearance of the Third does the ego thematize non-thematizable Others. When Levinas replies, "my definition of the other is completely different," he is saying that his philosophical definition of the Other does not rest on any nationality or kinship of the Other. Yes, the Palestinian can be the Other, but so too can the

---

[6] For example, Campbell (1999) concludes that Levinas' "notion of the Other is restricted to the neighbour in such a way as to keep the Palestinians outside of the reach of those to whom the I is responsible" (39), and Neumann (1999) writes "Levinas makes the political choice of first being a nationalist and only second a philosopher of alterity" (20).

Israeli, Saudi, or Iraqi. The Other is the neighbor, the one who approaches the ego. It is not thematizable. However, this non-thematizable ethical encounter is not the final word in Levinas' thought. His thought moves from ethics to politics with the introduction of the third person, the Third. Of necessity, then, the ego must resort to calculation, must compare previously incomparable others. As Levinas says, "If your neighbour attacks another neighbour or treats him unjustly, what can you do? Then alterity takes on another character, in alterity we can find an enemy." Only at the level of the Third, with the introduction of thematization, calculation, politics, and so forth, is the Other a Palestinian, an Israeli, a Tutsi, a Guatemalan street child, and so forth. At that level, the ego must weigh its responsibilities toward each Other. Here, the ego can discover an enemy but only reluctantly on the basis of the prior ethical relationship with the Other. "If your neighbour attacks another neighbour or treats him unjustly, what can you do?" (294).

THE INDIVIDUALIZED OTHER AND MERE "MOMENTS OF NEGATION"

Although this exchange does not mark a politically motivated hypocrisy, it is indicative of a more subtle and seemingly intractable problem in Levinas' ethical thought: the anonymity of the Other. Levinas' great accomplishment is to introduce ethics on a separate plane that intersects but is prior to ontology, politics, human rights, and law.[7] The exposure to the face of the Other calls into question or disrupts all politics, even an ethically justified politics. However, Levinas' failure to thematize the Other ultimately reduces the amount of normativity that can be derived from his thought.

As we have seen in his more formal accounts, he must insist that all Others have a face, even the Schutzstaffel (SS) guard. Levinas emphasized that the Other who appears before the ego appears denuded of all ontological categories. The face resists thematization and categorization. It is pure exposure, pure expression; it evinces alterity itself. It is only known through its call for a response. Insisting that the Other cannot be categorized, Levinas has abstracted the Other to the point that any specific Other would signify no differently than an infinite number of Others. Indeed, Levinas must hold that even the SS guard has a face and thus calls for an infinite ethical response from the ego (Levinas 1998f, 231). Levinas goes so far to say that placing the ethical relationship beyond thematization is the lynchpin for his philosophy. "The other must be received independent of his qualities, if he is to be received

---

7   For example, "Preexisting the plane of ontology is the ethical plane" (Levinas 1969, 201).

as other. If it weren't for this...*then the rest of my analyses would lose all their force....* [I]t seemed to me that forgetting all of these incitements to thematization was the only manner for the other to count as other" (Levinas 1998b, 80, emphasis added). So, it appears that when Levinas refers to the ethical relationship to the widow, orphan, and stranger in his more formal philosophical writings, such characters are metaphors for the nakedness of the face and not concrete widows, orphans, and strangers.

It is not that the Other who approaches is not unique. Paradoxically, each face that approaches, though denuded of categories, is absolutely unique. Levinas' innovation is that this uniqueness originates in proximity, not in thematization. The ego is drawn so close to the Other in proximity that it is unable "to take the distance necessary for the objectifying gaze" (Levinas 1998c, 194). The ego cannot separate from the Other. It is a hostage to the Other. "This not-being-able-to-stand-apart, this non-indifference with regard to the difference or the otherness of the other – this irreversibility is not a simple failure of an objectification, but precisely a doing justice to the difference of the other person...an otherness of the unique, exterior to all genus, transcending all genus" (194).

The Other is unique in its call for responsibility but remains non-thematizable, that is, until the entrance of the Third.[8] Only with the entrance of the Third is the destitute distinguished from the Rockefeller; only then "the face in its nakedness as a face presents to me the destitution of the poor one and the stranger" (Levinas 1969, 213).

Difficulties arise when we return to the metaphor of intersecting planes of ethics and politics, with the ethical plane pre-existing the political plane. At the line where the two planes intersect – where the ego is confronted clearly with the nakedness or potential death of the singular Other, the ego knows what to do; political calculations are unnecessary. It must be disinterested and respond infinitely to the Other. However, in Levinas' formulation, the ego is constantly being pulled away along the political plane from the line where ethics and politics intersect.[9] The ego is always confronted by Others; indeed, by all of humanity and thus it must constantly weigh its infinite

[8] Ajzenstat provocatively places responsibility for Levinas' ambiguity with regard to the singularity of the non-thematizable Other on the limits of philosophical language. "It sometimes seems as if the subject is responding to the same thing in every other, 'the trace' of 'otherness', and not to the particular person at all. But this, I believe, bespeaks a flaw in philosophical language rather than a flaw in Levinas' ethics. Levinas is not Shakespeare; he cannot describe the effect of the face without generalizing, even though the effect of any particular face is never general" (Ajzenstat 2001, 322).

[9] It should not be surprising that there have been debates among Levinasian scholars to what extent the ethical relationship is prior to the political realm.

responsibilities.[10] The ego, thus, is always already on the political plane, but this political realm must be answerable to the always receding original ethical relationship. The ego is left with concrete moments, experiences of the exposure to the face of the Other, that call into question the ego and its categories. These experiences like Derrida's desertified *tout autre* discussed earlier in the chapter might suspend the political briefly, but they will leave little ground for making normative judgments. Of course, because this transcendence stems from the face of the Other, there is a modicum of normativity as found in such commandments as "Thou shalt not kill," but beyond that, the ego is left with little from this ethical encounter to bring to political decision making, except the sense of having been disrupted. The judge's decisions remain madness with little direction, especially to call for the reinvigoration of politics or human rights law. As Levinas writes: "Anarchy cannot be sovereign like an arche. It can only disturb the State – but in a radical way, making possible *moments of negation* without any affirmation. The State, then, cannot set itself up as a Whole" (Levinas 1981, 194, emphasis added). Are these "moments of negation" enough to serve as the new guarantee for human rights that Levinas and Arendt seek?

These "an-archical" moments will quickly succumb to the contingencies and thematizations of politics. The ego who must translate these moments of negation into politics, into the comparison of incomparables, is caught up in a system based on an original violence filled with "unexamined prejudices, ancient battles, historical injustices, and sheer administrative fiat" (Benhabib 2004, 178). Complicating the task even further is the melancholy haphazardness (in Kant's terms) of the exposure of the Other. The ego may just as easily have been exposed to another Other or any set of Others. Politics will be disrupted by the proximity of the unique Other, but this is the Other who just happens to have approached the ego. In a segregated society, the Other who most likely approaches will be kin, or at least someone who shares many of the "unexamined prejudices" of the ego.

To counter these concerns, sympathetic Levinasian scholars have employed two main tactics. Many are all too wiling to overlook Levinas' more formal formulations with his insistence that the Other be non-thematizable and declare the Other to be "the stateless, the oppressed, the poor and the homeless, hungry widows and orphans. They are vulnerable people" (Herzog 2002, 207). Moreover, there are numerous examples in Levinas' writings where he makes such concrete claims. Unfortunately, the route

---

[10] "The third party looks at me in the eyes of the Other…the epiphany of the face qua face opens humanity" (Levinas 1969, 213).

from the non-thematizable Other of his formal writings to such concrete pronouncements is tenuous at best. Alford's (2002a) description is apt at least for his more formal philosophical writings: "Levinas was never interested in the concrete reality of the other person, whose fleshy reality can only get in the way of transcendence" (37).[11]

Other commentators have argued that Levinas' harsh view of politics must be tempered by a middle term between the infinite ethical responsibility and the violent order of political. Many propose a prominent place for more ethical political institutions, usually founded on some type of democratic legitimacy or some type of ethical encounter. Of course, a good argument can be made that such legal instruments as the Universal Declaration of Human Rights, the Genocide Convention, the South African Constitution, or even the Fourteenth Amendment to the U.S. Constitution are founded in some type of original ethical event. However, the analysis of the European Court of Human Rights decision in the *Sahin* case suggests that even the original violence of these more ethical institutions needs to be called into question by some type of originary ethics that is more than a moment of negation.

TOWARD A PHENOMENOLOGY OF THE SATURATED OTHER

In response to this dilemma, I propose that we not try to reform (at least initially) Levinas' conception of politics but to refocus his conception of transcendence found in the exposure to the Other. If politics cannot be trusted, then any reformation of politics cannot be trusted insofar as it is informed by mere "moments of negation." So, politics must be called into question more substantially, perhaps in a more sustained fashion. Is it possible to conceive of an exposure to the Other that calls into question the ego and its "unexamined prejudices" in a more radical fashion? I propose that we return to Levinas' less abstract conception of transcendence – the hyper-presence of the Other that is "the blinding bedazzlement of the gaze by an excess of light and a bursting of knowledge in adoration" (Levinas 1999a, 4). Can the hyper-presence of the Other bedazzle the ego in a more comprehensive and sustained way than the

---

[11] However, see Plant (2003b): "Alford overstates the otherworldly aspect" of "Levinas' ethics". Whereas Plant is quite right that corporeality is essential to Levinas' ethics, Alford's larger point seems to be that Levinas' account of the Other is not referring to a specific concrete Other, and "to render the other person absolutely other, not an alter ego, is to do violence to humans" (Alford 2002, 145). Eisenstadt (2007) writes in a slightly different context: "Certainly such arguments are worthwhile. But none of them has anything to do with Levinas."

more formal account of the Other denuded of ontological categories? In the next chapter, I use Dussel's writings on exteriority and Marion's writings on saturated phenomena to begin to develop a phenomenology of the Saturated Other that overwhelms the ego even more comprehensively and in a more sustained manner than the Levinasian Other.

4

The Saturated Other

Chapter 3 argued that human rights must be grounded in a transcendence of the Other but concluded that Derrida's and Levinas' conception of transcendence provided little ground for making complex political decisions. This inability was traced back to Derrida's reliance on the purified transcendence of the *tout autre* and Levinas' failure to conceive of an individualized Other, which was most apparent in not naming the Palestinian as an "Other." Two major questions present themselves: Is there a way of conceiving of the Other as transcendent, concrete, *and* individualized? Can a type of transcendence be conceived that will adequately deconstruct *and* reinvigorate human rights law; that will overcome the original violence of the hegemonic system and provide a new foundation for human rights?

In this chapter, I argue that Enrique Dussel's eclectic and voluminous writings provide a path for addressing one of the most intractable aporiai in heteronomic thought, namely the individuation of the transcendent Other, and thus moves us toward a deconstruction *and* reinvigoration of human rights law. I situate my interpretation of Dussel's theory of transcendence within the context of Jean-Luc Marion's recent phenomenologies of the saturated phenomena. I argue that Dussel's account of the Other closely resembles the hyper-presence of Levinas' writings and Marion's phenomenology of the saturated phenomena without much of Levinas' and Marion's noted theological baggage. Dussel's philosophy with its firm adherence to the marginalized human Other as individualized saturated phenomenon is able to make political judgments where Levinas was notoriously tongue-tied. In addition, Dussel's recent writings endeavor to synthesize this transcendental ethics of the Other with the participatory or discursive democracy advocated by Arendt, Benhabib, Habermas, and Karl Otto-Apel. Nonetheless, Dussel will insist that such a political thought must continuously be deconstructed by the a priori ethical relationship with the Other, thus addressing the propensity of discursive democracy to cauterize the Other, rendering him or her *aneu logou*.

JEAN-LUC MARION'S SATURATED PHENOMENA

Jean-Luc Marion's well-known debates with Derrida on the possibility of conducting a phenomenology of transcendence help clarify the two strands of transcendence in Levinas' thought and suggest a path for developing an ethics of the individualized Other in transcendence without theology. As we saw in Chapter 3, Derrida has argued for a more theological view of transcendence – what has been called a "desertified" (Kearney 1999) transcendence, a transcendence that is completely transcendent and thus never present. This transcendence is typified by the second step in Levinas' phenomenology, in which a trace of the divine comes to mind in the response of the ego to the Other. Marion, on the other hand, embraces the first strand of transcendence found in Levinas' writings: the appearance of the Other as hyper-presence. I will side with Marion that the *human* Other as transcendence is actually a form of hyper-presence – a presence that overwhelms the ego and its categories.

Marion explores transcendence through phenomenologies of "saturated phenomena" that structurally resemble the hyper-presence of the Levinasian face-to-face relationship. Marion argues that saturated phenomena "appear" to the ego but cannot be regarded in the sense of being gazed upon. They cannot be held in consciousness, as one would keep "objects in an objected state" (Marion 2002a, 214). As such, the saturated phenomena are known through counter-experience; the I "sees the superabundance of intuitive givenness; or rather, it does not see it clearly and precisely as such since its excess renders it irregardable and difficult to master" (Marion 2002a, 215).

This is similar to Levinas' appropriation of Descartes' idea of the infinite from the "Third Meditation" as "a thinking that finds itself thinking more than it can embrace, the blinding bedazzlement of the gaze by an excess of light and a bursting of knowledge in adoration" (Levinas 1999a, 4). The saturated phenomena as hyper-presence, as an excess of givenness, leave "the intention, meaning, or signification to rub its eyes in wonder, stunned and amazed by the visitation" (Caputo and Scanlon 1999, 6). So, a saturated phenomenon is paradoxically transcendent on account of its excess of presence. It cannot be contained by the ego's categories of thinking. It overwhelms the ego. The saturated phenomenon is not directly perceived but is known through the counter-experience of encountering it, an experience of the powerlessness to contain it. "The eye does not see an exterior spectacle so much as it sees the reified traces of its own powerlessness to constitute whatever it might be into an object.... [It] clearly experiences its own powerlessness to master the measurelessness of the intuitive given" (Marion 2002a, 216).

Marion's conception of transcendence is in stark contrast to Derrida's conception of the *tout autre*. Recall that the *tout autre* must be totally unknowable, unnameable, and undeconstructable; and most importantly, it must never be made immanent or come to presence. In their debates, Derrida was concerned that Marion's saturated phenomena as hyper-presence fail to break the hegemony of presence and are thus not truly transcendent. Marion, for his part, was concerned that Derrida's transcendence as *tout autre* is another in a long line of "poor phenomena" that "are distinguished...by their shortage of intuition, the poverty of their givenness, indeed the unreality of their objects" (Marion 2002a, 194–195). This distinction has been wonderfully summarized as follows: "In Marion we have to do with a dazzling glow, a glory which leaves the faculties of subjectivity stunned and silenced, but in Derrida we encounter the kenotics [emptiness] of faith, of a groping blindness, like a blind man feeling his way with a stick or a stylus, 'writing in the dark'" (Caputo and Scanlon 1999, 8).

Levels of Saturated Phenomena

Marion's most important theoretical moves for human rights of the Other are his development of a hierarchy of saturated phenomena or forms of bedazzlement and his carving out of a privileged place for the Levinasian Other within this hierarchy. The levels of saturated phenomena are differentiated based on their "degree of givenness" and their ability to surpass the categories (quantity, quality, modality, relation) described in Kant's *Critique of Pure Reason*. For example, an historical event would be a lower-order saturated phenomenon. It saturates the Kantian category of quantity because it cannot be known in its entirety as it admits an infinite number of interpretations. The painting, as idol, saturates more completely because in addition to the infinite number of interpretations we find with an historical event. "Each gaze at the painting fails to bring me to perceive what I see, keeping me from taking it into view as such – so that it always again conceals the essential from validity" (Marion 2002a, 230). Marion places the auto-affection of the flesh, as developed in Maurice Merleau-Ponty's phenomenology, as the third type of saturation in that "it saturates the horizon to the point that there is no longer any relation that refers it to another object" (Marion 2002a, 231). For Marion, the Other in a Levinasian sense is a higher-order saturated phenomenon because it gathers together the previous three types of saturation. The face of the Other, like the event, surpasses any attempt at interpretation or categorization; like the painting "it begs to be seen and reseen" (Marion 2002a, 233) and like the flesh it "shows itself only in giving itself" (232). The highest order of saturation, though, for Marion is the Revelation of Jesus as Christ. Revelation in the synoptic gospels appears as event, idol, flesh, *and* icon (the face of the Other) and thus overwhelms the four Kantian categories. The Revelation of Jesus was totally unforeseeable; the appearance is unbearable according to quality, overwhelms any possible relation, and is irregardable in terms of modality.

This focus on Revelation has opened Marion to charges of a "theological hijacking of phenomenology" (Caputo and Scanlon 1999, 7). By discussing God as present even as hyper-presence, Marion has been accused of impermissibly treating the ineffable as the subject of a phenomenological analysis (See Janicaud 2000). God as hyper-presence may not be a suitable subject for phenomenology, but Marion's account of the face of the Other as a higher-order saturated phenomenon may open a path for developing a heteronomic ethics more suitable for political judgment. I would like to "atheize" Marion's writings and concur with Levinas that the step toward God, Jesus as Christ, or to Derrida's *tout autre* is a second step, "and one must be careful to avoid stumbling by taking too large a step." Nonetheless, Marion's phenomenology of the Other as a higher-order (if not the highest) saturated phenomenon provides an account of the concrete human Other as transcendence that does not rest on theology or any conception of "pure" transcendence.

Marion and the Individuation of the Other

Nonetheless, Marion's philosophy of the Other, like Levinas' phenomenology, will have difficulty in individuating the Other. Although Marion has written about this issue at some length, he is ultimately unable to adequately tackle this intractable problem. His two major attempts at individualizing the Other are inadequate because they both over-emphasize the intentionality of the ego. He rightly doubts whether Levinasian ethics can find an "individuation of the Other" when "each and everyone can take on the face of the face" (Marion 2002a, 324). Of course, any heteronomic philosophy will run into difficulties when it is rooted in transcendence but still seeks to distinguish those that cannot be categorized. As soon as the ego assigns the Other any meaning based on an ontological characteristic, it moves away from considering the Other as a face, as hyper-presence (Marion 2002b, 121). However, any philosophy that does not allow for individualization of a specific Other leads to equivocity, "for another can always be substituted who can offer the face of the other" (Marion 2002c, 93).[1] This equivocity will prevent the ego from giving preference to the marginalized Other and will therefore be unable to distinguish the Guatemalan street child from the guard at Auschwitz. Further, such equivocity founded in radical transcendence will make any political formulations difficult except as a second step.

Marion first confronts this aporia by focusing on the events that happen to the face of the Other "or more exactly in what it becomes following what happens to it" (Marion 2002b, 122). Like the historical event, such categorizations are infinite and open to interpretation so that the ego undergoes an "infinite hermeneutic," endlessly attempting to piece together the story of the Other. Marion describes this superbly:

> Only the one who has lived with the life and the death of another person knows to what extent he or she does *not* know that other. This one alone can therefore recognize the other as the saturated phenomenon *par excellence*, and consequently also knows that it would take an eternity to envisage this saturated phenomenon as such – not constituting it as an object, but interpreting it in loving it. (Marion 2002b, 126–127)

Marion insists that this envisagement by the ego is not a seeing; that it does not constitute the Other as an object. It must be a "waiting," a "loving," a closing of one's eyes (Marion 2002b, 122). However, I am concerned that this envisagement remains reliant on the intentionality of the ego. The ego pieces together, or more accurately attempts to piece together, the story of the Other into a coherent whole. This formulation risks reducing the face of the Other to a category based on the ego's limited perception of the Other's experience, to what Kant might call the "melancholy haphazardness" of its being. Such a formulation built on the Other's unique history may open a space for the Other's individuation, but it may no longer radically call the ego and its categories into question. The ego, with its categories that are susceptible to reification, could reduce the infinite Other to a victim, or a

---

[1] This difficulty is especially acute in Marion's phenomenology as he widens the application of "the call" or command to the ego to the point that all saturated phenomena (the event, the idol, flesh, and the icon), all those phenomena that overflow intuition, would call the ego in their own way. For instance, the historical event calls the ego to an infinite hermeneutic as it surpasses all attempts to encompass it. Marion continues to hold a special place for the face of the Other because it "accomplishes the phenomenological operation of the call more, perhaps, than any other phenomenon (saturated or not)" (Marion 2002b, 118). Even here, though, Marion expands the contents of the face's call. Levinas claims that the summons of the face is straightaway ethical: "Thou shalt not kill"; but Marion argues the face's call can range from the *existentielle* ("become who you are!") to the religious ("love your God will all your heart, with all your soul and all your mind") to the erotic ("love me") (Marion 2002b, 118).

Tutsi, or a torture survivor. Marion needs to go further to ensure that any constitution of the Other is not susceptible to the branding or cauterization process of the ego.

Marion explores another alternative for individualizing the face, but this too ultimately risks relying on the intentionality of the ego. Here, Marion reverts back to the scholastic concept of *haecceitas*, the quiddity of the "as such," to individuate the Other. The *haecceitas* is the "atomic particularity" of the Other that is "beyond essence" (Marion 2002b, 95). Even the Other "knows nothing" of this *haecceitas* and literally jumps "into his alterity with a step that throws him into the final singularity" (2002b, 98). The Other loses himself into his or her *haecceitas*, and so Marion holds that it "marks the renunciation of intentionality" (2002b, 98), be it of the ego *or* of the Other. The ego experiences the Other's singularity as a call for a response, as an obligation that is unique to the ego. "No other than me will be able to play the other that the other requires, no other gaze than my own must respond to the ecstasy of this particular other exposed in his gaze" (2002b, 101). This obligation from the exposure to the unsubstitutable *haecceitas* of the Other is itself unsubstitutable.

Marion goes to great lengths to remove intentionality from this phenomenology, but ultimately the appearance of the face relies on the intentionality or will of the ego. He adds a step to this phenomenology that gives the ego the role of being a gatekeeper for the Other. The ego literally constitutes the Other. "To accept the other's face, or better, to accept that I am dealing with an other...depends uniquely on my *willing* it so" (2002c, 166, emphasis added). The ego can choose to ignore the Other or it can choose to open itself to the Other. If the ego refuses the command, the Other does not appear. "The other appears only if I gratuitously give him the space in which to appear" (2002c, 166). This clearing out of a space by the ego requires a form of charity that "empties its world of itself in order to take place there for what is unlike, what does not thank it, what – possibly – does not love it" (2002c, 167). To open up a place for the Other would require such an extra-human effort – what Levinas calls a disinterestedness – that it can only make sense through a theology of charity. This is a saintly act that is sustained ultimately by the love of God and would require thinking beyond phenomenology, to a love or faith (Morrow 2005). Such a formulation provides further credence to Badiou's original concern that "God the ineffable" ultimately sustains any ethics based on radical alterity. So, whereas Marion's phenomenology of the Other as a higher-order saturated phenomena and the ego's infinite responsibility for the Other is helpful in moving toward an individuation of the Other as hyper-presence, ultimately his account risks relying on the intentionality of the ego and falling into the abstract universalism of a theology.

DUSSEL'S OTHER AS AN INDIVIDUALIZED
SATURATED PHENOMENON

Dussel's writings on the Other provide a useful alternative for individualizing the Other as saturated phenomenon without reducing it to an object of intentionality and/or a theology. Is this possible? Can the nakedness of transcendence be clothed without making it immanent?[2] Does this knowledge (minimal as it perhaps could be), based on ontological categories, place the Other under the comprehending gaze of the ego?

Following Levinas and Marion, I argue that the human Other is a saturated phenomenon, in that it appears as hyper-presence and as such surpasses the Kantian categories. It overwhelms the ego's categories similarly to an historical event where each new interpretation breeds new interpretations. It upsets intentionality. Confronted by the Other, the ego experiences a "powerlessness to constitute whatever it might be into an object.... [It] clearly experiences its own powerlessness to master the measurelessness of the intuitive given" (Marion 2002a, 216). Contra Marion, it is not a matter of the will carving out a place for the Other through charity. The ego may choose to heed or not to heed the call of the Other, but the ego does not constitute the Other. Instead, as in Levinas' writings, the ego is a *sub-jectum*, it is constituted by its responsibility for the Other. The ego is so far from intentionality that it is a hostage to the Other. The accusation of the Other corresponds to the "de-substantiation of the subject, its de-reification, its disinterestedness, its subjection, its subjectivity. It is a pure self, in the accusative, responsible before there is freedom" (Levinas 1981, 127). The *call* of the Other may be known through the response, but the Other is always present, or more accurately hyper-present, whether the ego responds or not. The ego is not a gatekeeper for the Other, but the Other is a gatekeeper for the ego's subjectivity.

Levels of Exteriority

Here Dussel's conception of exteriority, what he calls "the most important category for philosophy of liberation" (1985, 39), becomes all-important for individuating this hyper-presence. In Dussel's work, the face of the Other appears as "exteriority" or transcendence, but the important point is that exteriority

---

[2]   Alford similarly suggests that a useful supplement to Levinas' thought would be to consider the other as "a passage to infinity and particular fleshy human being at the same time.... But, to experience it we will have to accept a lot more mixing and weaving of flesh with eternity than [sic] Levinas seems prepared for" (Alford 2002, 145).

appears to have a double meaning. In my reading, Dussel points to both an interior transcendence and an exterior transcendence where interior and exterior refer to the location of the Other in relation to the system that supports the ego. First, as in Levinas' phenomenology, the face of the Other is exterior to the ego. It overwhelms the ego. Second, in the language of his earlier works, the face of the Other overwhelms the system; it is exterior to the system. In *Philosophy of Liberation*, Dussel writes,

> The spatial metaphor of exteriority can be labeled by [*puede llamar a* (my translation)] more than one equivocation. We could also denominate the "beyond," vis-à-vis the horizon of Being of the system, an interior transcendentality, a "beyond" vis-à-vis the subject in the system, vis-à-vis one's work, one's desire, one's possibilities, one's *proyecto*. Exteriority and interior transcendentality have the same signification in this philosophical discourse. (1985, 39–40)

Exteriority signifies both beyond the subject who is within the system or interior transcendence and exteriority beyond the system.

Within the system (social, economic, political, racial, gendered, etc.) that sustains the ego, it is approached by "one absolutely *sui generis*, distinct from all the rest" (1985, 40) and that is the face of the Other. Dussel claims,

> No person as such is absolutely and only part of a system. All, *including even those who are members of an oppressing class*, have a transcendentality with respect to the system, interior to it.... [T]his internal transcendentality is the exteriority of the other as other, not as part of the system" (1985, 47–48, emphasis added).

In my reading, this internal transcendence corresponds to Levinas' description of the face of the Other in its bedazzlement, as abstract without ontological categories. In its internal transcendentality, the SS guard at Auschwitz, the member of the "oppressing class," would have a face and would signify a hyper-presence that overwhelms the intentionality of the ego.

There also appears to be a second moment of transcendence in Dussel's work. When the face of the Other (interior transcendence) is also the face of the marginalized Other that is exterior to the system (exterior transcendence?), it manifests alterity in a qualitatively different way or, in Marion's terms, in a more saturated way. This "metaphysical proximity materializes unequivocally, truly, before the face of the oppressed, the poor, the one who – outside all systems – cries out for justice, arouses a desire for freedom, and appeals to responsibility" (1985, 20). This more saturated exteriority interrogates the system as well as the categories of the ego. This formulation, in a way, turns

Levinas on his head. For Levinas, the Other imbued with ontological characteristics is a distancing from the proximity of the original ethical relationship toward politics and justice. For Dussel, the Other imbued with the ontological characteristics of poverty and oppression deepens, as in a higher-order saturated phenomena in Marion's analysis, the exteriority that founds ethics. The ego experiences a greater intensity of bedazzlement. Dussel writes, contra Levinas, "The metaphysical priority of the other...also has historical, political and erotic elements" (2003b, 143). In what I label "exterior transcendentality," "the Others reveal themselves as others in all the acuteness of their exteriority when they burst in upon us as something extremely distinct, as nonhabitual, nonroutine, as the extraordinary, the enormous ('apart from the norm') – the poor, the oppressed" (Dussel 1985, 43).[3]

The Saturated Other bedazzles the ego and overwhelms the ontological categories that support it and the oppressive system that accuses and cauterizes the Other. The Other cannot be comprehended by the ego's gaze, and when he or she draws near from outside of the system, the ego's entire frame of reference is shaken because such epiphanies "shake the very pillars of the system that exploits them" (Dussel 1985, 43).

Such a higher-order exteriority perhaps manifests itself most clearly in the effects on the ego's responsibility. As with Levinas' formulation, internal transcendentality calls for a concrete, asymmetrical, and infinite response from the ego. This is a provocation from the person behind the ontological categories; it is something of a blank slate, that which I owe a responsibility. The approach of the marginalized Other incessantly calls the ego *and* its system into question and thus calls the ego to a deeper or more saturated responsibility.

The ego is called, not only to respond directly to the Other, but "assuming the other to be the victim of an injustice insofar as, by virtue of being accused, the other has been marked [branded or cauterized] as the unjust, the guilty, the criminal – it is to come before that tribunal in the name of the other" (Dussel 2004, 330). The ego is called to work in solidarity with the Other to overturn the cauterization of the Other.

There appears to be even a third level of exteriority or saturated phenomena in Dussel's work. The ego's responsibility is heightened even further as the individualized Other shares ontological characteristics with an entire group. For Dussel, the person, with characteristics, can reveal an entire people, thus

---

3   Thus, Dussel can distinguish phenomenology, which deals with the things of the world and the system, from epiphany that is the revelation of the Other, which takes on special meaning when it comes from the marginalized. Epiphany is "the revelation of the oppressed, the poor – never a mere appearance or a mere phenomenon, but always maintaining a metaphysical exteriority" (Dussel 1985).

implicating a range of political positions: "each face, unique, inscrutable mystery of decisions not yet made, is the face of a sex, a generation, a social class, a nation, a cultural group, a historical epoch" (Dussel 1985, 44). A face can reveal a dominating group or "the withered face of the Bedouin of the desert, the furrowed and darkened skin of the peasant, the poisoned lungs of the miner whose face never sees the sun – these 'apparently' ugly faces, almost horrible for the system, are the primary, the future, the popular beauty" (1985, 44). For Dussel, this is more than individuation; this individuation is based on an infinite series of ontological categories that point to a community of others who are similarly oppressed. Dussel's Other is individualized, concrete, fully rational, and has his or her own voice. This voice can join with others to create an anti-hegemonic "community of victims." The ego, then, is called to a responsibility for the entire group – to work with the marginalized Others to reverse their cauterization.

The key point for understanding Dussel's contribution is that this responsibility for an entire group is founded in transcendence. For Levinas, only with the entrance of the Third, another Other, will his ethics move past this original equivocal stance and judgment be made possible and absolutely necessary. For instance, Levinas, in one of his many précis on the move from the Other to the Third, remarks,

> The third party, different from my fellowman, is also my fellowman. And he is also the fellowman of the fellowman. *What are they doing, the unique ones, what have they already done to each another?* For me, it would be to fail in my first-personal responsibility – in my pre-judicial responsibility with regard to the one and the other – fellowmen – were I to ignore the wrongs of the one toward [the] other because of this responsibility, prior to all judgment, of proximity.... [I]t means not ignoring the suffering of the other, who falls to my responsibility" (Levinas 1998c, 195, emphasis added).

Here we have a huge gulf between Dussel and Levinas. Dussel does not have to ask the question, "What have they already done to one another?" With his embrace of liberation theology's preferential option for the poor, Dussel already knows that one Other has been oppressed by another *and* cauterized by the system. For Dussel, there is no question that the suffering of the Other is the real concrete suffering that is often caused by the ego and/or the structural violence of the system. By extension, the ego is always already a concrete ego caught in the web of social, historical, economic circumstances. Dussel insists that this context – this system that supports the ego – must be called into question by the Other who is outside of the system. The ego must ask in what ways it has assumed a privileged position within the system and already marginalized the Other. The ego must deconstruct the system and its original violence to do justice for the Other. This call for a radical deconstruction does not come from a desertified Other as in Derrida's work; instead, it comes from the concrete marginalized Other who approaches from outside the system. In this way, the Saturated Other calls for a much more radical responsibility than even in Levinas' formulation. The ego is called to work with the Other to work to overturn the system in the name of the Other.

These various ways of responding to the Other will be made clearer by considering Dussel's much larger ethical framework. His grand synthesis will also show how theories of deliberative democracy such as those developed by Arendt and Benhabib, despite their shortcomings, can still play a prominent role in a phenomenology of the Saturated Other. Dussel will combine his phenomenology of the Other with the insights of deliberative democracy to argue for a new anti-hegemonic concrete universalism.

Dussel's Grand Synthesis: Ética de la Liberación

The phenomenology of exteriority is but one moment in Dussel's recent work. His work has achieved a grand synthesis, culminating in his 1998 work *Ética de la Liberación* (yet to be translated into English), which incorporates Levinas' ethics of the Other into a comprehensive architectonic with discourse ethics, the materialist writings of Karl Marx and Franz Hinkelammert, Charles Sanders Pierce's pragmatism, Dussel's own dazzling theory of world history, as well as the liberation writings of Rigoberta Menchú and Paulo Freire. Dussel divides his ethical architectonic between fundamental ethics, which is a synthesis of much of traditional ethical thought (discourse ethics, material ethics, and pragmatism), and critical ethics, which is the negation of the more traditional, fundamental ethics. Each of these is further divided into three parallel moments. As we shall see, the critical ethics, or what he will often call the ethics of liberation, is set in motion by what I have called the Saturated Other.

Fundamental ethics consists of three moments. The first is the formal principle of discourse ethics as developed by Karl Otto-Apel and Jürgen Habermas and which informs Benhabib's democratic iterations. This is a non-coercive community of communication reaching consensus on what is valid. Each participant attempts to provide a justification for their truth-claim that will resonate with others in the community and thus will achieve validity. As with Benhabib's democratic iterations, the only a priori content of such an ethics is compliance with the procedural rules needed to establish a non-coercive consensus. As Dussel writes, in the formal moment "the question of 'validity' has absolute priority with respect to the question of the 'content' of every ethics of the 'good'" (1997a, 3).[4]

Dussel insists that within fundamental ethics this formal moment requires a second moment guided by the universal material principle, which is "the reproduction and growth of human life" (1997a, 7) or more specifically "a concrete good human life" (1997a, 7). Even if a discursive democracy reached consensus on a set of norms, it "'loses legitimacy' once it does not acceptably treat and thereby maintain human life for its citizens" (1999b, 86). Dussel quotes Franz Hinkelammert, "A norm is valid only to the extent that it is applicable, and it is applicable to the extent that it allows us to live. ... A norm under which one could not live under any circumstance would be *a priori* invalid" (1997a, 5). At the same time, the material moment needs the formal moment of discourse. Dussel concedes that there will be disagreements about the material principle, about what constitutes the good life. Here, discourse will be needed "to explain its conflicts, contradictions, external confrontation with other conceptions of the ethical life, and exceptions, etc." (1997a, 9). Nonetheless, Dussel insists that the material moment must be originary to the formal or discursive principle or it will be subsumed by it. In this way, any discursive validity with foundations in poverty or oppression will be subject to critique by the material principle. For the sake of brevity I will omit a lengthy discussion of the third moment, feasibility, which resembles Aristotle's *phronesis*, or practical wisdom. It "takes into consideration concrete conditions at all possible empirical levels, of historical space and time, of social, technological possibilities, etc." (Dussel 1999b, 88).

The obverse of fundamental ethics is critical ethics or the "ethics of liberation." Each of the three moments (formal, material, feasibility) of fundamental ethics has a corresponding moment in critical ethics. Dussel begins from the material principle. Any system that violates the material principle and does "not allow its victims to live ... ought to be criticized" (1997a, 8). In the critical material moment, we realize that "the majority of this humanity finds itself sunk in 'poverty', 'unhappiness', 'suffering', under domination and/or exclusion" (1997a). The affirmation of the material moment leads to this discovery of an exterior to the system. From the perspective of the Other, such a system loses its validity just as any procedural rule in

---

4   Interestingly, Dussel traces this relegation of material ethics to Kant's concerns about melancholy haphazardness discussed in my Introduction: Kant writes, "All practical principles that presuppose an (material) object of the appetitive faculty as determining foundation of the will, are empirical and cannot give practical laws" (Dussel 1997a, 4).

fundamental ethics loses its validity if it deprives life. Deconstruction of the "hegemonic validity of the system" (1997a, 15) begins from the perspective of exteriority.

This critical material moment requires a critical formal moment (the flip-side of formal or discourse ethics), which establishes a "critical principle of validity." This is a new validity grounded in what Freire calls *concientiza-ção*, the raising of critical consciousness of those exterior to the system. From this awareness, the Others will use "consensual intersubjectivity" to develop an anti-hegemonic validity that begins from the realization that the Other is outside of the system. The claims of the community of victims will not be absolute truths but truth-claims that must be open to debate. This is the development of a new system, a new concrete universality that begins from the voice of the Other, those exterior to the original system. It aims toward a "future 'institutionality,' declared valid, consensually, by the new intersubjectivity" (1997a, 2).

Some commentators have underestimated the crucial role that Levinas' Other continues to play in Dussel's architectonic.[5] By prioritizing the material moment and devoting an extensive portion of his recent work to corporeal life, Dussel seems to be championing a philosophy similar to that of the young Karl Marx and minimizing the role of the Levinasian Other. However, it is clear that the face-to-face relationship with the Other remains the impetus for Dussel's critical ethics. He explains,

> The recognition of the Other . . . is prior to critique and prior to argument . . . is at the origin of the process, prior to the interpellation or the call of the poor to solidarity in the system. This "ethical consciousness' is attained, above all and before anyone else, in the intersubjective or communitarian subjectivity of the oppressed and/or excluded people itself. (1997a, 17)

The exteriority of the marginalized Other is more than exterior in a material way to the discursive community; it "is found already at another level" (Dussel 2000, 274). The material moment may provide its own criterion for judging the formal moment, but this is not the sole or even elemental criterion. The Other calls the truths of both the material and formal moments into question. Also, notice in the preceding passage that for Dussel this Levinasian a priori responsibility for the Other takes on a deeper meaning when it is saturated, that is, when it comes from the face of the "oppressed and/or excluded people."

---

[5] Cf. Marsh (2000) and Barber (2000). I develop this point further in Simmons (2007).

Dussel must hold on to the transcendence found in the exteriority of the oppressed Other or risk the formal moment of discourse ethics subsuming the material moment. Theorizing about an anti-hegemonic discourse without some type of transcendence risks privileging the formal moment of ethics, as in Benhabib's work; it could lead to a supra-communication community with anti-hegemonic movements co-opted/tamed as yet another competing faction arguing from their own competing perspective of the material principle. After all, the life claims of the oppressed can be disregarded by the communication community or even considered, weighed, and discarded by other members of the community.

In the spirit of Derrida's deconstruction, even the anti-hegemonic discourse needs to be constantly called into question by the marginalized and transcendent Other once it attains some power lest it devolve into yet another hegemonic discourse with its own outcasts. As Dussel writes in the context of Exodus, "But when the dreamed 'new' Jerusalem is finally built, it slowly transforms itself into Egypt, the 'second' Jerusalem, the Jerusalem to be deconstructed...and the history will continue, never repeating and always renewing itself, as the history of the politics of liberation" (Dussel 2006, 88).

With an origin in the two types of exteriority, Dussel can claim a concrete universality that is not merely the universality of the material principle, and it "is not claiming an abstract universalism. Rather, it is making claims toward a universality, but this claim is always to be placed in the vicinity of the victims" (Gomez 2001, 33). The universality founded on the claims of the victims – the marginalized Others – as an anti-hegemonic validity calls into question all other universalisms. Because it stems from the voice of the Other, such a social movement is, by itself, a critique of the system. Those external to the system can work together to create their own discursive community based on an "anti-hegemonic validity of the community of victims," such as that inspired by the work of Rigoberto Menchú. From this architectonic, the ego's various responses to the Other comes into sharper focus.

RESPONDING TO THE OTHER

The epiphany of the Other manifests itself most clearly in the effects on the ego. Like Marion, Dussel would hold that in the proximity of the face of the Other the proper linguistic case for the ego is the dative (the case of giving). With its very foundations shaken by this exposure of the concrete Other, the ego is called to be silent, to receive the word of the Other, and to serve as a witness for the Other. Baxi's (n.d.) description of the need to reform human rights education (HRE) is so appropriate I will quote it again at length:

Perhaps, the first step in the activist journey of huper solidarity is for HRE activists to *learn* from the victims of the perfidies of power *rather than to presume to educate them in the struggle for survival and justice. Which victim of land mines in today's world does not know the meaning, method and message of state terrorism? Which victim of ethnic cleansing and contemporary genocides needs to be educated in the HRE Decade Plan of action? Do the victims of militarized rapes need education in the CEDAW? Humility before the victims of gross and flagrant violations of human rights*, I believe, is critically indispensable for the would be HRE communities of the future. I hope I am wrong in saying this but from what I have seen of the evangelical militancy of some HRE endeavor[s] makes me think and *feel* anxious concerning what I must name *faute de mieux* as HRE "imperialism." If this is a proper diagnosis, the problem then becomes one of *how may we educate the HRE educators, rather than the people whom they so ardently wish to serve?* (Baxi, n.d.)

Tolerance and Patient Listening

At first glance, such listening resembles "tolerance," a fundamental tenet of discourse ethics, as advocated by Habermas, Otto-Apel, and Benhabib. All individuals must have equal access to the public sphere (e.g., Bohman 1997, 63) and must be respectful of one another's opinions. Instead of insisting on the intolerant truth of ideologues and absolutists, Habermas, Otto-Apel, and Benhabib refer to truth-claims, which "are always finite, partial, determined by a certain social, historical, psychological perspective" (Dussel 2004, 327). Such truth-claims are contingent; they remain open to falsification. Validity claims are then contingent truth-claims made in the public sphere and reinforced in an ensuing intersubjective dialogue. In tolerance the ego listens to the Other and thus treats the Other with some dignity; "who recognize each other reciprocally as equals" (Dussel 1997a, 10). Tolerance is the time between the announcement of a truth-claim and the ensuing intersubjective agreement. It is "the 'time' of the other's non-acceptance of one's truth" (Dussel 2004, 329). It is the waiting for the other's rationality to accept the ego's truth-claim.

Dussel, however, claims that tolerance is, in a way, "irresponsible"; it is an indifference to the situation of the Other. It is merely a welcoming of the Other into the discourse community of the system, where the ego and the system continue to use their rationality to determine the validity of the Other's truth-claim. Such a welcoming would further marginalize the Other as he or she must speak the language of the system – a system that, by its nature, excludes those who speak a different idiom. In a way, the indigenous people of the Americas were brought into the discursive community, but we must ask by what means and at what cost. Dussel writes,

> Amerindia or Hispanoamerica is not so much a brute, mute being as a being silenced and brutalized in the presence of an ear habituated to hearing other music, other languages, other harmonies. The Indian is not a being in the rough, but rather one brutalized in the presence of a unilateral consciousness of the conqueror, blind to Indian values. The Indian is the barbarian only for those who elevate their world into the only world possible. (quoted in Barber 1998, 58; cf. Lange 1998, 135)

An insistence that truth-claims must be based on the "unilateral consciousness of the conqueror" reinforces the ego's and system's rationality as the Other is treated "as a 'functional part' of a system" (Dussel 2003a, 1/1). Such cauterization of the otherness of the Other would even undergird justice-claims, even if they are made on behalf of the Other. So, justice (not in Derrida's transcendental sense) would be the perpetuation of the system's violence, such as the originary violence in human rights regimes. To require the Other to speak the language of the system, although satisfactory for a discourse ethics, would further serve to marginalize the Other. Such silencing disguised as tolerance can be seen in contemporary human rights institutions, which through their actions, in effect, tell oppressed groups that if you protest in the appropriate manner, we will listen, and if you suffer certain abuses that we define as abuses, we will respond (cf. Baxi 2002; Dawes 1999). What are the consequences of a right being recognized by international law? Or more poignantly, what is the cost of being excluded from the list? With such a potential for reproducing original violence through tolerance and justice-claims, it is imperative that the Other must continually question the system, its justice-claims, and its human rights from its exteriority.

Dussel develops his own conception of a tolerance beyond that of discursive democracy. I will call this Dusselian tolerance "patient listening." This patient listening is nicely described by Michael Barber: "One must commit oneself in humility and meekness to a pedagogic apprenticeship with the Other as master and to a following of the way that the Other's word traces, day in and day out" (Barber 1998, 53). Dussel uses Bartolomé las Casas' initial response to native American peoples as an exemplar of this patient listening. Whereas Juan Ginés de Sepúlveda and others advocated forceful intervention in the affairs of the native peoples in order to save the innocent victims of human sacrifice, Las Casas advocated patient listening to the voice of the anti-hegemonic community. He advocated a rational discussion of the truth-claim being made by the native peoples, based on their own *weltanschauung* (worldview). The

Spaniards should not expect the native peoples to renounce their truth-claim based on the word of the Spanish soldiers without further thought:

> They would act hastily and would be worthy of *admonition and punishment* if in something so arduous, so important and of such difficult abandonment...they lent faith to those Spanish soldiers, ignoring so many and so serious testimonies and of so great authority, *until with more convincing arguments, it will be demonstrated to them* that the Christian religion is worthier of being believed in, *which cannot be done in a short space of time.* (Dussel 2004, 329)

Solidarity with the Other's Proyecto

Dussel, with his embrace of what I call the Saturated Other, goes further. He calls for solidarity with the Other. Solidarity moves beyond tolerance because it does not share tolerance's "indifference before the Other." It is not based on the truth-claim of the ego or the system. It even goes further than patient listening. Instead, it is a concrete response to the Saturated Other. When the two types of exteriority converge, when the marginalized Others approach from outside of the system, they "shake the very pillars of the system that exploits them" (Dussel 1985, 43). The ego is called, not only to respond directly to the Other, but to represent the Other "before the tribunal of a system that accuses him or her" (Dussel 2004, 330). When the ego is confronted with both levels of exteriority, it is not only a matter of "knowing how to listen to the voice of the Other, but above all the knowing how to respond through a liberating praxis" (Dussel 2006, 80–81). Solidarity is "the affirmation of the exteriority of the other, of his life, his rationality, his denied rights" (Dussel 2004, 330), and this is a call for the ego to work "with the victim in order to stop him or her from being a victim" (2004, 332). Of course, patient listening remains crucial as the ego does not work with the Other based on the ego's *weltanschauung* but affirms "the exteriority of the other, of his life, his rationality, his denied rights" (Dussel 2004, 330). Patient listening would require that the Other self-ascribes her own identity and defines her own rights. The ego and the system's institutions are called to assist the Other in this process, but it is not through imposing their standards on the Other. It is "the fulfillment of the desire of the life-project the other cannot actualize" (Dussel 2004, 330).

Again, Dussel turns to Las Casas as an example. Not only did Las Casas leave open a space for the voice of the Other in the rational discourse, he took on the life-project of the native peoples. For Dussel, this is apparent in Las Casas' "recognition of the duty of the natives to wage a war in defense of their traditions against the European Christians, of whom Bartolomé is one" (Dussel 2004, 331). Las Casas is able to call a potential war waged against Christians "just" because the system has indeed silenced the voice of the Other, or more accurately Las Casas says it has "done nothing but tear them to pieces, kill them, distress, afflict, torment and destroy them by strange, new diverse forms of cruelty" (quoted in Dussel 2003a, 213). "To Batrolome...the whole system was unjust, starting from its basic intention...lust for gold" (2003a, 213). This situation will only be remedied by taking on the system itself. Las Casas was willing take on their life plan, even if it included human sacrifice, to work with the native peoples, even if it called into question the religious and political institutions that supported him.

TOWARD A HUMAN RIGHTS LAW OF
THE MARGINALIZED OTHER

The system cauterizes the Other and denies voice to those who would call it into question. Without voice the Other cannot interrogate the original violence of the system's institutions, including its human rights institutions that are set up to ameliorate the Other's suffering.

Thus, it is not surprising that the conservation of original violence in human rights law (as in the headscarf affairs) is associated with a cauterization of the Other. Even where the Other has a voice, it is often silenced by law's idiom; and because idioms will never completely overlap, there will always be violence. This violence will be intensified for the Other who is cauterized from the system (see the discussion in Chapter 5 and Conklin 1998). This suggests that extraordinary measures, beyond Benhabib's democratic iterations or Levinas' "moments of negation," must be taken to deconstruct human rights and restore the voice of the Other. If the starting point is the concrete Other, the Other must be in the courtroom, must have a voice, and must be allowed to define and perform her human rights. More than that, the system or singular judge must work with the Other to restore her rights.

Dussel's ethics of liberation turns the concrete universalisms of Arendt and discursive democracy on their heads. For Arendt, politics involves an agonistic battle and ultimate consensus between those who are *zoon ekhon logon*, the living animals with speech. This is best accomplished for Arendt when the politically irrelevant beings, the *aneu logou* (those without speech) are cauterized from the political sphere. Conversely, for Dussel, politics is only possible when the *aneu logou* are brought into the political process and when the hegemonic political actors are silenced by, and pay heed to, the voice of the Other. For Arendt, solidarity involves speaking for the Other, but not from their perspective as they are "never the best judges on the order of priorities in such matters." For Dussel, solidarity is patient listening to the *aneu logou* and working with them to realize their rights based on their own priorities. Whereas Arendt was reluctant to embrace a human rights institution such as an international criminal court because it did not have political legitimacy from the hegemonic powers, Dussel insists we must first ask whether the court would have legitimacy from the anti-hegemonic community. Such legitimacy could not be granted if it perpetuated the violence of the system against the oppressed. Likewise, Dussel turns discursive democracy on its head. Discursive democracy tolerates those who speak the hegemonic language of the political sphere, and thus it conserves the original violence of the system. Dussel insists that discursive democracy be at the service of the Other to aid in the creation of an anti-hegemonic validity that will undermine the original violence of the system, including its human rights institutions. These institutions must give priority to the voice of the marginalized Other. They must engage in patient listening to the provocation of the Other, and they must work with the Other to realize "the life-project the other cannot actualize" (Dussel 2004, 330).

PART III

Human Rights of the Marginalized Other

5

Learning to Learn from the Voice of the Other

Beasts have no praxis because they have no words.
– Seyla Benhabib

Part II developed a phenomenology of the Saturated Other, the marginalized Other who calls the ego to a deeper responsibility because it approaches from outside the system. This responsibility stems from the transcendence, or more accurately, the hyper-presence of the Other. Such a hyper-presence, like Derrida's undeconstructable justice, calls into question all pretensions of doing justice for the Other, including human rights law. The ego is called to an infinite responsibility to the Other that includes representing the Other at the system's tribunal. The ego must continuously critique all original and conserving violence, even of the institutions that are set up to serve the Other.

From Dussel's work, I derived three overlapping modalities of this responsibility. First, the ego is called to a patient listening to the voice of the Other. Second, the Other must be able to self-ascribe his or her identity and to identify his or her own rights. Finally, the ego is called to work with the Other to build the life-project that the Other is unable to complete because the Other is outside the system. This working with the Other for the realization of this life-project requires patient listening, self-ascription, and self-definition of rights so that "the dominated and/or excluded will be constitutive and participant agents in the justice that is also material" (21). In the three chapters of Part III, I employ the insights of theorists Jacques Rancière, Gayatri Spivak, Judith Butler, and others to explore how human rights law can better respond to the call of the marginalized Other through each of these three interrelated modalities.

Although human rights law has made great strides in rectifying human rights abuses, especially in the past decade, few are sanguine enough to admit that it is sufficient or even always helpful in ameliorating abuses. Human rights law has often been unable or unwilling to listen and learn from the Other. Indeed, human rights law often further cauterizes the Other. This cauterization process takes on myriad forms, some endemic to the abstraction and violence of law and others originating in the original violence of the human rights regimes stemming from such factors as geopolitical exigencies, cultural biases, and social norms. Some human rights institutions as well as some grassroots NGOs, however, have become increasingly conscious of the voice of the Other and have taken innovative procedural steps to ameliorate their suffering by working with the marginalized Other.

In this chapter, I first consider the insights of Jacques Rancière and William Conklin to show the various ways that law silences the voice of the Other through the operation of law itself. We cannot work for a reinvigoration of human rights law naively without considering the inherent weaknesses of law for serving the marginalized Other. Those who seek to serve the marginalized Other through law are using an instrument that by its very nature cauterizes the Other. Next, I turn to Gayatri Spivak's wonderful struggles to find a space for the voice of the Other in transnational discourses. From her works, I conclude that human rights law requires a ceaseless and patient listening to the Other. Human rights law must learn how to learn from below; it must constantly be educated by the Other.

I then consider this "learning to learn from the Other" in an empirical-legal context notable for its attempts to find a space for the voice and agency of the Other. I consider social action litigation (SAL) in India, where the courts have consciously adopted several methods to increase access to justice for marginalized members of society. Whereas SAL has benefited large segments of Indian society, the Indian Supreme Court's 2000 ruling on the Narmada River dam project has been condemned by human rights activists for failing to listen to the voice of the Other. I juxtapose the views of the Supreme Court with two groups that could claim, albeit imperfectly, to represent the voices of the marginalized. Although ultimately flawed, Indian SAL has broken new ground in allowing victimized Others to restore their voices through their own agency, and these lessons should be considered in other jurisdictions.

THE SILENCING OF THE OTHER IN HUMAN RIGHTS LAW

Law cauterizes. Rarely is law applied evenly or universally or even intended to do so. Law protects specific individuals and leaves others unprotected without a voice and therefore sustains previous partitions in societies. Law serves the hegemonic system.

Rancière and the Sans Part

French philosopher Jacques Rancière brilliantly argues that politics is not about who gets what within the polis but who is considered to be part of the polis and who are *sans part* (without a part), or in Aristotle's terms, *aneu logou* (without a voice). Most political philosophers from Aristotle through Arendt and Habermas have overlooked what Rancière calls the "misunderstanding" generated between those who are in the polis and those who are deemed to be *sans part*. This misunderstanding refers both to "the fact of not hearing, of not understanding" and to a "quarrel" or "disagreement" (1999, 5). Law not only reinforces the silencing of the Other, it must take the side of the system in the "dispute over the situation itself" (1999, 6). Those who are *sans part* are often not even "visible as an element of a situation" (1999, 6). They are not considered because they do not have a voice that can be understood by the system or by its law.

From the perspective of those in the polis and their law, the *sans part* only speak with "*to phôné*" (a voice) in Aristotle's sense that "serves animals in general to indicate or show sensations of pain or pleasure" (Rancière 1999, 21; cf. Aristotle 1932, 1253a). Or, to use Plato's language, the people (*hoi polloi*) resemble a great beast (Plato Bk. VI) that expresses nothing but mere opinion (*doxa*). Law is deaf to such animalistic "cries of hunger, rage, or hysteria" (Rancière 2004, 5). The *sans part* may understand the voice of reason, but they cannot exercise it. As Aristotle writes, "the slave is the one who participates in reason so far as to recognize it but not so as to possess it" (Rancière 1999, 17).

Because this disagreement is a "dispute over the situation itself," overturning this partition requires more than "a simple explanation of what the other's sentence is saying" (Rancière 1999, xi). The *aneu logou* must interrupt the situation; they must become parvenu and push themselves onto the stage and claim their voice, their right to be heard. For Rancière, this site where the inegalitarian logic of the common is confronted by egalitarian logic is politics. It is the opening of the situation itself. This "political subjectification" is a questioning of the original violence that determined who belongs within the polis – including the benefits of belonging and the consequences of exclusion.

Rancière provides "an extreme example" of the cauterization of the *sans part* and their political subjectification with the story of the debates on Aventine Hill during the Plebeian secession in 494 BCE. Rancière, following Ballanche's critique of Livy's classic account, holds that the battle between the patricians and the plebes was not a rebellion over material goods but a battle over who was allowed to speak. The patricians initially refused to make a treaty with the plebes because "to make a treaty meant giving one's word: since the plebeians did not have human speech, they could not give what they did not have. They possessed only a 'sort of bellowing which was a sign of need and not a manifestation of intelligence'" (Rancière 2004, 5). In response to this deaf ear from the patricians, the plebes formed their own assembly, their own government, and even consulted their own oracles. In Ballanche's terms, they wrote their "name in the sky" (Rancière 1999, 25). This establishment of an anti-hegemonic system in which the plebes could exercise their voice convinced the patricians to allow the plebes a voice in the Roman government with rights guaranteed through the Tribune of the Plebes. The Senators were forced to "conclude that, since the plebes have become creatures of speech, there is nothing left to do but to talk to them" (Rancière 1999, 25–26). Of course, this Tribune often served merely as a way of placating – or in Rancière's terms, policing – the plebes or as an instrument that could be manipulated to serve the interests of the patricians against the plebes. Undoubtedly Roman society continued to operate with fundamental partitions that separated Roman citizens from slaves and foreigners.

Even after gaining entrance to the polis, (some) citizens and their pleas can be systematically dismissed or misunderstood. This continued marginalization is enforced by what Rancière calls "policing." Not only does policing protect the common from politics by "suppressing surplus subjects" (1999, 8), it also continues to protect the hegemonic system once political subjectification is successful. Once admitted as citizens of the polis, those formerly *sans part* can be assigned a lesser place in the polis, and this assignment is aided by law in its policing function. Law defines "the allocation of ways of doing, ways of being, and ways of saying, and sees that those bodies are assigned by name to a particular place and task" (Rancière 1999, 29). Here, Jean-François Lyotard's work on the *differend* maintains its force. Any attempt to make a voice heard must encounter all of the original violences in law. They must encounter a "certain rationalism" of the system. This logic applies equally to human rights law, which claims to be egalitarian and claims to have welcomed all people and their torts into the polis.

Law's Categorization

Human rights law cauterizes. Even international human rights law, which purports to be in service to all Others to treat all others equally, cauterizes the Other. In Rancière's terms, human rights law polices. For instance, to recognize an abuse as a tort, human rights law must categorize and define human rights abuses. Abuses that do not fit pre-defined categories are, by default, sanctioned. Such categorization perpetuates the system's original violence as some abuses will not be considered torts to be addressed. For instance, Upendra Baxi rightly asks why isn't the Cold War named "an order of radical evil" (Baxi 2002, 19)? The encouragement, financing, arming, training, and operational support of proxy armies known to be committing grave human rights abuses surely constitutes a grave human rights abuse. Such actions as a matter of national policy clearly meet the international legal standards of aiding and abetting as determined by Allied judges at Nuremburg and elsewhere (see Simmons 2007). Yet, such abuses were calculatedly kept out of international human rights documents such as the Universal Declaration of Human Rights and the International Convention on Civil and Political Rights.

Similarly, we must ask why – in my own state of Arizona – are the deaths of over 200 migrants in the desert each year not treated as a human rights abuse? These migrants are "induced" to uproot their lives and traverse the border by U.S. economic and trade policies and (formerly) lax border enforcement, but concomitant nativist policies demand increased border enforcement that deliberately pushes the migrants into extreme desert conditions (Frey 2002; Failinger 2006). The failure to categorize such policies as human rights abuses works symbiotically with the silencing of the Other. The migrants' voices and their suffering rarely if ever are considered in the voluminous and vituperous immigration policy debates. Their anguish appears only to be animalistic cries of "feelings, pleasure, or pain, in the form of a cry, contentment or hate" and thus does not register to the courts. Instead, the law reinforces the partition by prosecuting those who attempt to reach out and recognize the humanity of the migrants and ameliorate the suffering of those lost in the desert. For example, in 2005 two college-aged students were indicted for aiding and abetting migrants because they drove three migrants in medical need to a Tucson clinic. In this case, the system sustains the partition in society by censuring any response to the *to phôné* of the *aneu logou*.

Law's Silencing of the Other

Legal abstraction cauterizes. Even when human rights law reaches out and considers such anguish as a tort to be addressed, the Other can remain silenced because of the universalization process inherent to law. The instruments, institutions, and practitioners of law, because they necessarily deal with the universal, must abstract (etymologically: to pull away) the concrete experiences of the victim. As James Dawes (1999) writes,

> Replacing the particular with the general, the private with the common, and the subjective with the objective, international law (it can be argued)

invokes the participation of selves devoid of personhood, and of cultural
and linguistic thickness.... [I]t institutes an empty formalism that obliter-
ates the space of difference, of the individual, of the unique, and the con-
text-dependent. (244)

In a way, then, human rights instruments perpetuate violations by treating
the victim as an object. Human rights abusers that aim to turn the individual into a cipher have an ally in international human rights law when the
individual becomes part of the moral calculus of formalism and categorical
imperatives.

Canadian legal scholar William Conklin (1997, 1998) explores how the
inherent abstraction of law teams with the nomenclature of law and the previous partitions in/of the polis to further silence the Other by requiring the Other
to speak in a peculiar idiom, the idiom of the "master discourse." The experience and discourse of the victims, "the non-knowers," increasingly becomes
abstracted or disembodied to fit the "secondary genre" or discourse of those in
the legal profession ("the knowers"). To participate in the discourse of knowers, victims must be represented by experts who are charged with interpreting
the text and their experiences. However, law's prolixity requires abstraction of
the suffering. Even though the legal text may have been written with the best
of intentions and the knowers (the attorneys) are seeking, with good intention,
to remedy a tort, "the harm" of the human rights abuse "is doubled" as the
harm is translated into the legal discourse. In this translation, "the aggrieved,
as a judicial person, became 'alive' with lawyers' meaning. The aggrieved, as
an embodied participant, was forgotten" (Conklin 1997, 234). Conklin calls
the resulting gap between the two idioms a juridical *differend*.

This abstraction process – the translation of experience into the language
of law – reinforces and is intertwined with the cauterization of law. This differend is exacerbated when the victimization is part of systemic oppression.
The victim's narrative will not be heard as it will be in an idiom that does not
register with the hierarchy. Indeed, the testimony of the Other is always put
on trial to determine its legitimacy.[1] Translation cauterizes, and yet it is necessary. Without this translation, the aggrieved will be cauterized from the legal
process. "If a court of appeal finds that one is not a juridical person, then the
claimant does not possess standing before the representers of the secondary
language" (Conklin 1997, 241).

Movingly, Conklin describes the original cauterization from the polis and
the subsequent abstraction process in the case of the Innu community of

---

[1] Henderson, for example, argues "that the testimony of black women in a sexist and racist
culture is always on trial, always put to a test, always suspect" (Oliver 2001, 99).

Davis Inlet on the Newfoundland coast. For decades, the community had literally been *sans part* in the Canadian polis (cf. Hanrahan 2003). Formerly a nomadic tribe centered on the hunting of migratory caribou herds, in the 1950s they were pressured to settle along the coast at Davis Inlet, a place they called Utshimassits. However, when they refused to register under the Indian Act and did not meet the criteria to be covered under a Municipality Act of Newfoundland, they were ineligible for most government services. Deprived of their life-project and with nowhere to turn, the community fell into despair with rampant unemployment, extreme alcoholism, squalid living conditions, and drug use that led to what was labeled the "highest suicide rate on earth" (Survival International 1999, 5). Their pleas were not heard by the Canadian polis until video was released of six children after an unsuccessful group suicide attempt by sniffing petrol. "The graphic pictures of wild-eyed children hurling themselves against the wall and screaming 'Leave me alone! I want to die!' shocked Canada and made Utshimassits, after years of official neglect, the focus of national and international media attention" (Survival International 1999, 6).

Once a community forces itself into the polis and such a tort is recognized in need of remedy, the cauterization process can continue through the judicial differend that develops as community members' decades of suffering must be translated into a legal idiom. "The lawyers, social workers, police and judges had to classify the behaviour of the indigents in a manner which made sense to others in the secondary genre" (Conklin 1998, 85). To best translate their multifaceted experiences, the translator will reduce their suffering by "isolate[ing] one part of the residents' experience" (86). The story that will be told is not the one chosen by the community but will be one that the translator believes will resonate with others in the secondary genre. However, this initial choice, whether to frame the tort to be addressed as a group suicide attempt or the misdeeds of young offenders, or as an Indian problem, will dictate how the case will be handled, which will in turn determine the outcome of the case.

This reduced experience will then be attached to "chains of signifying relations" that will be connected to the "authoritative signs" of legal discourse. The legal community then is confronted with a series of "juridical facts" that may not even be recognized by the Innu as representative of their own experiences. "As I engage in dialogue with other lawyers in our search for the authority of our interpretations, the individual Inuit child with a biography slips from my face-to-face relations with others" (Conklin 1998, 90). Further, the experiential time of the victim is reduced to linear time by the legal process through a series of depositions and testimonies. "Reported judicial decisions do not describe the non-knower's long moments of intense anxiety, short moments of sharp psychic pain, and the exhausted silences which the non-knower and his or her family members experienced" (94). The ensuing legal analysis then becomes a balancing of abstracted rights claims by experts who are rewarded for their ability at "applying the law" through tying the reduced experience to statutes, precedents, and so forth. Legal analysis "idealizes the indigenous event itself. Indeed, the event is dispersed, and my production of signs becomes the event" (88). Hobbes' famous dictum rings true: "*Auctoritas, non veritas facit legem*" (authority, not truth makes law).

Reclaiming voice was made more complex in the case of the Innu because of a cultural differend. The Canadian government insisted on the election of a community chief with an elected council, but the Innu have traditionally had a dispersed hierarchy with decision making by consensus within familial bands. Moreover, their culture tends to eschew conflict and assertiveness, which have traditionally been used to stimulate social movements. Not only did the Innu not speak in a manner that would resonate with the hegemonic system, they did not play the role of the parvenu in the proper manner as defined by the system.

Since the well-publicized group suicide attempt, the Canadian government has responded in many ways. The Innu were recognized under the Indian Act and, after several delays, relocated to new land called Natuashish in 2002 and 2003 with better housing and sanitation at a cost of $152 million. Governmental services were stepped up. The eventual cost of the relocation has been estimated at $280 million, or $400,000 for each of the 700 members of the community. Extensive reports on their living conditions were submitted to the Canadian Human Rights Commission in 1993 and 2002. However, the Innu have been unable to reclaim their life-project that was taken away by colonization. They have not been able to remedy the "loss of cultural continuity in daily life" (Burns 2006, §4). Governmental support has often been stymied by bureaucracy, and attempts to reintegrate a nomadic lifestyle have been halted by pressure from mining and logging companies. Although the community had significant input in the relocation plans, requests to build more culturally sensitive homes with large meeting rooms and utility rooms for processing caribou were ignored (Burns 2006, § 24). The 2002 report to the Canadian Human Rights Commission concluded: "The machinery of the governmental bureaucratic processes does not always seem attuned to responding to Innu needs and problems" (Backhouse and McRae 2002, 60). The community is again in despair with rampant alcoholism, drug use, and domestic violence. Tragically, four children hanged themselves within a short period in 2004. On January 31, 2008, the community voted to outlaw the possession of alcohol, and they will soon have their first high school graduate.

However, the underlying causes of the despair have not been addressed, and the voices of the Innu are still ignored: "We were never given a chance to have a say in the past, but now we do have a say. But we still are not being listened to" (Penashue, n.d.). The Innu have not been able to claim substantial political subjectification.

SPIVAK AND THE IMPOSSIBILITY OF "ENTERING THE OTHER'S SPACE"

Perhaps no thinker has struggled with the intractable problems of voice, idiom, and counter-hegemony as Gayatri Chakravorty Spivak. From her justly famous essay "Can the Subaltern Speak?" through her wonderfully opaque magnum opus *Critique of Postcolonial Reason* to her recent writings on globalization and human rights, Spivak has meditated on the various ways that hegemonic discourses, including human rights law, silence the subaltern even when they attempt to speak for the subaltern.[2] Hegemonic systems are adept at reproducing their hierarchies in the name of beneficence.

Spivak shows the utter impossibility of speaking for the subaltern due to the inevitable, un-sheddable position of privilege of the academic, the activist, the attorney, and the judge. She relentlessly questions the ability of the ego to empty itself of itself to serve the Other. These intractable difficulties in speaking for or serving the Other may threaten to reduce us to quietism, but Spivak insists that this Sisyphean task must be continuously undertaken. The ego and the hegemonic system that sustains it must be unremittingly deconstructed through a very patient learning from below, that is, learning to learn from those who have been excluded from the hegemonic discourse. She aptly writes, "Finding the subaltern is not so hard, but actually entering into a responsibility structure with the subaltern, with responses flowing both ways: learning to learn without this quick-fix frenzy of doing good with an implicit assumption of cultural supremacy which is legitimized by unexamined romanticization, that's the hard part" (Spivak 1995b, 293).

Representing the Other

According to Spivak, many who mistakenly maintain they speak for the Other have conflated two notions of representation. The first, corresponding to the

---

[2] Spivak's understanding of the subaltern has evolved over time, but the term generally refers to the individual "where social lines of mobility, being elsewhere, do not permit the formation of a recognizable basis of action" (2005, 476). In this work, I will, too quickly perhaps, equate the subaltern with the marginalized Other.

German word *darstellen*, is signification or portrayal as in art or philosophy. This is the realm of subject-predication where identity is determined and almost always fixed.[3] The second is a speaking-for as in political representation, corresponding to the German *vertreten*. Spivak claims that many of those who claim to represent or speak for the Other, such as Arendt's judge that we met in Chapter 1, have already imposed their portrayal of the Other. The judge drafts a portrait of the Other based on his or her predilections and then speaks for that portrait. The Other is ventriloquized more than given voice. Examples abound of this colonial authorization. Spivak points out that the British chose an elite Indian class to be their intermediaries to implement indigenous law within strictures pre-established by the British. Thomas Babington MacCauley famously said, "We must at present do our best to form a class who may be interpreters between us and the millions whom we govern; a class of persons, Indian in blood and colour, but English in taste, in opinions, in morals, and in intellect" (Spivak 1999, 268). Spivak insists that we must constantly deconstruct all claims of speaking for the Other by deconstructing all portrayals of the Other and all those ideologies that sustain our perceptions.

Her critique of Michel Foucault and Gilles Deleuze, whom she praises as "the best prophets of heterogeneity and the Other" (Spivak 1999, 272), is especially cogent for understanding the difficulties in representing the Other. Spivak takes special umbrage with Deleuze's claim that "there is no more representation; there's nothing but action" (1999, 256). Any occlusion of representation allows for a "subject-privileging" in which the intellectual can claim that he or she correctly represents (speaks for) the subaltern, and thus "the intellectuals represent (claim) themselves as transparent." Thus Deleuze and Foucault, though usually sensitive to the invisible ideologies that sustain power relationships, fail to recognize that they are involved in the reproduction of a system (rooted in the international division of labor) that silences Europe's Others. Imperialism and colonialism and all those ideologies and laws that support them and silence Europe's Others remain un-interrogated.

While disavowing representation, Foucault and Deleuze valorize the concrete experience of the subaltern as when Deleuze writes, "Reality is what actually happens in a factory, in a school, in barracks, in a prison, in a police station." To reduce the subaltern to concrete experience is too often to make the experience another data point to be portrayed from the perspective of the hegemonic discourse. Any representation of the concrete experience will

---

3   The performativity of identity will be discussed in detail in the next chapter in the context of Judith Butler's works.

almost always be contaminated by the privileged position of the academic or colonialist who reports it. And yet, the appropriator or narrator of this experience, be it an academic, NGO, or activist, does not question the accuracy of their portrayal or the uses of this valorized concrete experience. Such a strategy continues to be employed by such organizations as the World Bank through their "Voices of the Poor" project (e.g., Narayan et al., 2000). Instead, the academic's theories are marshaled to make sense or bring order to the concrete experiences of the Other. Spivak is especially critical of those, such as feminists and cultural studies scholars, who previously summoned a marginalized person to appear at an academic conference in "a politically correct ritual moment" only to be dissected and understood by imperial knowledge. In such performances, the Other is essentialized as a subject and becomes a constative. Ironically, Foucault, who famously calls attention to the performativity and fluidity of the subject, risks eliding the social determination and fluidity of the Other when he valorizes concrete experience. Such privileging often "essentializes the oppressed as nonideologically constructed subjects" (Alcoff 1991–1992, 22).

We now see the seemingly intractable difficulties in speaking for the Other. The voice of the marginalized will be represented (signified or portrayed) through micrological and macrological discourses that reinforce the hegemonic power structure. The strategy of relying on the concrete experiences of the Other, acting as if we are transparent, often serves to make invisible our collusion in the marginalization process. Even the voice of the Other is prone to be interpreted or theorized by academics and activists through the lens of the hegemonic discourse. To "speak for" would require a deconstruction of both the intellectual and the situation of the marginalized; but such a deconstruction would be nigh impossible, because the theory, method, and practitioners of deconstruction itself are tainted by the hegemonic discourse that have already represented/portrayed the Other and its concrete experience. As a marginalized Other, the Other cannot speak or be heard. The Other remains *aneu logou* and *sans part*. Spivak sighs, "No one can say 'I am a subaltern' in whatever language" (2005, 476).[4]

Spivak's exasperation at the impossibility of the subaltern who is "on the other side of the international division of labor" speaking in a way understandable to the hegemonic discourse is the subject of her famous accounts of widow sacrifice (sati). Both imperialists and nationalists created narratives

---

[4] John Beverly writes: "If the subaltern could speak in a way that really mattered to us, that we would feel compelled to listen to, it would not be subaltern" (Beverly 1999, 66). Spivak's famous statement that "the subaltern cannot speak" has been so misunderstood that she would later call it "an inadvisable remark" (Spivak, 1999, 308).

for the widows. The imperialists saw the outlawing of sati as a noble cause of "white men saving brown women from brown men" (Spivak 1999, 297). The Indian nationalists emphasized the brownness of the women, that their sacrifice was an anti-imperialist political or religious gesture, and thus concluded that "the women actually wanted to die" (297). Amidst such representations or ventriloquizations, the widows' voices are not heard. Spivak was exasperated:

> The rhetoric of the ending is a rhetoric of despair. It was at that moment, right after the story, when I said, throwing up my hands, "the subaltern cannot speak." (Spivak 1990, 89)

Nevertheless, the widows, like the Plebes at Aventine Hill and the Innu of Newfoundland, can speak, but they are met with interpreters who refuse to listen because they are embedded within the hegemonic system.

Spivak is not claiming a privileged place for herself from which she can accurately represent the widows' voices. She readily admits that any solution she offers will be tinged by a colonial discourse – even for the most radical among us: "All speaking, even seemingly the most immediate, entails a distanced decipherment by another, which is, at best, an interception" (1999, 309). As such, the subaltern's voice remains something of a secret.[5]

In a poignant essay, Spivak assumes the role of an assimilated ex-colonial who has checked into a hotel room on a sojourn to open oneself to the Other without bringing along the baggage of western hegemonic thought. As such, "she 'knows' nothing on the other side" (Spivak 1991–1992, 1345). The best she can do is "the most literal-minded 'hanging out', resisting anthropology, resisting history, resisting revolutionary tourism" (1991–1992, 1347). But ultimately she cannot shed her privileged position:

> Keeping her presuppositions examined, her theoretical nose clean, the only way she can question the woman it seems eerie to call the 'subaltern', when one is face to face, when the moment seems right in her hanging-out times, are by way of questions cooked on the hot plate in the hotel room. (Spivak 1991–1992, 1347)

All attempts at representation (either as *darstellen* or *vertreten*) are enmeshed in the hegemony. They are part of a "vast aggregative violating systemic work which is precisely from that hotel lobby that she is trying to leave" (1347).

---

5   As Rigoberta Menchú writes, "I'm still keeping my Indian identity a secret. I'm still keeping secret what I think no-one should know. Not even anthropologists or intellectuals, no matter how many books they have, can find out all our secrets" (quoted in Spivak 1999, 245 n73).

Learning to Learn from the Other

Despite these seemingly insurmountable difficulties, Spivak has recently provided a sketch of how the subaltern can gain voice in transnational discourses such as human rights law. First, Spivak argues for a new sense of human rights starting from a "Levinasian"[6] obligation for the Other; that is, a call *of* the ethical as opposed to a call *to* the ethical from rationally derived principles à la Alan Gerwith. The responsibility for the Other calls the ego to a constant, vigilant negotiation with the structures of violence that will allow us to "open ourselves to an other's ethic" (Spivak 1993, 177). However, this responsibility must stem as much as possible from an Other that is untainted by our representations of the Other. It requires a suspension, a bracketing of the theoretical and the hegemonic, knowing that they can never be completely bracketed. Such a constant critique, Spivak argues, requires an education that reorients our thinking toward the Other. We must not just learn from below, but we need to learn to learn from below.

Spivak proffers the teaching of humanities as a metaphor for learning to learn from below. She has in mind a humanities-to-come – a humanities that is rarely taught. This is not the education in western liberal values advocated by Richard Rorty or even the education of the poor in Dickens undertaken by Martha Nussbaum.[7] Such an education, Spivak fears, "will continue to provide justification for international control." Instead, a humanities education is marked by "an *uncoercive* rearrangement of desires" (Sharpe and Spivak 2003, 615). This rearrangement of desires is not imposed by the teacher but takes place in a manner analogous to the reading of texts; not as "analyzing and diagnosing" but as a "no holds barred *self-suspending leap into the other's sea* – basically without preparation" (Spivak 2004a, 207–208, emphasis added).

Learning to learn from below requires what Spivak calls *teleopoiesis*. While "poiesis" is "imaginative making," Spivak borrows from Derrida's work to find both performativity and distance in the term teleopoiesis. The Greek stem *teleo-* stresses the bringing to completion, but Derrida invigorates the meaning by deliberately conflating it with the unrelated stem *tele-* (at a distance, mostly in time). So, for Derrida, *telepoiesis* becomes the process of creating toward an ever-distant future (*a-venir*). Spivak tweaks this formulation by adding an

---

[6] Spivak has difficulty in giving credit to Levinas because of what she sees as his "unquestioning support for the state of Israel" and his views on women as criticized by Irigaray.

[7] Rorty famously wrote "producing generations of nice, tolerant, well-off, secure, other-respecting students of [the American] sort in all parts of the world is just what is needed – indeed all that is needed – to achieve an Enlightenment utopia. The more youngsters like that we can raise, the stronger and more global our human rights culture will become" (1993, 127).

emphasis on spatial distance. Telepoiesis becomes creating toward a distant future with a "distant other." It suggests that the gap between the ego and the Other will never be bridged. Awareness of this distance leads to humility and suspension of certainty.

Imagination is indispensable for implementing telepoiesis. This is not Arendt's account of imagination (discussed in Chapter 1) as the judging of "objects that are no longer present" by "thinking in my own identity where I am not." Unlike Arendt where "I try to think in the place of the slum-dweller" but "still speak with my own voice," Spivak is trying to imagine a learning that requires turning off my own voice. Imagination is a material working with the Other through the Other's eyes as much as possible. There is no formula for such learning, for such exercise of imagination. Instead, Spivak refers to "a slow mind-changing process [that] can be used to open the imagination to such mindsets" (Spivak 2004b, 533). This is teaching and learning as ethnographic field work working with materially, in the field, to change the hegemonic system. It must be based on patient listening, "is never accurate, and must be forever renewed" (2004b, 529). One must leave the hotel room as much as possible and "involve yourself into the life detail of these women" (Sharpe and Spivak 2003, 613) all the while knowing that such work will forever be tainted by portrayals "cooked on the hot plate in the hotel room." To learn to learn from below is not to appropriate indigenous knowledge to add to, or even revise, hegemonic theories. A "self-*suspending leap into the other's sea*" (Spivak 2004a, 207–208) is an embrace of a different episteme, which requires a suspension of the hegemonic language and "a sustained institutional practice of diversified language learning in imaginative depth" (Spivak 2006, 1612). Language learning is not only being fluent in the subaltern's language, but also to reorient the language of beneficent human rights institutions into the idiom of the subaltern. Only in this way can the original violence of the hegemonic system that cauterizes the Other be addressed.

The ego must work with the Other, from the Other's perspective, to claim political subjectification for the Other, in Rancière's sense. This requires the self-ascription of the Other in order to claim a collectivity based on their own representations (Spivak 2005, 483, see Chapter 6 for a sustained discussion of self-ascription). Spivak remains skeptical of movements and countermovements that attempt to speak for the subaltern. "In general, the leaders of collectivities – good or bad – have the right to the metonym/synecdoche complex. That the rank and file do not, sometimes gets overlooked. That I believe is the difference between 'good' and 'bad' movements" (Spivak 2005, 481). Indeed, Spivak is skeptical of all collectivities that form a synecdoche. Spivak's definition of the subaltern now assumes a different facet: The subaltern is someone who lacks "the power to self-synecdochize" (2005, 482). A series of subalterns too quickly can be made into the universal or a "people" instead of a series of singularities creating themselves into a multiplicity while retaining the right to withdraw their affiliation lest it become "confused with identity" (2005, 482).

Toward a Human Rights Tribunal of the Other

Is it possible to "create a stage on which problems can be made visible" (Rancière 1999, 7) but that does not cauterize the Other or re-victimize the victim by imposing its idiom on the victimized Others? Ultimately, if law and its idiom reinforce the hegemonic system, law must be stopped or at least suspended. A space must be opened where jurisgenerative/anti-hegemonic communities can evolve and speak and where the plebes can form their community to demonstrate that they have a voice. This voice must be constantly critiqued to determine whether it metonymizes the voices of the subaltern. The subaltern must self-synecdochize. Instead of putting the voice of the Other into question or on trial, a human rights of the Other requires that the system's tribunal and all those who claim to speak for the Other be put into question. A tribunal must critique its own rules of standing to determine if the definition or representation of a juridical person is already imbued with structural violence that determines who is *sans part*. It must learn to learn from below what is a human rights abuse to avoid categorizations that are cauterizations. It must allow a prominent place for the voice of the Other throughout the proceedings and, as far as possible, allow the other to speak in his or her own idiom. If law will ultimately abstract the experiences of the Other and insist on its own idiom, the judge must at least linger with the face of the Other as long as possible, to linger in the language of the anti-hegemonic discourse in "a sustained institutional practice of diversified language learning in imaginative depth." The tribunal must involve itself in "the life detail" of the marginalized Other.

SOCIAL ACTION LITIGATION IN INDIA

India's evolving jurisprudence of social action litigation (SAL)[8] represents one of the most dramatic examples of attempting to learn to learn from below, to set up a system against the "traditional judiciary poster where

---

[8]   Baxi (1988) and others insist on the term SAL to differentiate the Indian experience from Public Interest Litigation in the United States and elsewhere.

people's causes appear merely as issues, argued arcanely by lawyers and decided in the mystery and mystique of the inherited common-law-like judicial process" (Baxi 1988, 388). SAL was consciously developed in the early 1980s through "a series of unprecedented and electrifying initiatives" (Galanter and Krishnan 2004, 795) by the Indian Supreme Court (and the High courts) to give agency to those most marginalized in society through liberalized rules of procedures for human rights abuses. The roots of SAL are found in the Indian Constitution, especially Article 32, which guarantees the right to seize the Supreme Court for violations of the "Fundamental Rights" included in Part III of the 1949 Constitution, especially the "protection of life and personal liberty" guaranteed in Article 21. These provisions were reinvigorated by their interpretation in a post-emergency era 1977 report by Justices Bhagwati and Krishna Iyer. Through this report and numerous subsequent decisions, the justices developed a specifically Indian approach to working for the rights of the marginalized as distinguished from much of western law, which Justice Bhagwati describes as "transactional, highly individualistic, concerned with atomic justice incapable of responding to the claims and demands of collectivity, and resistant to change" (quoted in Agarwal 2004, 691).

Under SAL, any individual can directly petition the highest courts to investigate a human rights abuse. Such petitions need not be formal legal briefs but could be a note or even a post card. In one famous example of what has become known as epistolary jurisdiction, the Court initiated a full investigation when it received a newspaper clipping that documented the working conditions of bonded laborers (*Mukesh Advani v. Madhya Pradesh* 1985).

If the individual or group of individuals suffering the abuse is "by reason of poverty, helplessness or disability or socially or economically disadvantaged position, unable to approach the Court for relief, any member of the public can maintain an action for an appropriate direction, order or writ" (*S.P. Gupta v. Union of India* 1982). Thus, cases have been brought by academics, activists, and journalists on behalf of the marginalized in society who normally would not have access to the courts – often called, in terms that invite the Spivakian critique, *representative* standing. At times, the cases seem to be instigated by the courts themselves, or at least the courts have encouraged the bringing of claims on specific issues (Baxi 1988, 398).

SAL cases are not heard in the usual adversarial fashion. The Court recognized that normal judicial procedures would create what Conklin labeled a *juridical differend* whereby the testimony of the Other would need to be translated into legal discourse, and in such a format the victim would be severely disadvantaged.

It must be remembered that the problems of the poor which now coming before the court are qualitatively different from those which have hitherto occupied the attention of the court they *need a different kind of lawyering skill and a different kind of judicial approach*. If we blindly follow the adversarial procedure in their case, they would never be able to enforce their fundamental rights and the result would be nothing but a mockery of the Constitution. (*Bandhua Mukti Morcha v. Union of India* 1984, emphasis added)

Instead, because the government through the Indian Constitution has pledged to protect a wide range of human rights, it is assumed that the victims and the government both are seeking to rectify the abuse. Thus, a commission of inquiry is often established in which (theoretically at least) the victim and the government work collaboratively to find a solution. In this way, the victims are not required to marshal the evidence to make the case. The state works with the marginalized by taking affirmative actions to aid in the preparation of the case. The commission also is tasked with preparing a list of remedies that are then given the force of law by a ruling from the Court. Most interestingly, these commissions often undertake fact-finding missions that have been described as "intensive fieldwork" (Baxi 1988, 405 n. 81); that is, in Spivak's terms, involving themselves in the lives of the marginalized.

On the issue of remedies for human rights abuses, the Court "has all incidental and ancillary power including the power to forge new remedies and fashion new strategies designed to enforce the fundamental rights" (*M.C. Mehta v. Union of India* 1986). Vandenhole (2002) provides a sense of the wide range of remedies ordered:

The court has sometimes given orders or recommendations to the executive branch, for example to provide for a sufficient number of homes for the mentally ill, to set up an effective implementation scheme for the minimum wages act, to create juvenile courts, to release adequate funds to improve the management of a psychiatric hospital, to release adequate funds for the rehabilitation of released bond labourers, to prosecute police officers for murder, or to convene a meeting for the elaboration of principles and a policy on the progressive elimination of child labour. (160)

The courts have also often taken on a role in overseeing the implementation of the remedies, that is, working with the marginalized to realize their life-projects.

Not surprisingly, SAL has been harshly criticized by some for creating an overly activist judiciary that impinges on the powers of the other branches of government.[9] The Court is effectively drafting policies and, with its oversight of remedies, potentially usurping the discretion of administrative agencies. Further, as expected, this technique has been increasingly appropriated by interest groups, businesses, and others for their own ends to the detriment of marginalized populations.

From the standpoint of human rights of the Other, other drawbacks need to be negotiated. First, despite the procedural shortcomings, it is probable that different groups will take it upon themselves to represent the marginalized members of society based on their own representations (portrayals) of the Other. As much as possible the courts would need to take steps so that the marginalized could self-synecdochize. Second, like all structures created to give voice to the marginalized, SAL must be subject to continuous critique as it is susceptible to appropriation and original violence. SAL was crafted in one of the most highly politicized periods of Indian history, and thus the justices have had to be very cognizant of their position in government, especially on such sensitive issues as international security and economic development. Also, environmentalism became something of a mantra, especially after the Bhopal tragedy, and could usurp the rights of the marginalized as has been seen in recent pro-environmental decisions that have resulted in the displacement of tens of thousands of marginalized peoples. For instance, in the "Delhi polluting industries" cases the Court's orders, intended to benefit the poor by improving their environment, will ultimately force the removal of tens of thousands of people from their homes (Hosbet 2000). These potential pitfalls combine to silence the voice of the Other.

Narmada: The Limits of the People's Court

The Indian Supreme Court's 2–1 decision in *Narmada Bachao Andolan v. Union of India* (2000) is perhaps the most controversial of all SAL cases. It has been called "a shockingly bad judgment, a negative answer to those who sought relief, and a severe blow to people's movements" (Iyer 2000). The Court allowed the completion of the controversial and massive Sardar Sarovar dam on the Narmada River with minimal oversight despite the spirited and decades-long protest of several groups fighting on behalf of the adivasis (tribal peoples) to be displaced, including the Narmada Bachao Andolan (Save the Narmada Movement, hereinafter, NBA). The NBA had reason to believe that

---

9   "The Supreme Court and the high courts have now become a part of the system of governance monitoring official actions giving, from time to time, such fiats as they think proper, expecting unquestioned allegiance to every word that falls from the lips of these superlords" (Hosbet 2000).

the Supreme Court would be receptive to their SAL petition as it had previously ruled in favor of the oustees and had halted the construction of the dam from 1994 to 1999. Further, in an unrelated case, the court made it clear that "no developmental project, however laudable, can possibly justify impoverishment of large sections of people and their utter destitution" (Kibreab 2000, 293). Instead, the Court in this case not only allowed the completion of the dam, but the logic of its decision has been rightly characterized as an "erasure" of the views of the adivasis (Routledge 2003).

Project Background

The Sardar Sarovar dam is the lynchpin of one of the largest and most politicized hydrology projects in history, involving 30 large dams, 135 medium-sized dams, and more than 3,000 small dams. It promises to harness huge amounts of water from the Narmada River that is relatively under-developed with only 4 percent being used before reaching the Arabian Sea. The terminal dam at Sardar Sarovar was to be built to a height of 138 meters and stretch over 1,200 meters across the river. With the completion of the dam, the water would be diverted into a maze of 75,000 kilometers of canals, including a 532 kilometer cement-lined main canal. The dam would also create 1,450 megawatts of much-needed electricity. This project promised to provide irrigation, drought control, electricity, and clean drinking water that would supposedly benefit millions of mostly marginalized people, most of whom live in drought-prone areas. Nonetheless, many commentators argue that the greatest beneficiaries of the irrigation system will be the large sugar cane plantations, and most of the drinking water will service large cities in the region. The human and environmental costs for the project have been much debated, but a governmental tribunal in 1979 estimated that 248 villages consisting of 66,593 people would ultimately be submerged by the reservoir. Tens of thousands of others would be displaced by other aspects of the project such as the construction colony at the dam site, the canal systems, and the resettlement of the original oustees. A vast majority of the oustees are adivasis, including almost all those from the states of Gujarat and Maharashtra, who maintained traditional lifestyles with close connections to the river (Parasuraman 1999, 180).

The project is even more complicated because it involves three large Indian states with different interests that will be differentially impacted by the project.[10] The project has also intersected with contentious party politics at the

---

[10] Ultimately, a fourth state, Rajasthan, was added to the award as it received some of the irrigation water.

state and national levels and various ethnic and class divisions. The dam itself is in the state of Gujarat, but most of the lost land and displaced villages from submergence are in Madhya Pradesh, and most of the displaced would be relocated to the state of Maharashtra. The people and government in Gujarat have generally been well-disposed to the completion of the dam, with much less support in Madhya Pradesh and Maharashtra.

After years of failed negotiations, the federal government created the Narmada Water Disputes Tribunal (NDWT) in 1969 to mediate between the affected states. Its five-volume decision, produced after ten years of hearings, fact-finding missions, and numerous extensive technical reports, tried to balance the costs and benefits for each state. The magisterial decision mainly dealt with dam specifics and other technical details, but it also included a policy on resettlement and rehabilitation that was actually quite progressive for the time. It set the final height of the Sardar Sarovar dam at 138.68 meters (455 feet), submerging 37,533 hectares, and dividing the water and electricity between the affected states, with a majority of the water and electricity going to Madhya Pradesh. Gujarat would see its share of the Narmada water increase substantially and receive a substantial boost in electricity without suffering much loss of land and thus was required to pay the lion's share of the resettlement and rehabilitation (R&R) costs of the oustees.

The project-affected families (PAFs) would receive R&R based on a progressive (for its time) formula in which they would receive land, money to build a house, and other monies for resettlement costs. All adult sons would be treated as separate families and thus receive their own land and money. Also to be provided were drinking wells, primary schools, and other village amenities, including a seed store and children's park for every 500 families. The award stipulated that "no submergence of any area would take place unless the oustees were rehabilitated" (*Narmada Bachao Andolan v. Union of India* 2000). The NDWT also established the Narmada Control Authority that would oversee the implementation of the Award and could commission subcommittees as needed. Ultimately six subcommittees were constituted, including two on R&R and one on the environment.

Although the Tribunal's ruling was progressive for its time, it continued to reflect the top-down development discourse of its time. The voices of the marginalized Other were not considered. The Tribunal "did not hold public hearings or consult the people most affected by the construction, those who would be displaced by the reservoir, the dam site, or the canals" (Wood 2007, 112). Environmental costs were also not considered in the debates or even mentioned in the final five-volume decision.

Two major problems soon became apparent. First, each state developed separate and evolving R&R plans, and these were implemented unevenly depending on state-specific political pressures. Madhya Pradesh generally dragged its heels in implementing its plans, and the piecemeal process exacerbated the chaos of the displacement with thousands of people being relocated without the necessary land allocated for resettlement or without necessary amenities provided. In some cases, the promised subsistence allowances were not made and the allocated land was difficult or impossible to cultivate. Many adivasis who were relocated eventually moved back to their original lands, necessitating their re-removal.[11] Originally, the adivasis had little ability to voice their complaints, but several newly created NGOs were able to win some improvements in the implementation plans. Most notably, Arch-Vahini, a group most active in Gujarat, successfully fought for the rights of title-less adivasis and for full implementation of the R&R plans. These improvements often came after extensive and prolonged non-violent resistance, international pressure, and lengthy legal battles (Parasuraman 1999, 192).

Second, the Tribunal's definition of PAFs left out thousands of people who would be affected by the project. They were literally considered *sans part*. Those displaced by the vast construction colony near the dam were not included nor were people displaced by the building of the vast irrigation canal network (estimated at 157,000 people). The original award did not grant any compensation to the thousands of adivasis who did not have formal land deeds but relied on customary law for their property rights. These were officially branded as encroachers. Thousands more, such as fishermen, shop owners, and peddlers, had no formal title to land and thus received no compensation. Similarly, little provision was made for communal property. Again, these policies changed over time and varied between the three states.

The Counter-Hegemonic Struggle

The counter-hegemonic struggle for the displaced adivasis has been multifaceted and has played out in many forums at the local, national, and transnational levels. It became a global cause célèbre that ultimately led to crucial changes in the World Bank's policies and spurred the creation of the World Commission on Dams, but ultimately this only led to moderate improvements in the conditions of the adivasis. In the decades-long struggle, the voices of the adivasis were often silenced by the hegemonic system, and they

---

[11] See Parasuraman (1999, 183ff) for a detailed case study of an alleged model village that actually should serve as an example of how not to do R&R.

were often cauterized in the comprehensive way developed earlier in this book. However, there have been occasional instances where scholars, activists, politicians, and judges have suspended their own episteme and patiently listened to the voices of the Other. This has required what Spivak called "a sustained institutional practice of diversified language learning in imaginative depth" (Spivak 2006, 1612).

Early protests centered on the displacement from the massive construction colony but spread quickly once the extent of the planned displacement became clear. The World Bank, which had promised to bankroll a large segment of the project, became concerned and sent Dr. Thayer Scudder, a western anthropologist, on well-publicized fact-finding missions to examine the resettlement issue. Scudder was intent on hearing the voice of the adivasis. "Tell me whatever you want, give me in writing whatever you need...because there is going to be a loan agreement with the World Bank and all the governments in India, and I am going to write that part of the agreement" (quoted in Khagram 2004, 213). His scathing reports resulted in the World Bank conditioning its loan on successful resettlement plans (Khagram 2004, 213–214). Under continued monitoring by the World Bank and numerous high-profile international NGOs, the R&R plans became more inclusive and the Narmada Control Authority created an environmental subcommittee. As a result of a court ruling stemming from an SAL petition, an R&R subcommittee was also formed. Also, at the instigation of the national government, the project now required environmental clearance that was finally approved in 1987 with several conditions, notably that "that environmental safeguard measures are planned and implemented *pari passu* with progress of work on project" (*NBA v. India* 2000).

Continued uneven implementation of the R&R plans was met with continued protests and the founding of the NBA in 1989. With a slogan of "we want development, not destruction," the NBA organized countless protests, sit-ins, hunger strikes, and road blockages to stop construction of the dam. The resulting international attention led to U.S. Congressional hearings in 1989, which spurred the World Bank to undertake its own independent assessment, the first of its kind by the Bank. After a ten-month investigation, the final report, known as the Morse report, recommended that the World Bank "step back" from supporting the project unless several conditions were met. At India's request, apparently to avoid further controversy and embarrassment, the World Bank withdrew its support from the project; and Japan, the other major international donor, followed suit.

The Narmada campaign, at this stage, was hailed as the model of indigenous social movements developing an anti-hegemonic discourse in partnership with international groups and successfully shaping development policies of governments and intergovernmental organizations (IGOs). The movement innovatively advanced international norms in such areas as indigenous rights and environmental rights. It succeeded in changing the way the World Bank and bilateral donors conducted business and ultimately led to the creation of the World Commission on Dams made up of government ministers, scientists, and activists, including Medha Patkar (the founder of the NBA) and anthropologist Scudder.

Nevertheless, the Indian government forged ahead with the project using its own funds. This decision necessitated changes in the anti-hegemonic movement as international norms and coalitions could no longer be employed as effectively (see, for example, Rajagopal 2005). Recourse had to be sought in domestic politics, especially the courts.[12] The NBA, with some assistance from the state of Madhya Pradesh, filed an SAL petition to the Supreme Court in 1994 that argued, inter alia, that the Tribunal's Award of 1979 failed to take into account the voices of the PAFs and thus was fundamentally flawed. It asked for a halt in construction until proper environmental clearance was granted and the costs and benefits of the entire project could be re-evaluated in light of the new perceptions of social and environmental costs. They also alleged that the relief and rehabilitation of the oustees violated ILO Convention 107 (which provides that displaced indigenous peoples should be "provided with lands of quality at least equal to that of the lands previously occupied by them"), read through Article 21 of the Indian Constitution. In 1995, the Court ruled that a review of rehabilitation procedures were needed and ordered a halt to the construction until it could issue a final judgment.[13] The Court appeared willing to re-open the entire issue. The other states and the federal government "contended that the cause of the tribals and environment was being taken up by the petitioners not with a view to benefit the tribals but to see that a high dam was not erected per se." Further, they argued that it was much too late – violating the principle of *laches* – to bring such a case, as the Award had been issued fifteen years earlier and substantial construction had been completed. Such a procedural objection to substantive human rights violations would seem to be just the type of objection that would not be allowed in a SAL case. As Justice Verma once wrote, "We have to rise above the law for the protection of human rights" (in Rajagopal 2005, 370 n.123).

---

[12] She concludes: "The struggle from 1994 to 2000 had been waged in and through the Supreme Court and it had proved to be very costly" (Rajagopal 2005, 374).

[13] In 1999 without much explanation, the Court without ruling on the merits allowed construction of the dam to continue from a height of 80 m to 88 m.

The Supreme Court Decision

In a 185-page decision including a 32-page dissent issued in late 2000, the Indian Supreme Court ordered the building of the dam "as expeditiously as possible" but with several conditions to ensure the proper implementation of the R&R plans (*NBA v. India* 2000). The opinion was greeted enthusiastically by the national government and the government of Gujarat, but the NBA concluded that the opinion

> overlooks critical facts, is illogical, places complete and unjustified faith in the Government's machinery and assurances, and takes on [sic] overly legalistic and technical view over human and environmental concerns. It is nothing short of an anti-people judgment and clearly the institution of the Apex Court has failed miserably in safeguarding the rights of the common people of this country. (Narmada Bachao Andolan 2000, part A)

In Spivak's terms, the Court created a portrait of the petitioners, the NBA, and the adivasis without much consideration of their own self-representation; and this representation sustained the hegemonic discourse of the judges. Indeed, it appears that the Court gave little credence to anything the NBA or adivasis said whereas accepting almost all arguments in favor of the dam. It even disregarded the state governments when they were self-critical of their own performance in implementing the R&R plans. Further, their opinion was overly formalistic and ran counter in obvious ways to the spirit of SAL. Indeed, it turned SAL on its head.

First, the Court branded the NBA "an anti-dam organization" that was "opposed to the construction of the high dam" when the NBA's petition did not call for the dismantling of the dam but argued for a lower final dam height and additional oversight of the R&R plans. The motives of the NBA were also called into question as the Court referred to the bringing of the case as "publicity interest litigation" instead of public interest litigation. Such an accusation seems odd when the Court had agreed to hear the case and had stayed the construction of the dam for almost five years. Alternatively, the NBA could have been just as validly portrayed as a Gandhian organization or an indigenous rights organization. The Court also branded the traditional livelihood of the adivasis as backward with little to recommend it: "The tribals who are affected are in indigent circumstances and who have been deprived of modern fruits of development such as tap water, education, road, electricity, convenient medical facilities, etc." (*NBA v. India* 2000, at 145). Nothing is said of the value of their communal livelihoods, religions, or attachment to the river.

With these portraits of the NBA and the affected adivasis, the Court accepts the hegemonic discourse of the unmitigated positive effects of development. In a way, the Court plays the role of Indian nationalists who extol the virtue of the sacrifice of widows for the greater good.[14] In this instance, the savior is not the colonizer or the anti-colonizer but development itself, especially the majesty of dams. Indeed, the last section of the opinion has been rightly characterized as an elegy to big dams. It includes the wholly unbelievable statement that "the Petitioner has not been able to point out a single instance where the construction of a dam, on the whole, had an adverse environmental impact. On the contrary the environment has improved." Therefore, the precautionary principle, which was routinely applied in Indian environmental cases, need not apply because "the experience does not show that construction of a dam . . . leads to ecological or environmental degradation."

Finally, the Court, counter to its precedents, allowed formalistic rules to block substantive rights. The NBA was chastised for violating the principle of laches for not filing their petition earlier. They only objected to the 1979 NWDT Award in 1994 after much construction had taken place. "It is against national interest and contrary to the established principles of law that decisions to undertake development projects are permitted to be challenged after a number of years during which period public money has been spent in the execution of the project (*NBA v. Union of India* 2000 at 45)." Further, the Court goes against previous SAL cases by not allowing human rights challenges to administrative decisions. It frowns on attempts by the NBA or any third party "to challenge the correctness of an issue decided by the Tribunal."

Despite the court's questionable portrayals of the NBA, adivasis, and large dams, and despite allowing procedural barriers to bar substantive human rights claims, the Court was willing to consider whether the implementation of the R&R plans was in violation of Article 21 read along ILO 107 (para 47). These rights, however, were not viewed in isolation. Against the rights of these oustees, the Court also considers the rights of those who will benefit from the dam. Stopping the dam at this point would risk the "fundamental right to life of the people who continue to suffer due to shortage of water to such an extent that even the drinking water becomes scarce." Also weighing against the rights of the oustees are the other putative benefits of the dam.

---

[14] Rajagopal (2005) has dissected the many hegemonic discourses underlying the Court's opinion. She finds that the opinion is rooted in modernism, nationalism, developmentalism, statism, legalism, judicialism, and selective cosmopolitanism (cf. Baxi 1988 who argues that SAL, even at its height, gave deference to development and national security concerns).

The Court was impressed with the progressive nature of the Tribunal Award, especially when weighed against the "indigent" circumstances of the adivasis. Not only would the R&R not violate their rights under the ILO, but it would improve their living conditions. "At the rehabilitation sites they will have more better amenities than which they enjoyed in their tribal hamlets. The gradual assimilation in the main stream of the society will lead to betterment and progress (see para 60)." The Court also used its own portrayals of the affected persons and development when considering whether the Tribunal's definition of PAFs was comprehensive. The Court concluded that other categories of affected families, such as those affected by the construction colony or those displaced by the vast canals, should not receive compensation because their lives were not adversely affected even though they were to be displaced or, at minimum, lose land. These costs were outweighed by the future benefits they would receive from the project. "Most of the people falling under the command area were in fact beneficiaries of the project and their remaining land would now get relocated with the construction of the canal leading to greater agricultural output."

The next question was whether existing implementation procedures for R&R could be remedied without radical changes. The Court discounted the claims of the NBA that an independent commission should be established to oversee implementation and concluded that "there is a system in force which will ensure satisfactory resettlement and rehabilitation of the oustees" (378). The Court, though, was aware that the states had not done enough to implement the R&R plans, so it directed them to adequately implement previous R&R plans under direction of the NCA or the Grievance Redressal Authorities GRAs. Further, the Court required the drafting of an action plan by the NCA within four weeks for ensuring future compliance. The Court concluded, "There is no reason now to assume that these authorities will not function properly." From a cursory view, the majority opinion may seem reasonable with adequate safeguards, but the implementation structure is basically the same that has been in place for years; the NBA contended that "this arrangement has clearly failed, and failed abysmally to ensure even proper R&R" (Narmada Bachao Andolan 2000, part B). The Court was aware of many of the delays in implementation of the R&R, especially in Madhya Pradesh, and proper R&R was not in place for the 90 meter height.[15]

---

[15]   "The reports of the Grievances Redressal Authorities, and of Madhya Pradesh in particular, show that there is a considerable slackness in the work of identification of land, acquisition of suitable land, and the consequent steps necessary to be taken to rehabilitate the project oustees" (*NBA v. Union of India*, at 5). The dam is currently 121 meters in height.

However, still the Court ordered construction to 90 meters as "expeditiously as possible." Many PAFs would be harmed by the renewal of construction, but the Court was gambling that the states would step up quickly and implement R&R plans in time to save them. It set up a situation in which the PAFS will "suffer for the 'non-cooperation' of the State" (Narmada Bachao Andolan 2000, part B).

REPRESENTING THE RIGHTS OF THE OTHER

Rights talk has become so pervasive that human rights are routinely used to justify all sides of global problems. The question becomes: Who should define what are the fundamental rights at stake? A new hierarchy of rights is needed. A human rights of the Other calls for a preference for the rights of the marginalized based on their life-project as they define it. In the Narmada case, however, all sides were justified by reference to the rights of the marginalized. It is imperative that the rights of the marginalized are accurately portrayed. The Court took sides between two groups who claimed to represent the rights of the adivasis without asking the adivasis. The NBA concludes that the Court had "completely ignored the submissions made by the Petitioners about the reality of the tribal areas, which may seem poor to outsiders but have their own rich resource base, skills, culture, systems and so on." Of course, it would be absurd to expect thousands of affected persons to desire the same life-project, but it is safe to assume that the river and their pre-dam livelihood meant more to most adivasis than the Court assumed. Paul Routledge wrote, "People who live beside the Narmada feel a deep sense of attachment to the particulars of the landscape – to the sounds, the smells, the look, the feelings that are engendered by living in the place.... People's language, their sense of community, their faith in the bonds of kinship, and the structures of material and emotional aid given to one another, the memories of people's ancestors evoked by particular settings, are tied to the place of their inhabitancy" (2003, 251). However, following Spivak, one must ask whether such accounts are tainted by different ideological positions.

Representation of the adivasis was ubiquitous during the decades of the struggle. The Tribunal and the Supreme Court both spoke for what they portrayed as their best interests. However, Spivak teaches us that representation or synecdochization even occurs by those who are close to the tribals and attempting to advance their rights by the creation of an anti-hegemonic discourse.

After renewed protests by the NBA, the government of Maharashtra created an independent committee headed by retired Justice S. M. Daud to study the

effects of further increases of the dam height. The committee concluded that
the PAFs, especially the tribals, had not been adequately re-settled, even for
the dam height of 90 m.

> Even those brought into the rehabilitation sites, a large number of them face
> severe privations such as no land being allotted to them or those with allot-
> ments have to put up with less land or land unsuitable for cultivation, lack of
> water etc. This deprivation goes to the extent of water required for drinking.
> If there be a shortage of drinking water it goes without saying that noth-
> ing like water for irrigation of the lands allotted to the tribals exist. (Daud
> Committee 2001, "Issues Section")

The Daud Committee's attempts to listen to the adivasis were remarkable.
They made countless visits to the submergence and resettlement areas in both
Gujarat and Maharashtra. For the most part, they conducted village assem-
blies known as "gramsabhas" with participation open to all villagers. These
were conducted almost entirely in the tribal languages, as Justice Daud and
many other committee members were fluent in several tribal languages.
When necessary they also relied on translations notably done at the time by
Medha Patkar of the NBA. The transcription of the testimonies was done in
an open manner, and the ensuing report included many of these testimonies.
Even the ultimate recommendations of the Committee called for full participation of the adivasis. They recommended that further development be "done
in effective collaboration with the 'Gramsabhas' of the villages" because "the
tribals lack the skills to communicate with the officialdom, which also has a
tendency to ignore their grievances."

   A human rights of the Other would insist on a critique of even this meth-
odology. The Daud Committee, by working through the gramsabhas, was
relying on a mechanism that has had mixed reviews for hearing the voices
of the marginalized. These assemblies were formalized in 1993 in the 73rd
Constitutional Amendment in order to create a "deliberative space" (deSouza
2003, 111) that would check official and unofficial forms of hegemonic power
in the villages. To date, and not unexpectedly, the results have been mixed. It
appears that the meeting times and places of the assemblies have been manipulated by those in power, and women, dalits, and adivasis all seemed to have
been marginalized in the deliberations (deSouza 2003). It also appears that
marginalized people who have tried to make use of the assemblies and other
innovations have been stymied by violence from dominant groups. Once
again, we are confronted with the "primary" problem of discursive democracy:
"How more of the people who routinely speak less ... might take part and be

heard and how those who typically dominate might be made to attend to the views of others" (Sanders 1997, 352).

Recently, several scholars have also explored whether the NBA, despite its notoriety, adequately represents the adivasis. None of the following is meant to take away from the enormous sacrifices that the NBA and its leader Medha Patkar have endured and the enormous gains they have achieved, especially in publicizing the plight of the adivasis.[16] They have worked with the adivasis by involving themselves in their life-projects. They have undergone detention, hunger strikes, and beatings on behalf of the adivasis. However, it is important to show that such efforts too, in Spivak's words, risk being cooked on the hot plate in the colonial hotel room.

The leaders of the NBA are generally not adivasis but well-educated urban dwellers who have taken up the cause. These leaders often had to take on the role of spokespersons because they are more media savvy or spoke the dominant languages. Further, because the NBA operates on local, national, and global stages, it has had to make very difficult decisions about how to represent itself and the adivasis. It chose, as most NGOs must do, to repress some internal dissent in order to maintain an external appearance of unity. As the global movement has shifted from a human rights stance, focused on this specific issue, to a larger anti-development perspective, the NBA has had to appeal to groups that praise indigenous knowledge such as the International Rivers Network and the Environmental Defense Fund. These decisions led to a rift between the NBA and groups such as the Arch-Vahini that didn't oppose the dam but were pushing for better implementation of the R&R plans. Instead, the NBA indeed became, as the Supreme Court had branded it, an anti-dam organization.

Further, to appeal to the larger international community, the NBA chose to project a specific portrayal of the adivasis. The "adivasi identities within the NBA have tended to get strategically essentialised and homogenized, in order to be contrasted with the destructive character of the development being undertaken in the Narmada valley" (Routledge 2003, 265–266). The NBA could appeal to a worldwide audience with the view that adivasis were "'ecologically noble primitives', who lived in self-sustaining communities

---

[16] Routledge is on point here: "I think that it is important for academics to be critically with resisting others as well as for them, engaging in collaboration as well as criticism and analysis" (2003, 267). He ultimately calls for a "relational ethics" as well as an "embodied collaboration with struggles in situ" as well as "being constructively critical" with regard to "relational ethics" where "such connections are invariably enacted in an asymmetrical way…whose interactions are forged under unequal relations of power."

that were 'naturally' conservationist" (Whitehead 2007, 412). Such a view was embraced by many activists drawn to the movement, such as author Arundhati Roy. Such an image also resonated with the Gandhian leanings of the activists with their embrace of an ascetic life.

Yet, strong evidence suggests that the adivasis were not opposed to dams per se and were not adequately represented by the NBA's portrayals. Indeed, the decisions to move away from the core concerns of the adivasis, coupled with the weariness of a decades-long struggle and the Supreme Court's adverse ruling, have alienated the NBA from many adivasis. Many former NBA-affiliated adivasis have since received land and have now abandoned the cause of the NBA. One scholar concluded that "pushed from above and below, the NBA movement lost support even of the adivasis it claimed to represent" (Whitehead 2007, 399).

CONCLUSION

Human rights law, established to "give voice to human suffering, to make it visible, and to ameliorate it" (Baxi 2002, 4), often further cauterizes the Marginalized Other. This cauterization is, in part, endemic to the abstraction process inherent in law as seen in the case of the Innu peoples of Canada. At other times, human rights institutions such as the Supreme Court of India, even after it developed Social Action Litigation, have been unwilling to listen and learn from the Other. This unwillingness is clearly manifest in the controversial Narmada River decision. The Court's unwillingness to listen, to heed what Rancière calls the "animalistic" cries of the *aneu logou*, further reinforced the previous partitions in society.

In the place of the voice of the Other, the Indian Supreme Court and other groups created a representation of the adivasis that dovetailed with hegemonic discourses. These essentialized synecdoches categorized the adivasis as anti-development or as "ecologically noble primitives." Adivasis that did not fit these portrayals were branded as not fully adivasi. Their identities are frozen across time and space and not allowed to develop.

Human rights law is so enmeshed in the cauterization process that extraordinary measures are needed for its continuous deconstruction and progressive development. Human rights law requires a ceaseless and patient listening to the Other. It must learn how to learn from below. It must constantly be educated in the episteme of the Other.

A human rights of the Marginalized Other will require that the Other is able to self-ascribe her own identity, to define which groups she belongs to while retaining her singularity. The Other must be able to speak in an idiolect, that is, with her own voice that is part of a larger dialect. The next chapter adds insights from Judith Butler's writings on identity formation in the context of hegemonic narratives to further explore the need for self-ascription of identity in human rights law. Concretely, self-ascription will be examined through recent asylum cases from a range of jurisdictions.

6

Self-Ascription by the Marginalized
Other in Asylum Law

Hegemonic systems, including legal systems, cauterize the Other; that is, they brand some individuals as "so far inferior that they ha[ve] no rights which the [white] man [is] bound to respect" (*Scott v. Sandford* 1857). Once branded as inferior, they become *aneu logou* (without a voice) and *sans part* (without a part) in the polis. To reverse this cauterization process, the previous chapter argued it is imperative that the Other reclaim a voice; that human rights law must learn to learn from the voice of the Other. Once the Other has a voice, the deconstruction of cauterization must continue by overturning the branding or categorization of the Other. The Other is categorized, or placed into an essentialized synecdoche where he or she is labeled as a permanent part of a group. In the example from the last chapter, the Indian Supreme Court portrayed the adivasis as anti-dam and anti-development whereas pro-adivasi NGOs represented them as "ecologically noble primitives." In Chapter 2, we saw that young French Muslim women were branded as victims of patriarchy or as uneducated immigrant girls that were excluded from l'affaire du foulard. A human rights of the Marginalized Other must call for the continuous deconstruction of the identities that are imposed on marginalized Others. Again, the branding will not be overturned by scholars, attorneys, or judges, but by self-ascription by the Other.

Some political theorists of group rights have also recently called for an important role for self-ascription (Benhabib, Gutman, and Valadez).[1] Yet,

---

[1] Group rights theories that begin with such claims as a "flexible, open-ended view of culture" (Carens 1997, 44), the original inequality of the political space, and the claim that democracy be conducted in the "language of the vernacular" (Kymlicka 2001) will most likely require the self-ascription of group identity. Group-specific rights such as special provisions for self-government, exclusion from citizenship duties (conscription, clothing restrictions, etc.), and support for cultural or religious practices are vital for overcoming original political inequality (Kymlicka 2001); strengthening an individual's sense of self-worth, meaning, and agency; and for ameliorating extremism. Group rights and cultural identity claims (indeed, any theory of

many tensions inherent to self-ascription remain unexplored, and these theories too often have relied on the Cartesian view of the individualized autonomous subject free to initiate action. Rarely have such calls for self-ascription
begun from a more nuanced view of the self. Self-ascribed identity is often
multifaceted and fluid, and rarely is it completely voluntary, being constrained
by societal norms and various power structures. For instance, Upendra Baxi
argues for a new discourse of group rights that would account for the fact that
"being human is itself a process of continual redefinition" (2002, 79), what
[Naomi] Mezey (2001) has nicely called "the dance of mutual constructedness." However, this redefinition is constrained, sometimes severely, by existing power structures. Baxi poignantly asks: "Are all identities fluid, multiple,
and contingent? If however, you can place yourself in the non-Rawlsian original position of a person belonging to an untouchable community would you
find it possible to agree that caste and patriarchical identity has become fluid,
multiple, contingent? As an untouchable, no matter how you perceive your
identity…you are still to be raped." (Baxi 2002, 83–84). Any theory of self-
ascription must consider "the dance of mutual constructedness" of individual
identities and the hegemonic power structures that cauterize the Other and
provide a central place for the voice of the Other so that human rights law is
based on a learning to learn from below.

In this chapter, I first turn to Judith Butler's nuanced theory of self-ascription
that focuses on the fluidity of selves and the constraints to autonomy posed
by the social construction of identity. I am especially intrigued by her most
recent works that struggle to merge her earlier, more Foucauldian work on
identity formation with a Levinasian view of ethics based on the ego's infinite
responsibility for the Other. A human rights of the Marginalized Other must
be informed by both Foucault's work on hegemonic power structures and
Levinas' ethics of the Other. Butler's work shows the multifaceted ways that
identity is interpellated onto the Other and the near impossibility of overturning that identity. Within Butler's work is a space for the near-Sisyphean task
of deconstructing prescribed identities through the ego becoming a social
theorist in service to the Other. However, a close reading of Butler's work
shows that the appearance of the Other as well as the ego's response will be
ultimately determined by the hegemonic system.

I then apply Butler's views on self-ascription and ethics to recent asylum
law in the United States and elsewhere. Asylum law, replete with so many

differentiated citizenship) hinge on the prior delineation of individual and group identity. If
a group deserves preferential treatment, it is imperative to clearly demarcate the boundaries
to determine who does or does not belong to that group.

examples of inhumanity, brutality, and neglect, may seem like an unusual place to turn, but self-ascription is pivotal for many asylum claims. If an asylum seeker claims to have been persecuted based on "membership in a particular social group," she must self-ascribe herself as a member of that group. Each of the two main theories used to mark particular social groups in the asylum context (immutable characteristics and social perceptions) can be usefully reinvigorated by focusing on the important role of self-ascription. Nonetheless, self-ascription in the asylum context, like Butler's account of the Other, needs to be supplemented with Spivak's work on learning to learn from below and provide a central place for the Other to define his or her rights.

BUTLER AND THE SOCIAL CONSTRUCTION OF IDENTITY

From her earliest writings Butler has argued that the subject's identity is contingent; it is created through social discourse. For example, in *Gender Trouble* she argued that prevailing notions of sexuality and gender are created by the social discourse, which determines what is proper and what is not. Thus, there is no permanent conception of gender based on biology. Instead, we are categorized by society; some behaviors and subjectivities are branded as inappropriate and must be cauterized from the social sphere (see Butler 1997a, 133). In this way, the temporality of the subject is diachronous to the temporality of norms that precede it and persist after the demise of the subject. The norms remain neutral and mostly untouched by the appearance of the subject, whereas the norms accuse or interpellate the subject in an Althusserian sense. The norms operate, for the most part, covertly. Indeed, "this normative exercise of power is rarely acknowledged as an operation of power at all," as Charles Taylor says. "It is carried in patterns of appropriate action" (Butler 1997a, 134).

Just because "the subject is constituted by social discourse does not mean that the subject is determined by social discourse" (Magnus 2006, 83). Language fails to completely capture reality and "that lack of capture (between the term and its referent) constitutes the linguistic possibility of a radical democratic contestation, one that opens the term to future rearticulations" (Butler 1997a, 108). Though there is an endless repetition or reiteration of the subjectification process, there is a gap in language and thus, "the repetition, or, better, iterability thus becomes the non-place of subversion, the possibility of a re-embodying of the subjectivating norm that can redirect its normativity" (Butler 1997b, 99). The hegemonic discourse has fault lines, spaces, and states of exception where the self can perform subversive acts to rebel against the cauterization process. So the cauterization process, what Butler calls the production of foreclosures, also creates the potential for a future of language through re-significations of the hegemonic discourse. Paradigmatic "re-significations" in Butler's work include the re-appropriation of the appellation "queer" by the LGBT community and the polysemy of the N-word in hip-hop culture. This re-signification as a breaking of normative violence is a demand for recognition that may create "a livable life" for those previously interpellated (Butler 1999, xxvi). Butler praises Rosa Parks because "in laying claim to the right for which she had no prior authorization, she endowed a certain authority on the act, and began the insurrectionary process of overthrowing those established codes of legitimacy" (1997a, 147).

Many commentators have wondered whether Butler's account of performativity provides even a modicum of agency for the ego. Butler argues for performativities of self-ascription, parodying the name that one is called; but following Foucault she ultimately concedes that these parodies are still born within the hegemonic discourse (1999, 138). Indeed, in *The Psychic Life of Power* Butler follows Nietzsche and argues that a subject's conscience is an internalization of social subjection, so that the subject appears to be determined by discourse. By admitting the hegemonic system is ubiquitous even within the parodying process is to admit that all we can throw back at the hegemonic system is more hegemonic system. Even self-ascription would be a repetition of the hegemonic discourse. "If we are formed in language, then that formative power precedes and conditions any decision we might make about it, insulting us from the start, as it were, by its power" (Butler 1997a, 2). However, Butler still insists that there are "faultlines" in the hegemonic discourse that can be used against the system: "Agency begins where sovereignty wanes" (1997a, 15–16). In this waning of sovereignty, which recalls Levinas' "moments of negation," the subject can work through its trauma "through the arduous effort it takes to direct the course of repetition" (Butler 1997a, 38). This arduous effort is made more difficult by the constant repetition and reiteration of the hegemonic discourse that will seek to close any gaps between the term and its referent.

This longing for fault lines and the Sisyphean task of working within these fault lines to re-signify ascriptions in the face of a hegemonic discourse undergirds Butler's analysis of hate speech laws and anti-obscenity ordinances in *Excitable Speech*. Butler takes on Catharine MacKinnon's arguments that pornography is a form of violence (not that it may lead to violence, but that its very existence is a form of violence) and should therefore be regulated by the state. Butler counters that language or expression is rarely violence by itself and any banning of language might usurp a place where women could express their agency by re-signifying the discourse. Butler chides MacKinnon's emphasis on pornography and similar calls for rating systems for music that contain violent imageries in terms reminiscent of the critiques of l'affaire du foulard discussed in Chapter 2. "The dignity of women is understood to be under attack not by the weakening of rights to reproductive freedom and the widespread loss of public assistance, but primarily by African-American men who sing" (Butler 1997a, 23). As in the headscarf affairs, women are allegedly empowered by removing an opportunity to signify their identity. Butler warns against any censorship because it will feed the monster of the state. The state, or the hegemonic discourse, will remain the final arbiter of what is pornography or hate speech or proper attire and will be able to wield censorship laws to repress any outlaw speech such as re-significations of the discourse itself. Censorship will exacerbate the original violence of the hegemonic discourse. Butler, like Levinas and Derrida before her, is arguing for a suspension of the law, but this must be done by those whose identity is interpellated by the system.

The "Don't Ask, Don't Tell" Policy

Butler's analysis of the U.S. military's "don't ask, don't tell" policy is especially on point as it exemplifies the government's banning of a specific type of self-ascription. This policy was drafted in 1993 to negotiate a compromise between President Clinton's campaign promise to allow gays in the military and a recalcitrant Pentagon. The resulting statute is remarkable because it does not ban the use of the word "homosexual" – indeed the word must be used in the statute, and the ensuing dialogue undoubtedly led to more uses of the term than ever before – but only one use of the word, in the context of a self-ascription. The statute calls for the dismissal of someone who

> has stated that he or she is a homosexual or bisexual, or words to that effect, unless there is a further finding, made and approved in accordance with procedures set forth in the regulations, that the member has demonstrated that he or she is not a person who engages in, attempts to engage in, has a propensity to engage in, or intends to engage in homosexual acts. (10 U.S.C. 654)

This denial of self-ascription relies on the operation of the hegemonic discourse that will, quite blatantly, decide whether someone is a homosexual. The regulation defines a homosexual act as "any bodily contact which a reasonable person would understand to demonstrate a propensity or intent to engage in an act." Of course, the reasonable person who is charged with defining homosexual acts and persons would most likely be "one who embodies homophobic cultural norms" (Butler 1997a, 106).

These norms, Butler argues, relying on Freud's *Totem and Taboo*, are part of a "'homophobic phantasmatic' according to which homosexual proclamations are regarded as 'contagious acts'" (Stevens, 1999, 346). Thus, as contagious acts, they must be stopped from spreading by being cauterized from the military. How can the military claim that a self-ascription of sexual preference is a contagious act that "would create an unacceptable risk to the high standards of morale, good order and discipline, and unit cohesion that are the essence of military capability?"

Butler argues that the self-ascription of homosexuality actually is a form of solicitation – a solicitation that disrupts the social regulation of the homoerotic, which creates the needed esprit de corps. The subjectification of the ideal military man requires the simultaneous presence and sublimation of homosexual desires. A self-ascription of homosexuality would wipe the veneer off of what has been sublimated. "'I am a homosexual,' is fabulously misconstrued as, 'I want you sexually'" (Butler 1997a, 113), or at a minimum, I will want someone sexually, which will disrupt the cohesion we need. "The speakability of the term breaks a taboo within public discourse, the floodgates open, and expressions of desire become uncontrollable" (114). The homosexual "becomes taboo himself because he possesses the dangerous quality of tempting others to follow his example" (115). Ultimately, the banning of self-ascription of homosexuality tells us much more about "straight" military personnel who will be easily seduced by those who "engage in homosexual acts."

The military's censorship of this one self-ascription takes away any room for re-signification. One can only self-ascribe as a homosexual on the government's terms; as an asexual homosexual. Butler concludes with a plea that we must "forestall" the "final word" on homosexuality (126), but it is difficult to see whether the limited agency she grants the subject will be able to successfully mobilize against the hegemonic discourse. The oppressed can re-signify an interpellation, but this example shows that the hegemonic discourse can also successfully mobilize against the subversive act. A mantra of the LGBT community, "I am gay," was successfully cauterized (branded as a contagion that must be sealed off from the polis) from military discourse despite the wishes of the president and powerful members of Congress.

SELF-ASCRIPTION, RESPONSIBILITY, AND THE SOCIAL THEORIST

The address of the Other plays a major role in Butler's earlier writings, but it is almost always as interpellation, as an imposition of normative violence on the ego during the subjectification process.[2] After 2003, especially in *Giving an Account of Oneself*, Butler increasingly relies on Levinas' and Jean Laplanche's writings to re-conceive the address of the Other as a call for an ethical response. Butler, though, struggles to reconcile her previous more Foucauldian writings on self-ascription with their view that the exposure to the Other calls the ego into existence. It will be helpful to explore this tension in some detail as it haunts any theory that attempts to concretize Levinas' writings.

The call of the Other for Levinas is non- or even anti-interpellation; it doesn't reproduce the system. It doesn't impose a discourse of power on the ego. It doesn't seek to cauterize any specific identity or subjectification. Instead, the face of the Other "addresses me in a way that is singular, irreducible, and irreplaceable" (Butler 2005, 91). The face of the Other "makes an ethical demand upon me" (Butler 2005, 90). It calls for the ego to provide a response. When exposed to the face of the Other, the ego is called to give an account of itself.

Butler's use of Levinas is made more interesting as she clings to her Foucauldian roots. The I who is called to account by the Other "is already implicated in a social temporality that exceeds its own capacities for narration" (Butler 2005, 8). This social temporality is a truth regime that has constrained the subjectification of the ego. So, "when the 'I' seeks to give an account of itself, an account that must include the conditions of its own emergence, it must, as a matter of necessity, *become a social theorist*" (Butler 2005, 8, emphasis added). To give an account, the ego must take on the role of social theorist to deconstruct the societal norms. "In this sense, [Levinasian] ethical deliberation is bound up with the operation of [Foucauldian] critique" (Butler 2005, 8).[3]

The ego as social theorist in service to the Other must deconstruct its own identity and the societal norms that have shaped it. The ego must ask whether its privileged position is at the expense of the Other, and it must relieve the societal interpellation of the Other. As in Enrique Dussel's formulation: The ego is called, not only to respond directly to the Other, but to represent the Other "before the tribunal of a system that accuses him or her" (Dussel 2004, 330).

---

[2] For example, "to be addressed is not merely to be recognized for what one already is, but to have the very terms conferred by which the recognition of existence becomes possible. One comes to 'exist' by virtue of the fundamental dependency on the address of the Other" (Butler 1997a, 6).

[3] Butler claims that Foucault misses the rupture that is called by the Other; he does not ask the question "Who are you?" (Butler 2005, 25).

Combining Foucault and Levinas Butler finds that the narrative that comprises the account of oneself does not belong to the ego in two senses. The hegemonic discourse interrupts the ego's narrative; it dispossesses the narrative from the ego. Moreover, the narrative belongs, in a sense, to the exposure to the Other. "It is effectively exported and expropriated from the domain of what is my own" (Butler 2005, 36–37). It appears that Butler's famous ethical self-making has taken on a completely new guise with her emerging indebtedness to Levinas. Ethical self-making, the performance of identity as a subversive act, now appears to be in service to the Other. Just as the gap between term and referent previously provided a space for alterity to appear, the face of the Other now provides a gap in the hegemonic discourse that calls for the ego to assume the task of a social theorist. Levinas' call for a radical passivity of the ego surprisingly opens up another much-needed place for agency within Butler's enterprise.

If Butler remains faithful to the ego as a social theorist in response to the Other, the Other must be seen as primary, as the impetus for all accounts of the self. However, it appears that Butler is unable or unwilling to fully recast many of her previous insights within this more profound Levinasian light.[4]

Butler and Levinas

Butler shares with Levinas an emphasis on the interruption that occurs when the self is exposed to the face of the Other. The ego is shaken to its foundation because it is unable to comprehend or grasp the Other. This infinitude reveals an opacity, an uncertainty, that calls into question the self-assured knowledge of the ego. Butler, however, strains to make this opacity into an ethics. She deduces that ethics comes from opacity because they both have a common antecedent in relationality. Because relationality leads to self-opaqueness *and* relationality leads to ethics, she incorrectly deduces that self-opaqueness *by itself* leads to ethics (Butler 2005, 20). Self-opaqueness at most could lead to toleration and a suspension of judgment, but for Levinas the infinitude of the Other that calls into question the certainty of the ego is supplemented by a phenomenology of the face of the Other. The face expresses a vulnerability, a mortality, that calls the ego to respond concretely, infinitely, and

---

[4]   Butler consciously eschews a seamless integration of Levinas' thought with that of Foucault, Nietzsche, and Laplanche. "I do not attempt to synthesize them here," but "each theory suggests something of ethical importance that follows from the limits that condition any effort one might make to give an account of oneself" (Butler 2005, 21).

asymmetrically. Because Butler does not appear to take this second step, her account of relationality remains rooted in reciprocity and not asymmetry.

Following "a certain post-Hegelian reading of the scene of recognition," she finds ethics in reciprocity, in the "shared and invariable, partial blindnesses about ourselves" (Butler 2005, 41). Faced with the Other, the ego becomes aware of its own inability to form a coherent narrative because of its inability to grasp the Other and its inability to remove societal norms from its own account of itself. The ego faced with this self-opacity assumes that the Other is undergoing a similar crisis.[5] In this reciprocity Butler finds ethics, not based on the difference with the Other, but on equivalences. "The uniqueness of the other is exposed to me, but mine is also exposed to her.... [M]y singularity has some properties in common with yours and so is, to some extent, a substitutable term" (Butler 2005, 34). Levinas, on the other hand, insists that the ego is called into existence by the persecution it undergoes for the Other, and this relationship is asymmetrical. "A uniqueness without inwardness, an ego without rest in itself, a hostage for everyone, turned away from itself in each movement of its return to itself – man is without identity" (Levinas 1987, 130). The ego discovers itself as a subject literally when it is subjected to the Other. Butler's ego, on the other hand, appears to be able to find itself outside the context of the Other. The Other is not primary. The ego tells its story to another but not always as a response to the Other, let alone as a social theorist for the Other. She writes, "We can surely tell our stories, and there will be many reasons to do precisely that," and these can even be told "over wine" (Butler 2005, 37). A prominent role remains for giving an account of oneself in order to "find a living place for this 'I'" (Butler 2005, 8). Levinas, on the other hand, calls for an ethics based in "a perpetual duty of vigilance and effort that can never slumber.... Love is the incessant watching over the other; it can never be satisfied or contented with the bourgeois ideal of love as domestic comfort" (Levinas and Kearney 1986, 30).

This reciprocity colors Butler's account of the approach of the Other. Following Arendt, when confronted with a newcomer, the ego must ask "Who are you?" "This question will open relationality" (Butler 2005, 31) and will place the ego in the mode of patient listening à la Dussel – a listening that does not expect a final answer from the Other. In this way, "we let the other live" (Butler 2005, 43). Simultaneously, the ego is being called by the Other to

---

5 Butler mobilizes Hegel's logic of the "this": Every "this" can be broken down further, which means that every 'this' has some sort of universality. So "this" fact of singularizing exposure...is one that can be reiterated endlessly, it constitutes a collective condition, characterizing us all equally, not only reinstalling the "we," but also establishing a structure of substitutability at the core of singularity (Butler 2005, 34–35).

give an account of itself, that is, to answer the question "Who are you?" When approached by the Other, to ask "Who are you?" is to call the Other, in a very non-Levinasian way, to give an account of themselves.[6] This demonstrates attentiveness to the Other, a listening to the Other, but it also resembles a mutual recognition or an interpellation more than an unconditional hospitality. Indeed, to ask "who are you?" is antagonistic to traditional conceptions of hospitality as epitomized in the Odyssey (Reece 1993). As Derrida writes, "Unconditional hospitality implies that you don't ask the other, the newcomer, the guest, to give anything back, or even to identify himself or herself. Even if the other deprives you of your mastery or your home, you have to accept this. It is terrible to accept this, but that is the condition of unconditional hospitality; that you give up the mastery of your space, your home, your nation. It is unbearable" (Derrida 1999, 70).

Truth Regimes

For my purposes, Butler's important contribution is to add a Foucault-inspired analysis of truth regimes to Levinas' ethics. It is instructive to ask how truth regimes and their norms affect the original ethical relationship. Do they cloud the ego, the Other, the relationship with the Other, the response to the Other, or all four? Butler does not spell this out specifically, but it appears that the hegemonic discourse is ubiquitous in this relationship. It is clear that the ego will be caught up in a web of social norms. When approached by the Other, I am already entangled in a normative web that necessitates me becoming a social theorist in service to the Other. Further, the ego's response will be colored by these norms; "our capacity to respond to a face as a human face is conditioned and mediated by frames of reference that are variably humanizing and dehumanizing" (Butler 2005, 29). It follows then that the ego's narrative (52), even its unconscious (53), will be tainted by this normative violence. These norms are so overpowering that the ego even "becomes an instrument of that norm's agency" (26).

Not so clear is whether the exposure to the Other is colored by these norms. For Levinas, the face of the Other precedes all norms, all politics, and all law. The face is naked without ontological characteristics. It cannot be categorized; it cannot be cauterized. In this way, the Other and the ethical call interrupt the hegemonic system even if this may only be a moment of negation. Butler, however, seems to claim that the perception of the Other already takes place within, and is colored by, a web of norms. As she says, the recognition

---

[6] Butler later elaborates on this reciprocity in the context of the analyst-analysand (2005, 55).

of the face takes place, Butler says, "within an operation of power " (Butler 2005, 29). "There is a language that frames the encounter, and embedded in that language is a set of norms concerning what will and will not constitute recognizability" (Butler 2005, 30). So norms precede the Other, but at the same time, in some sections of the text, it appears that the Other precedes the social norms. The Other "mark(s) a site of rupture within the horizon of normativity and implicitly call for the institution of new norms, putting into question the givenness of the prevailing normative horizon" (Butler 2005, 24).[7]

   This apparent incongruity most likely stems from the fact that for Butler it is not the face of the Other that breaks down the hegemonic discourse, it is the ego's response to the Other that has the power to break down the discourse. "Could it also be true that I would not be in this struggle with norms if it were not for a desire to offer recognition to you?" (Butler 2005, 26) What leads to ethics beyond the norms is not the face of the Other but the relationship with the Other that necessitates an account of the self that cannot be completed. I cannot know the Other, and I cannot know the exposure completely in that I cannot narrate it, because it is already enmeshed with a regime of truth, because the "norms by which I seek to make myself recognizable are not fully mine" (Butler 2005, 35). So, the relationship with the Other provides another site of opacity that allows for the ego to perform its narrative. This account is not prior to the norms but is posterior. At the same time, the Other does not appear to have an ontological status prior to the norms.

   If this is the case, what deconstructs the original violence of the system? In Butler's formulation, the face of the Other disrupts the ego. The ego must stop eating good soup (Levinas' trope) or drinking wine (Butler's), listen to the Other, and give an account of itself. The ego must also allow the Other to identify herself, allow her a voice. However, this entire relationship is conditioned by the system itself. The Other is not beyond the system, nor is the ego or its relationship or response to the Other. The ego who is called to account for itself should allow the Other to self-ascribe its identity (and vice versa), but the Other's identity will be determined both by the ego and the system. Problematically, though, if the ego is constituted by the hegemonic discourse, it will only accept a finite set of answers to the question of "Who are you?" As Butler writes, "We feel more properly recognized by some people than we do by others" (2005, 33). The ego, enmeshed within the system, risks cauterizing certain responses to the query and thus cauterizing certain behaviors as well as individuals and their identities.

---

7   This incongruity also could refer to a double origin following Levinas' and Descartes' formulations.

Summary

In her analysis of the exteriority of the Other to the ego, Butler has found another fault line in the hegemonic discourse. However, the ego is not confronted with anything that is beyond the hegemonic system; and therefore all it throws back at the system, whether for its ethical self-making or in response to the face of the Other, is more system. In contrast, the phenomenology of the Saturated Other that I developed in earlier chapters begins with the vulnerability of the face that calls the ego to an infinite responsibility. The Other as well as the response are pre-ontological; they call into question all categorizations, all typologies, and all interpellations of the Other. This responsibility takes on deeper meaning when it is confronted by the face of the Other who has been marginalized by the hegemonic discourse. It is not clear that Butler's ego, enmeshed in hegemonic norms, will be able to recognize the marginalized Other. The Levinasian ego is called from beyond the truth regime to a responsibility for the Other. As a second step, the ego will need, as Butler argues, to find a way to combat the system, which will require the ego to become a social theorist. To take on the system is to fight the interpellation being done to the Other, to stop the Other from being called Other. At its best, this is working with the Other in service to the Other – to facilitate the Other becoming a social theorist. This is working with the Other to aid in the creation of an anti-hegemonic validity that will undermine the original violence of the system. The ego must work with the Other to realize "the life-project the other cannot actualize" (Dussel 2004, 330).

SELF-ASCRIPTION IN ASYLUM LAW

It is more than a bit peculiar to turn to asylum law in the United States (and elsewhere) for lessons stemming from Butler's and Levinas' work on ethics and self-ascription. The U.S. asylum system, along with the U.S. immigration policy, is broken. The sheer numbers of asylum seekers along with concomitant budget cuts and neglect have taxed the system beyond the breaking point. Further, the conflation, in a post-9/11 world, of asylum seekers with immigrants (legal and illegal) and terrorists has thwarted any political will to reform the system. The U.S. government continues to give lip service to its official policy of welcoming legitimate asylum seekers, but the asylum system can most accurately be described as a state of exception where functionaries of the state fill the interstices of law by crafting their own law (cf. Benjamin 1996). Instead of evincing a Levinasian-type of hospitality, every day the lives of countless marginalized Others are "ground to bits in the bureaucratic mill" (*Benslimane v. Gonzales* 2005).

This state of exception is made clear in a massive 2007 study fittingly called "Refugee Roulette" (Ramji-Nogales et al., 2007). Approximately 35 percent of all applications for asylum heard by immigration judges are granted, but there are vast disparities between different immigration courts and individual judges. The disparity in asylum grants is so stark that the random administrative selection of judges to hear a particular case appears to be the determining factor in whether a grant is received. Nationwide, some judges granted asylum in more than 90 percent of their cases, whereas other judges granted asylum in less than 10 percent of their cases. The disparity is also striking between courts. Chinese asylum seekers had a 7 percent chance of being granted asylum if their case was heard in Atlanta, but their chance rose to 76 percent if their case was heard in the Orlando court. The authors of the study controlled for different types of cases by looking at disparities between judges in the same courts on cases from the same countries. In one court, one judge granted asylum to 94 percent of Chinese asylum seekers, whereas another judge granted less than 10 percent. In another court one judge granted asylum to Albanian nationals at a rate of 1,820 percent more than another judge from the same court (Ramji-Nogales et al., 2007, 40).

The U.S. asylum system is further broken by the failure to follow Constitutional due process guarantees as evidenced by the recent battle between immigration judges, the Board of Immigration Appeals (BIA), and circuit court judges.[8] Circuit Judge Posner recently concluded that "the adjudication of these cases at the administrative level has fallen below the minimum standards of legal justice" (*Benslimane v. Gonzales* 2005). He goes on to compare the asylum process in this case to being "ground to bits in the bureaucratic mill against the will of Congress" and the ultimate rationale of the BIA's decision in the case at hand "to have been completely arbitrary." Posner cites a vast array of opinions in other cases to show the process to be fundamentally flawed. Here are just a few:

- "The [immigration judge's] opinion is riddled with inappropriate and extraneous comments" (*Dawoud v. Gonzales* 2005).
- "This very significant mistake suggests that the Board was not aware of the most basic facts of [the petitioner's] case" (*Ssali v. Gonzales* 2005).

---

[8]   The rulings of immigration judges can be appealed to the Board of Immigration Appeals, and the BIA's rulings can be appealed to the circuit courts. Space prevents a thorough overview of the asylum process. Details are provided in the text as needed.

- "The procedure that the [immigration judge] employed in this case is an affront to [the petitioner's] right to be heard" (*Sosnovskaia v. Gonzales* 2005).
- "The immigration judge's unexplained conclusion is 'hard to take seriously'" (*Grupee v. Gonzales* 2005).
- "The elementary principles of administrative law, the rules of logic, and common sense seem to have eluded the Board in this as in other cases" (*Niam v. Ashcroft* 2003).
- "The tone, the tenor, the disparagement, and the sarcasm of the [immigration judge] seem more appropriate to a court television show than a federal court proceeding" (*Qun Wang v. AG of the United States* 2005).
- "The [immigration judge's] assessment of Petitioner's credibility was skewed by prejudgment, personal speculation, bias, and conjecture" (*Lopez-Umanzor v. Gonzales* 2005).

One study found that of the decisions appealed to the circuit courts, fully 40 percent were vacated. This is all the more shocking when one considers the gravity of these decisions and the fact that most asylum seekers are not represented by attorneys who would assist in appealing these cases to the BIA and then to the circuit courts.[9] Cases appealed to the BIA are almost always given only cursory attention. One circuit court opinion noted that "the Board member who denied [this] appeal is recorded as having decided over 50 cases on October 31, 2002, a rate of one every 10 minutes over the course of a nine-hour day" (*Albathani v. INS* 2003). In 2005, responding to a backlog of almost 5,000 asylum appeals, the Second Circuit instituted a non-argument calendar for these cases, which mandates that oral arguments will not be heard except in special circumstances. So not only do particular judges jeopardize the "right to be heard" (*Sosnovskaia v. Gonzales* 2005), the overwhelming number of cases silence the Other.

Silencing of the Other in U.S. Asylum Cases

The voice of the Other is silenced throughout this broken process, but one judge, Donald V. Ferlise, has epitomized this silencing. His behavior is so remarkable that it deserves to be recounted in some detail.

---

[9] Legal representation has been found to be an important factor in determining whether an application is granted. One study found that those without attorneys were denied 93% of the time, whereas those with attorneys were denied in 64% of the cases.

In a case, later vacated and remanded by the Third Circuit (*Cham v. Attorney General* 2006), a remarkable exchange occurred between Ferlise[10] and Abou Cham, a 27-year-old Gambian, who was the nephew of the former president of The Gambia. The former president's political party had been banned, and several of Mr. Cham's relatives had been attacked or imprisoned – seven had previously been granted asylum in the United States. Though Mr. Cham was provided a Wolof-English translator, the official language of the country is English and the working language in school is English, so he would clearly be proficient to testify in English. It is important to note that The Gambia is a polyglot nation, with conversations frequently shifting seamlessly from one language to the next without any apparent cue to an outsider (author's observations from frequent trips to The Gambia). The ensuing confusion in the oral proceedings was exacerbated by the court assigning a translator from neighboring Senegal, where a different dialect of Wolof is spoken that is often intermingled with French. Further, Senegal and The Gambia are heavily Muslim with many words known mostly in Arabic. For example, neither Mr. Cham nor the translator knew the Wolof words for most months and dates, because they were mostly spoken in English, Arabic, or French. It must also be noted that the judge's credibility determination is a key component of any asylum decision, and judges often look to the applicant's testimony on one or two factual points to determine credibility. When asked the date of his birth, Mr. Cham answered in English, but was reprimanded by Judge Ferlise:

JUDGE: All right. Remember what I told you, Mr. Cham? Mr. Cham, these instructions are not really earth shattering. They're not that complicated. We are going to stay totally in the Wolof language, now. All right?

A. Okay.

Q. Just, just answer in the Wolof language. It's rather simple. All right. What's your full date of birth, sir?

A. 1979.

Q. All right. Did you not just tell me 1978?

A. '78.

...

JUDGE: Mr. Cham, the question is a rather basic question. When were you born? You said in English, 1978. You said to interpreter in the Wolof language, 1979, or at least that was interpreted as 1979. I just brought that to your attention. Now, we're back to 1978. When were you born, Mr. Cham? Give me your date of birth?

---

[10] Ferlise was the judge who berated Fauziya Kassindja in her asylum case made famous by her heart-wrenching book (Kassindja 1998; see *In Re Fauziya Kassinga* [sic] Interim Decision).

A. I, I cannot count it in Wolof. That's the reason why I'm a little confused.

Q. I want to know the date you were born, sir.

A. 1978.

Q. What date? Give me a month.

A. September. September 28.

Q. And, please -

A. I'm sorry, sir. I'm sorry.

Q. Would you, please, remain in the Wolof language? I don't know why you're doing this. I'm giving you instructions to speak only in Wolof and you keep intermingling English and Wolof.

A. When it comes to counting, Your Honor, I am, I'm not very, very good at it in Wolof. I am better at counting in English than I am in Wolof. I'm very sorry.

The interpreter tells Judge Ferlise that "they use the Arabic [names for the] month" and Judge Ferlise asks the interpreter if he knows the Arabic names – but the interpreters says "I know few of them. I don't know all of them. . . . I use the French or the English."

The hearing continues:

Q: Mr. Cham, do you have a problem following directions?

A: I'm sorry, sir. I'm sorry.

Q: Well, I'm, I'm tired. I'm sorry. And I'm tired of hearing you say I'm sorry. I don't want you speaking English."

. . .

Q. I don't want you speaking English. I gave you the opportunity and you flubbed the opportunity. You were tripping all over the words in English. Your English is not that good. I thought it was better. Now, instead of using your native language with the interpreter that I've provided at some cost to the Government, you want to impress me with your English. Stay in that Wolof language.

A. Okay, sir.

Q. You're just delaying everything here.

A. I'm sorry, sir. I'm sorry. I'm very sorry. Forgive me.

In his oral opinion, Judge Ferlise concluded: "There is no portion of the respondent's testimony that makes sense to this Court" and concluded that he had "fabricated his entire case in chief."

On appeal, Judge Barry of the Third Circuit concluded: "From the very beginning of the two-day hearing in this matter until the very end, Judge

Ferlise continually abused an increasingly distraught petitioner, rendering him unable to coherently respond to Judge Ferlise's questions" (691). She concluded that this case "exemplifies the 'severe wound...inflicted' when not a modicum of courtesy, of respect, or of any pretense of fairness is extended to a petitioner and the case he so valiantly attempted to present. Yet once again, under the 'bullying' nature of the immigration judge's questioning, a petitioner was ground to bits" (686).

Judge Ferlise's tactics are not isolated to this case. On the same day, the Third Circuit vacated another decision in which they concluded Judge Ferlise's decision did not flow logically from the facts (*Shah v. Attorney General* 2006). The petitioner presented evidence that her father had been killed, and the government attorney even conceded as much. But outrageously,

> in his apparent zeal to deny relief to petitioner, however, the Immigration Judge, Donald V. Ferlise, came to the conclusion that the father is alive. In concluding that the father is alive, Judge Ferlise utterly ignored undisputed evidence of the father's death and shored up his conclusion with evidence he had excluded, evidence that actually corroborated the fact of the father's death.

In another shocking case, Judge Ferlise incessantly berated a woman who claimed she had served as a ritual sexual slave by her father in a Ghanaian sect, who abused her for more than ten years from the age of seven (*Fiadjoe v. Attorney General* 2005). In a decision subsequently upheld by the BIA, Ferlise found her testimony not credible and ruled that the government was unable to find that the government was "either unwilling or unable to control her father's sexual abuse," which is requisite in these cases. While awaiting her court date Ms. Fiadjoe was seen by a psychologist who "found that Ms. Fiadjoe was withdrawn and highly anxious, made almost no eye contact, kept her head down, spoke very softly and frequently dissociated." After several sessions with a psychologist Ms. Fiadjoe made significant improvement. However, at her hearing, Judge Ferlise's questioning reduced her to dissociation once again:

JUDGE TO MS. FIADJOE: How [long] did this go on?
A: It, when I left to Accra it stopped, but when I came back to my father again then, at the age of 18 it continued from there.
Q: All right, (indiscernible) at age seven, did your father beat or rape you at age
seven?
A: Yes.

Q: For how long of period of time did that go on?

A: For, til I was seven, I know my father was raping me.

Q: Ma'am, you're not making any – -

A: – - For it went –

Q: – - Ma'am, you, you can cry, that's fine, but your not making any sense, and the tears do not do away with the fact that your [sic] not making any sense to me. Now, rather than crying, just answer the question. You said, your father raped you at age seven and he would beat you, correct?

A: Yes, but I didn't tell anybody.

Q: I don't care if you did or not. At age seven, how long did this go on that he was raping you and beating you?

A: In fact, he was doing that to me when I cried to my auntie, I want to – -

Q: – - Ma'am, I don't like it when someone beats around the bush, okay, when they don't answer me. Another thing I don't like is when somebody makes sounds as if their crying and their eyes stay dry, all right. It's a form of histrionics, stage (indiscernible), I don't like that. I want straight answers and I want straight answers right now. You said, your father beat you and raped you at age seven, how long did that go on while you were age seven?

After that exchange Ms. Fiadjoe was unable to coherently relate her narrative, and several contradictions appeared in her testimony. The judge continued to press for details of other traumatic events including her boyfriend's murder by her father. On appeal, the Third Circuit wrote that "the concluding portions of the hearing further demonstrated the [immigration judge's] continuing hostility towards the obviously distraught Ms. Fiadjoe and his abusive treatment of her throughout the hearing. *He had succeeded in returning her to the condition which Ms. Jansen had enabled her to overcome after repeated therapy sessions, breaking down and dissociating*" (emphasis added). This is quite apparent in the reading of the oral decision by Ferlise:

JUDGE TO MS. FIADJOE: Ms. Fiadjoe, you've heard my decision, you've heard what I've just said?

A: (No audible response).

Q: Oh, you were sleeping there, you fell asleep didn't you?

A: (No audible response).

Q: You fell asleep during my decision?

A: No, I'm feeling headache.

Q: Did you hear what I said or were you asleep?

A: I wasn't asleep.

Q: Did you hear what I said?

A: I thought that you (indiscernible), so I didn't.

Q: Okay, all right, well, what I said was, that first of all, I don't believe your testimony, I think that you were making up your testimony as you were going along. Your testimony is contradicted by, much of it is contradicted by your own witness, Ms. Jansen, her, her the letter that she wrote, your testimony generally doesn't make any sense. I further found, and I denied it, basically because of that, I further found that if I had found that you were credible, that you were telling me the truth, I do not find that – -

(OFF THE RECORD)

(ON THE RECORD)

JUDGE TO MS. FIADJOE: I don't find that you have been persecuted and on one of the five statutory grounds . . I don't find that they've been persecuted pursuant to definition of persecution. And for that reason, I've denied your application, do you understand, now?

A: Yes.

Q: Okay, the answer is yes.

The very day that oral argument was heard in the circuit court, Attorney General Gonzales issued a statement that said: "I have watched with concern the reports of immigration judges who fail to treat aliens appearing before them with appropriate respect and consideration and who fail to produce the quality of work that I expect from employees of the Department of Justice." He concluded by reminding immigration judges, without irony: "To the aliens who stand before you, you are the face of American justice" (quoted in *Cham v. Attorney General* 2006).

The U.S. asylum process is not only broken, it is a place where the voice of the Other is routinely cauterized. It is a state of exception. It is the converse of Judge Edwards' famous conclusion that in the American judicial system "it is the law – and not the personal politics of individual judges – that controls judicial decision making" (Ramji-Nogales et al., 2007, 4). Nevertheless, most theories of heteronomic ethics, including Butler's and the human rights of the Saturated Other developed here require that the law be suspendable. Butler's philosophy requires a state of exception or fault line within the law where self-ascription is possible or where the ego can respond to the address of the Other. Asylum law, mired in a state of exception, is also one of the few areas of law in which an individual is given great latitude to self-ascribe her identity. By examining this area, we can further understand the tensions between self-ascription, normative violence, and the possible place in law for an ethical response to the marginalized Other.

Membership in Particular Social Groups

According to the 1951 Convention Relating to the Status of Refugees, expanded by the Refugee Protocol of 1967, a persecution claim requires the refugee seeker to show that he or she has been persecuted or has a well-founded fear of persecution "on account of race, religion, nationality, *membership in a particular social group*, or public opinion" (emphasis added).[11] Extensive case law has recently examined what constitutes membership in a "particular social group" (MPSG), and the courts in the United States and elsewhere have been surprisingly open to allowing individuals to self-ascribe their social group. Whereas originally holding that particular social groups must be based on some immutable characteristic, the courts have now allowed for a greater fluidity in the self-definition of groups.

An eye-popping range of different self-ascriptions have been granted the status of an MPSG, including "Cuban homosexuals," "upper-class Iranian women, who supported the Shah of Iran and are Westernized free-thinking individuals," "Iranian women who advocate women's rights or who oppose Iranian customs relating to dress and behavior," "parents of Burmese student dissidents," "Pakistani women falsely accused of adultery and unprotected by the state," "gay men with female sexual identities in Mexico," "young women who are members of the Tchamba-Kunsuntu Tribe of northern Togo who have not been subjected to female genital mutilation, as practiced by that tribe, and who oppose the practice," "women of the Tukulor Fulani tribe who have suffered FGM," and "educated wealthy, landowning, cattle-farming Columbians targeted by FARC."[12] At the same time, a host of proposed particular social groups (PSGs) have been denied, including "young, working class males who have not served in the military of El Salvador," "campesino cheese makers who have provided the El Salvadoran guerillas with food on occasion," "drug traffickers," "member of [an] Irish terrorist organization sentenced to death by the organization for complicity in assisting escape of hostages," and "Guatemalan women who have been involved intimately with Guatemalan male companions who believe that women are to live under male domination." Due to the confidential nature of immigration proceedings, some judges have likely relied on even more wide-ranging and innovative PSGs that have not been publicized.

[11] Incorporated into U.S. law through the Refugee Act of 1980 as 8 U.S.C. § 1101 (a)(42).

[12] Although these ascriptions have all been found to meet the definition of a PSG under the meaning of the Convention, not all of these individuals received asylum as they may have been unable to convincingly meet other tests under the Convention, such as whether they were in fact a member of the PSG or that the government played a role in their persecution.

Protected Characteristics and Social Perceptions Approaches

The definition of a permissible PSG differs between countries and between
courts within countries because there is very little to guide its interpretation.
The text of the Refugee Convention provides no clarification, and there are
no analogous definitions in international law (Aleinikoff 2003, 264). Unlike
other treaty controversies, the *travaux preparatoire* (preparatory works) are
"unhelpful" (Aleinikoff 2003, 265) as there was minimal mention of the issue
in the drafting debates for the 1951 Convention and the U.S. Congress did
not address this issue in its ratification debates.[13] With such a state of exception, courts in the United States and elsewhere have struggled to develop a
test for delineating a PSG. Most commentators have now accepted the distinction drawn by Alexander Aleinikoff between the protected characteristics
approach and the social perceptions approach.

The protected characteristics approach usually requires that the group
share a "common immutable characteristic" or a shared experience that "the
individual should not be required to change because it is fundamental to their
individual identities or consciences" (*Matter of Acosta* 1985). This approach
is now used in most U.S. circuits, New Zealand, the United Kingdom,
and elsewhere. The protected characteristics approach is praised because it
"is sufficiently open-ended to allow for evolution...but not so vague as to
admit persons without a serious basis for claim to international protection"
(Hathaway 1991, 161). However, several groups that suffer persecution would
most likely not qualify under such an approach, including union members,
students, those fearful of persecution based on their opposition to the Chinese
sterilization policy, and wealthy landowners targeted by rebels. Further, the
protected characteristics approach is "arguably in tension with a common
sense meaning of the term social group" (Aleinikoff 2003, 294), which does
not require an immutable characteristic.

In response, several courts have embraced the social perceptions approach.
In *Applicant A. v. Minister for Immigration and Ethnic Affairs* (1997), an
Australian Court considered an asylum claim based on fear of forced sterilization in China. Courts in many jurisdictions have struggled with these cases
as this fear is not based on an immutable characteristic and in general persecution itself cannot define the group. In *Applicant A* the court concluded
that a PSG can be based on "a common attribute and a societal perception

---

13   The minutes of the meeting only mention that the Swedish delegate said, "Experience has
     shown that certain refugees had been persecuted because they belonged to particular social
     groups. The draft Convention made no provision for such cases, and one designed to cover
     them should accordingly be included."

that they stand apart" (*Applicant A v. Minister* 1997, at 265–266). Society's perception of the individuals as a separate group fits the plain reading of the Convention text as "membership of a particular social group implies that the group must be identifiable as a social unit" (at 264). The U.S. Ninth Circuit embraced a variation of the social perceptions approach in *Sanchez-Trujillo* (1986), in which it concluded a PSG "implies a collection of people closely affiliated with each other, who are actuated by some common impulse or interest. Of central concern is the existence of a *voluntary associational relationship* among the purported members" (emphasis added).[14] Sanchez-Trujillo differs from the Australian case in that the perception of a distinct social group resides with the individuals voluntarily associated into a group and not with society's or the persecutor's perception of the group. The social perceptions approach has been praised for being more humanitarian than the protected characteristics approach as "any group, of any size, that is set apart from society and is targeted for persecution on account of this separateness is cognizable" (Inlender 2006, 700). Unlike the protected characteristics approach, "it does not rely on a value-laden assessment of the fundamental nature of the group's shared trait" (Inlender 2006, 700). This is especially the case in Sanchez-Trujillo, where the self-ascription of the group by itself constitutes the group.[15]

Other U.S. courts have been reluctant to follow the social perceptions approach, claiming that the *Sanchez-Trujillo* approach might omit some groups that would be covered by the protected characteristics approach, especially women and homosexuals. The Ninth Circuit remedied this defect by simply combining the social perceptions approach of *Sanchez-Trujillo* with the protected characteristics approach of *Acosta* in *Hernandez-Montiel* (2000). A PSG now is "one united by a voluntary association, including a former association, or by an innate characteristic that is so fundamental to the identities or consciences of its members that members either cannot or should

[14] The Court said that the "prototypical example of a 'particular social group' would consist of the immediate members of a certain family, the family being a focus of fundamental affiliational concerns and common interests for most people." However, this prototypical example is in conflict with the very definition it seeks to support because most family relationships are not voluntary. "As a contrasting example, a statistical group of males taller than six feet would not constitute a 'particular social group' under any reasonable construction of the statutory term, even if individuals with such characteristics could be shown to be at greater risk of persecution than the general population."

[15] A PSG is a "group of persons who share a common characteristic other than their risk of being persecuted, or who are perceived as a group by society. The characteristic will often be one which is innate, unchangeable, or which is otherwise fundamental to identity, conscience or the exercise of one's human rights" (UNHCR 2002). Notably, the UNHCR did not include the voluntary association definition from *Sanchez-Trujillo*.

not be required to change it" (*Hernandez-Montiel* 2000, 1093). Similarly the UNHCR embraced a combined approach in its most recent guidelines (UNHCR 2002).

An asylum law that begins from the perspective of the marginalized Other would require the widest possible definition of a PSG, such as the combined approaches of the UNHCR and the Ninth Circuit. Further, within both the protected characteristics approach and the social perceptions approach there needs to be a privileged space for self-ascription, a patient listening to the voice of the Other.

Self-Ascription of Immutable Characteristics

Under the protected characteristics approach, the Other should be able to self-ascribe the characteristic that is immutable or fundamental to his or her identity. These characteristics should not be circumscribed by the law or by a judge, especially by a judge thousands of miles away from the applicant's country of origin who might not understand the applicant's culture. Such judgments would risk being interpellations of subjectification where the subject's identity is circumscribed by truth regimes in Butler's terms. Instead, judges should be open to the way that applicants define their identity and look past societal authentication of particular identities. A recent U.S. case, *Hernandez-Montiel v. INS* (2000), is especially on point here.

Geovanni Hernandez-Montiel applied for asylum in the United States after enduring years of persecution in Mexico because of his homosexual orientation and the fact that from the age of twelve he often dressed as a woman. Expert testimony concluded that in Mexico a homosexual man who takes on the "passive, role in these sexual relationships" can be "ostracized from the very beginning and is subject to persecution, gay bashing as we would call it, and certainly police abuse." In his teens, Hernandez-Montiel's family attempted to "cure" him of his homosexuality several times, and they eventually kicked him out of the house. He was also persecuted at school before being expelled and harassed by the police. He was violently raped by police officers twice two weeks apart when he was fourteen.

The U.S. immigration judge found him to be credible and concluded he had been persecuted but held that he was not being persecuted on the basis of a PSG. The judge characterized his PSG as "homosexual males who *wish* to dress as a woman [sic]" (emphasis added). His membership in this group was not judged to be based on an immutable characteristic because "respondent's decision to dress as a women [sic] is volitional, not immutable, and the fact that he sometimes dresses like a typical man reflects that respondent himself may not view his dress as being so fundamental to his identity that he should not have to change it."

The Ninth Circuit, on the other hand, looked past the hegemonic discourses in Mexico and the United States. They began their analysis by stating that "sexual orientation and sexual identity are immutable; they are so fundamental to one's identity that a person should not be required to abandon them" (at 20–21). They then changed the description of the PSG to "gay men with female sexual identities in Mexico." This reconfiguration more accurately described Geovanni's self-ascribed identity. The court stated that members of this group "outwardly manifest their identities through characteristics traditionally associated with women, such as feminine dress, long hair and fingernails." This sexual identity is not "volitional" but is "so fundamental to their human identities that they should not be required to change them." Finally, the court was especially swayed by Geovanni's self-ascription of his identity: "Geovanni's credible and uncontradicted testimony about the inherent and immutable nature of his sexual identity compels the conclusion that Geovanni was a member of the particular social group of gay men in Mexico with female sexual identities."

Voluntary Association as Social Perceptions

To further irrupt the hegemonic discourse, we need to consider the role of self-ascription in defining the social perceptions of a group. To date, most courts have relied solely on the perception of society or the perception of the persecutor. To do so is to follow the interpellation of the oppressor. Instead, space should be allowed for voluntary association or self-perceived membership in a social group.[16] Some scholars have suggested that such a standard would allow trivial groups to be defined as PSGs, whereas other approaches would insist that the group was defined by a "truly important trait" (Aleinikoff 2003, 299). Inlender (2006) asks, "Why, for example, should trombone players be able to present a colorable claim to refugee protection?" However, if individuals are being persecuted because of possessing a common trait, such as being a trombone player, it must be non-trivial. Inlender (2006) responds: "If members of a social group of trombone players *were* to be singled out for persecution, why should they not be able to seek relief under the Refugee Convention?"

Voluntary association is especially important to counter the belief that the persecution cannot define the PSG. Almost all courts and the UNHCR have

---

[16]   Inlender (2006) cogently argues that the "relevant referent for the perception of separateness" could be answered differently for different circumstances.

held that the group must exist in some form before the persecution. However, Butler's insistence that identity is performed through resistance to discourse would suggest that resistors to persecution should be able to self-ascribe their identities through their very resistance. For example, those who oppose China's one-child policy have not usually been considered a social group under either the protected characteristics or social perceptions approaches. However, from Butler's perspective they are creating their individual and group identities through a "dance of mutual constructedness" (Mezey 2001) aimed at overturning a hegemonic discourse. The most progressive innovations in this direction have been seen in several recent Australian cases. In *Applicant A*, Justice McHugh wrote: "While persecutory conduct cannot define the social group, the actions of the persecutors may serve to identify or even cause the creation of a particular social group. Left-handed men are not a particular social group. But, if they were persecuted because they were left-handed, they would no doubt quickly become recognisable in their society as a particular social group." Here we see a tension within Butler's theory of performativity. Is it the persecution or is it the resistance to the persecution that is defining the group? Is it possible for a group of resistors to form without being defined in some way by the persecution itself?

The Social Theorist and the Narcissist

When exposed to the face of the Saturated Other, the judge is called to be a social theorist, to deconstruct societal norms both within U.S. law and within the sending country. Here, it is important to note how important context is under the social perspectives approach. One commentator wrote, "The social perceptions approach acknowledges and responds to the rich diversity of social and cultural practices and beliefs that have an impact on the lives of individuals and groups" (Inlender 2006, 700). When the social perceptions approach is taken seriously, the judge is required to delve into the political, social, cultural, and economic characteristics of a country to understand why a specific individual was (or will be) persecuted. "A fact specific inquiry meets the humanitarian aim of the Convention by ensuring that each claim is comprehensively considered, rather than dismissed on the basis of an imported and arbitrarily applied limiting principle. Heavily fact and context-specific inquiries also promote accountability of decision-makers by requiring them to reflect meaningfully on country conditions and articulate how the applicant's claim fits within those conditions" (Inlender 2006, 701). The social perspectives approach also fosters a progressive development of human rights as the judge is called out of his or her preconceived notions to freshly consider the persecution context. For example, depending on the context, wealthy landowners may or may not qualify as a particular social group, and that may change over time. Lord Hope of Craighead wrote in a UK case: "The phrase can thus accommodate particular social groups which may be recognizable as such in one country but not in others or which, in any given country, have not previously been recognized" (*Regina v. Immigration Appeal Tribunal* 1999, 297).

However, the judge as ego is embedded within a truth regime that could prevent his taking on the role of social theorist. The judge may not feel any need to give an account of himself or his identity, perhaps because he has already cauterized the Other and will not grant the applicant a voice in the courtroom. This may even be a reaction to the applicant as a contagion that must be stopped from spreading, similar to the proclamation "I am gay" by a service member in the United States. Just as gay service members would open the floodgates to unrepressed expressions of homoerotic desire, admitting asylum applicants may open the floodgates to those who are carriers of a contagion, such as communism, extremism, terrorism, and so forth. In these cases, the self-ascription of an asylum applicant is an essentializing process that can take on the form of an interpellation or condemnation. In condemnation, "we establish the other as nonrecognizable or jettison some aspect of ourselves that we lodge in the other" (Butler 2005, 46). Instead of responding to the Other, the ego "moralize(s) a self by disavowing commonality with the judged" (Butler 2005, 46). This condemnation is a form of what Freud calls the narcissism of minor differences. The ego looks to the Other to form a "this" or a "we." In order to solidify this identity, some Others must be purged as different. The ego and its identity will be threatened by what is most alike and seize on minor differences to set up a barrier between us and them. This seems apparent in Judge Ferlise's demand that Abou Cham speak Wolof and not English. Not surprisingly, another of Judge Ferlise's cases epitomizes this narcissism of minor differences (*Sukwanputra v. Gonzales* 2006). Once again, the Third Circuit had to vacate his order because he "interjected intemperate and bias-laden remarks...none of which had any basis in the facts introduced." Most telling, Judge Ferlise interrupted the applicant from Indonesia:

> Ma'am she has no right to be here. You have no right to be here. All of the applicants that are applying for asylum have no right to be here. You don't come to the United States to look for a job! That's not the purpose of asylum. You don't come here to look for a job, or look for a house, or look for a better car, and then as an afterthought say, well, the only way I'm going to be able to stay here is if I can convince a Judge that I'm going to be persecuted. It's not the way the law works. Now, if you're telling your sister to come to the United States to pretend to be a student to have her come here, you're guilty of visa fraud. That is a felony. You can go to jail for that! *You have to understand, the*

whole world does not revolve around you and the other Indonesians that just
want to live here because they enjoy the United States better than they enjoy
living in Indonesia. It is not a world that revolves around you and your ethnic
group (*Sukwanputra v. Gonzales* 2006, emphasis added).

What makes this tirade all the more remarkable is that "there was no evidence
adduced at the hearing that petitioner was seeking asylum only because she
enjoyed the quality of life here better than that in Indonesia, nor was there any
basis for the IJ's remarks that petitioner might be guilty of visa fraud." Judge
Ferlise's tirades expose much more about his narcissism than about the facts of
the cases, just as the "Don't Ask, Don't Tell" policy reveals more about straight
military personnel than homosexual personnel.

Judge Ferlise is just a particularly troublesome example of a larger structural problem – the systematic cauterization of the refugee. In this text, we
have seen refugees or asylum seekers in a range of contexts systematically
branded as inferior and as deserving of fewer rights, of being silenced, and
having their suffering ignored. Refugees or foreigners, under the category of
Muslim women, were almost completely silenced from the headscarf debates
in France. Palestinian refugee camps were sealed off by Israeli forces that
looked away during a notorious massacre of men, women, and children.
Asylum seekers in the United States face a game of "refugee roulette" in which
their fate rests on random bureaucratic decisions. Far from Benhabib's ideal
of "just membership" for refugees and asylum seekers or Derrida's "unconditional hospitality," refugees today, like refugees in the inter-war years described
by Arendt, exist in "a peculiar state of nature" (Arendt 1951, 300).[17]

CONCLUSION

Giorgio Agamben wrote, "The refugee is perhaps the only thinkable figure for
the people of our time and the only category in which we may see today . . . the
forms and limits of a coming political community" (Agamben 1996, 159). If a
coming political community or legal system is to be built on human rights of
the Marginalized Other, the normative violence of law must be suspendable.
When the judge is exposed to the face of the Other, he or she must engage in
a patient listening, even work with the applicant to overturn the hegemonic
norms. However, as Butler reminds us, these norms are so overpowering that

---

[17] A plethora of recent reports have also documented the continuing inhumane treatment
of immigrants and asylum seekers in the United States, especially in Arizona (e.g., Inter-
American Commission on Human Rights 2009).

the ego, even a well-intentioned ego, risks becoming "an instrument of that norm's agency" (2005, 26).

Even the most progressive interpretation of a PSG is bound by the original violence of the 1951 Refugee Convention. Whereas some countries pushed for a treaty that would allow the protection of any refugee who faced persecution in any way, the United States and France refused to sign a treaty that did not have substantial restrictions limiting the time period and geographical locations of who would qualify as a refugee. They were only willing to accept refugees from the war in Europe and were reluctant to open their doors to future refugees or refugees displaced by World War II from Africa and Asia.

Every year thousands of refugees are sent back to their countries to face a very uncertain future even though they have credibly shown in a court of law that they have a well-founded fear of persecution. However, their persecution does not fit one of the five original Convention grounds. They will not be persecuted "*on account of* race, religion, nationality, membership in a particular social group, or public opinion" (emphasis added). This nexus requirement, including the determination of what constitutes a particular social group, has been subject to the interpretations of "reasonable persons" embedded in a truth regime as with the legal definition in the "Don't Ask, Don't Tell" policy.[18]

To craft an asylum law from the perspective of the Other would be to break down this original violence of the Convention's founding moment and grant asylum to anyone facing persecution whether or not it is "on account" of these five grounds.[19] Some jurisdictions have taken small steps to break down this original violence. A New Zealand judge opined that "refugee law ought to concern itself with actions which deny human dignity in any key way" (*Re GJ* 1995). As one commentator said, "It is profoundly irrational to differentiate between the types of arbitrary and capricious persecution that an oppressive regime may impose" (Helton 1983, 59).

To break down this original violence will require more than self-ascription of identity; it will require a redefinition of the fundamental right at stake. This redefinition should not be done by the hegemonic powers who will not understand the myriad ways that persecution is experienced. Nor should it be done by scholars, activists, attorneys, or judges. It must be done through exposure to the face of the Other, through a learning to learn from the voice of the

---

[18] Several scholars have found biases in these cases based on whether a country was communist (Helton 1984; Griffin 1995) and an ally in the war on terrorism (Swanwick 2006). Others have found a general class bias in determining a PSG (Fullerton 1993).

[19] For a heart-wrenching case that dealt with this very issue, see *In re R-A-* (Vacated by Attorney General, January 19, 2001).

Other. This re-conception of the fundamental rights at stake will require a far-reaching reorientation about the meaning of persecution. Persecution, in a Levinasian sense, is not just what the Other undergoes but is the very account of subjectivity where the ego is persecuted by the suffering of the Other. As Levinas writes: "The more I return to myself, the more I divest myself, under the traumatic effect of persecution, of my freedom as a constituted, willful, imperialist subject, the more I discover myself to be responsible" (Levinas 1981, 112). As responsible for the Other's persecution, the ego must work with the Other to realize the rights of the Other as they are defined by the Other.

7

Heteronomic Rights and Duties

This chapter further translates the phenomenology of the Saturated Other into the language of human rights law, that is, the language of legally enforceable rights and duties. I argue that the content of human rights law needs to be fundamentally expanded and redefined, but this should not be done a priori by scholars (including the present author), activists, or attorneys; this should be directed by the Marginalized Other. When the rights of the Marginalized Other take priority over Arendt's call for a right to have rights (see Chapter 4), it follows that the Other should have a legally enforceable right to define his or her rights, which would include the right to determine a hierarchy of rights, that is, to determine which rights are most fundamental. I will label rights developed in this fashion *heteronomic rights*, etymologically meaning rights based on a law (*nomos*) of the Other (*heteros*). The establishment of rights hierarchies based on a law of the Other will lead to what I call *heteronomic tiered scrutiny*, where more fundamental rights, as established by the Other, will require the strictest scrutiny as to whether they may be infringed by the hegemonic system. To self-ascribe one's identity (discussed in Chapter 6) and define one's rights is to overturn the categorizations or interpellations of the hegemonic narrative and to begin to establish a new anti-hegemonic validity in which the Other assumes control of his or her *proyecto de la vida* (life project).

Concomitantly, the duties of states (and other institutions) are expanded and transformed by the phenomenology of the Saturated Other. Expanding on emerging models of affirmative duties in international law that rely on the tripartite duties to respect, protect, and fulfill human rights, I argue for what I call *heteronomic duties* for the Other. States and other actors have the affirmative duty to work with the marginalized to realize their *proyectos de la vida*. Because their *proyectos* are obstructed by the structural violence of the system, the state can be held accountable – in violation of human rights law – for creating and maintaining the structural violence that deprives the Other of his or her rights. States can be held legally accountable for perpetuating such structural barriers as illiteracy, gender discrimination, hunger, and disease. States must continuously critique all original and conserving violence, even of those institutions like human rights tribunals that are established to serve the Other. Because a hegemonic discourse, in the form of an invisible ideology, often facilitates the marginalization of the Other, the state's affirmative duties must also include the duty to work with the Other as a social theorist to deconstruct the interpellation of the Other by the hegemonic discourse or, in Paulo Freire's language, to work with the Other to raise their consciousness. Consciousness raising must not be an education in the hegemonic discourse but will require the suspension, as much as possible, of the invisible ideologies of the system. It requires facilitating the development of the marginalized Other's episteme. The state is legally bound to learn to learn from the voice of the Other. If a state is found in violation of these norms, human rights institutions should issue reparations orders that require the state to work with the marginalized Other, and these orders should be overseen by the human rights institutions working hand in hand with the Other.

This chapter begins with a brief discussion of current jurisprudence drawn from regional human rights bodies, especially the African Commission on Human and Peoples' Rights, which expands traditional thinking about the content of rights and the affirmative duties of states. The African Commission, more than most human rights bodies, has moved beyond the Enlightenment emphasis on negative rights and civil and political rights and embraced state duties to fulfill economic, social, and cultural rights. I then discuss recent Canadian jurisprudence where courts have struggled to define aboriginal rights and redefine state duties while respecting the perspectives of aboriginal peoples. I will argue that recent attempts to define aboriginal rights have been unable and unwilling to truly consider their perspectives as the Canadian courts have failed to deconstruct the original violence of the hegemonic system. The courts have also struggled to define the duties of the state vis-à-vis aboriginal peoples. The heteronomic duty that I call for goes even beyond the Canadian conception of the state as fiduciary or trustee acting in the best interest of the aboriginal peoples as well as the recent jurisprudence that the state has a duty to consult with, and accommodate the interests of, aboriginal peoples. The Canadian courts have eschewed opportunities to facilitate the development of the aboriginal's episteme and thus have failed to sufficiently learn to learn from the voice of the Other.

The final section analyzes recent groundbreaking jurisprudence from the Inter-American Court of Human Rights. The Inter-American Court has recently changed its rules of procedures to better provide a forum for the voice of the Other, especially when considering reparations for human rights violations. This patient listening to the voice and episteme of the victims, especially vulnerable populations, has led to "perhaps the most comprehensive legal regime on reparations" (Grossman 2007, 1376) with many groundbreaking orders that require a state to work with the victims or their families to continue their life-project. I conclude with a discussion of the groundbreaking case of *Moiwana v. Suriname*. Here the Court, especially Judge Trindade in his concurring opinion, patiently listened to the Other and then worked with the victims to realize their life-project based on their self-defined fundamental rights, which included, for the first time in international law, a right to a life-project after life. The Court ordered Suriname to work with the marginalized to realize their *proyectos*, but to what extent Suriname has taken on the heteronomic duty to be a social theorist to deconstruct the hegemonic discourse remains to be seen.

RIGHTS AND DUTIES IN THE AFRICAN HUMAN RIGHTS SYSTEM

When we begin from a right of the Other to define his or her rights, all a priori categorizations of rights dissolve. No longer is the suffering of the Other cauterized because it does not fit a priori distinctions developed by the hegemonic discourse.[1] The previous chapter, for example, showed how the international legal definition of persecution denies asylum to countless victims because their well-founded fear of persecution is not on account of the designated reasons (race, religion, etc.). Likewise, the suffering of the Other does not neatly fall into "generations" of rights, so the artificial distinction, deriving in good part from Cold War politics, between civil and political rights and economic, social, and cultural rights vanishes. Further, the "western" liberal distinction between negative and positive rights also becomes tenuous. The

---

[1] A major effort, although ultimately flawed, by the World Bank to catalog the suffering of the poor in their own voices surveyed more than 20,000 poor people – "poverty experts" – and concluded that powerlessness "consists of multiple and interlocking dimension of illbeing or poverty" (Narayan et al., 2000). These were roughly categorized into ten dimensions, such as "Livelihoods and assets are precarious, seasonal and inadequate," "Places of the poor are isolated, risky, unserviced and stigmatized," "The body is hungry, exhausted, sick and poor in appearance," and "Gender relations are troubled and unequal." Cf. Koch (2005), "The closer one gets to the complexity of the problems of everyday life the more frequently one will encounter the fact that the response to a concrete social demand requires measures of considerable complexity sometimes defying classification as relating exclusively to either respect, protection, or fulfillment" (93).

state is not called to merely refrain from interfering with individual rights, but it is also called to perform positive duties in service for the Other.

Several scholars and human rights jurists have also moved beyond these artificial Cold War-era distinctions and have embraced a tripartite typology of state duties, namely the duties to respect, protect, and fulfill human rights (cf. Shue 1996; Koch 2005). These include more than the duties to respect and protect civil and political rights such as the freedom of speech, providing for legal counsel, a jury of one's peers, and fair voting procedures. The state's duties extend now to fulfilling economic, social, and cultural rights, including, inter alia, the rights to food, shelter, health, and a healthy environment. Regional human rights institutions, especially the African Commission on Human and Peoples' Rights, have perhaps gone the furthest in pushing for such innovative expansions of human rights and state duties.

Affirmative Duties to Fulfill Economic, Social, and Cultural Rights

Enmeshed in Enlightenment rights frameworks, most international human rights bodies only hold states accountable for violations of civil and political rights. For instance, the European Convention of Human Rights does not include any economic, social, and cultural rights (ESCRs), and only Article 26 of the American Convention on Human Rights mentions ESCRs. The European Court and the Inter-American Court have recently both developed a robust jurisprudence on the affirmative duties of states, but these cases mostly focus on the state's duty to investigate, prosecute, and punish violations of civil and political rights. For example, the Inter-American Court of Human Rights reasoned in its first contentious case that the general affirmative duty under Article 1 of the Convention to *ensure* rights and freedoms of the Convention requires that "the States must prevent, investigate and punish any violation of the rights recognized by the Convention" (*Velasquez-Rodriguez Case* 1988). A similar calculus has been used extensively by the European Court of Human Rights to create affirmative duties to investigate and punish violations of fundamental civil and political rights (see, for example, *McCann v. United Kingdom* 1995 and *Sabuktekin v. Turkey* 2002).[2] Many commentators have heralded recent cases where the European Court codified the responsibility of a state for the actions of private individuals (e.g., *X and Y v. Netherlands* 1985),

[2]   Recently the European Court has been more willing to take steps into the realm of economic and social rights, as "the mere fact that interpretation of the Convention may extend into the sphere of social and economic rights would not be a decisive factor against such an interpretation: there is no water-tight division separating that sphere from the field covered by the Convention" (*Airey v. Ireland* 1979, para. 26).

but in these cases the Court relied on the same calculus – that the state had failed to set up institutions or create laws that would provide proper investigations or provide remedies to ensure basic civil and political rights guaranteed in the Convention. To date, these courts constrained by the original violence of their founding documents have not fully embraced a state's duty to fulfill ESCRs.

The African Charter on Human and Peoples' Rights (entered into force in 1986) breaks new ground in affirmative duties for states, individuals, and communities. It includes, as does the European and Inter-American conventions, the responsibility of state parties for a series of civil and political rights; that is, "to guarantee the independence of the courts" and "to ensure the elimination of every discrimination against women and also ensure the protection of the rights of the women and the child." Strikingly, the Charter also lists a series of obligations to fulfill ESCRs, including, inter alia, "to assist [and protect] the family," "the right to enjoy the best attainable state of physical and mental health," "to ensure the exercise of the right to development," and "to eliminate all forms of foreign economic exploitation." Articles 27–29 even lay out a host of responsibilities for individuals, including "duties towards his family and society," the duties "to serve his national community by placing his physical and intellectual abilities at its service," and "to contribute to the best of his abilities, at all times and at all levels, to the promotion and achievement of African unity."

Despite this long litany of affirmative duties, until recently, the African Commission's few rulings on affirmative duties mostly mirrored those of the Inter-American and European systems; that is, states are held responsible when they have failed to take the necessary affirmative steps to fulfill civil and political rights.[3] In recent cases, the Commission has expanded a state's affirmative duty to include the fulfillment of ESCRs. Here I will discuss two landmark cases in which the Commission fashioned new rights to protect the marginalized and held states responsible for fulfilling these rights.

Constructing the Rights to Housing and Food: SERAC v. Nigeria

In its most expansive ruling to date, *SERAC v. Nigeria*, the Commission ruled that Nigeria was in violation of several provisions of the African Charter for abuses suffered by the Ogoni people due to the immense oil extraction industry in the Niger Delta region. A public-private consortium involving the

---

[3] In a notable early exception, Zaire was found to have violated the provisions of Article 16 that individuals have the "right to enjoy the best attainable state of physical and mental health," because the state had failed to provide safe drinking water, electricity, and medicine.

military-led government and Shell Oil had developed the oil fields with little regard for the health of the citizens or the damages done to the local environment. When the local people banded together to create the Movement of the Survival of Ogoni People (MOSOP) to engage in non-violent protests, the "Nigerian security forces…attacked, burned and destroyed several Ogoni villages and homes under the pretext of dislodging officials and supporters of the Movement of the Survival of Ogoni People (MOSOP)." This terror campaign left thousands homeless. The military systematically destroyed crops and the Ogoni's livestock. Exacerbated by the extensive damage to the environment from the oil industry, thousands were left without an adequate food supply and were near starvation.

The Commission framed its inquiry of specific rights in the context of two principles, each of which move us beyond the classic Enlightenment understanding of human rights. First, it considered state responsibilities under human rights law and concluded that states must not only respect human rights but they also have an affirmative duty to take positive steps to ensure that human rights including ESCRs are not interfered with by third parties. Indeed, the Commission made intimations that states have a positive duty to fulfill economic, social, and cultural rights, especially the right to a healthy environment. Further, states are responsible not only for their own actions but for the actions of private actors, such as in the instant case where "the Nigerian Government has given the green light to private actors, and the oil Companies in particular, to devastatingly affect the well-being of the Ogonis."

The state was found to be in violation of a series of Articles of the African Charter. It violated Article 16's "right to enjoy the best attainable state of physical and mental health" and Article 24's "right to a general satisfactory environment." These rights require positive steps by the state. The state must "take reasonable and other measures to prevent pollution and ecological degradation, to promote conservation, and to secure an ecologically sustainable development and use of natural resources." Guaranteeing these rights includes such measures as "undertaking appropriate monitoring and providing information to those communities exposed to hazardous materials and activities and providing meaningful opportunities for individuals to be heard and to participate in the development decisions affecting their communities."

Most interestingly, the Commission went beyond the original limitations of the African Charter and developed new rights. It derived the right to housing from a progressive combination of Article 14's right to property, Article 18's protection for the family, and Article 16's right to physical health. The government was in violation of this implied right to housing for destroying Ogoni homes and preventing them being rebuilt as well as the forcible evictions of thousands. Similarly, the Commission developed a right to food through a combination of the right to life in Article 4; the right to health in Article 16; and the right to economic, social, and cultural development in Article 22. "The government has destroyed food sources through its security forces and State Oil Company; has allowed private oil companies to destroy food sources; and, through terror, has created significant obstacles to Ogoni communities trying to feed themselves" and was thus in violation of the implied right to food.

State Duty to Provide Mental Health: *Purohit v. Gambia*

The duty to provide for mental health was established in the pioneering case of *Purohit v. Gambia*. The Commission found that that The Gambia's mental health legislation (the outdated Lunatics Detention Act) and its treatment of the mentally ill at its Campana psychiatric unit violated several provisions of the African Charter such as Article 2 (equal protection), Article 5 (human dignity), Article 6 (right to liberty and freedom from arbitrary detention), and Article 16 (the right to enjoy the best attainable state of physical and mental health). Several parts of the final decision stand out particularly in relation to the theoretical framework developed in this book.

The government was found to have cauterized the mentally ill in the manner described in earlier chapters. The Commission was troubled by the manner in which the mentally ill were labeled or branded by Gambian law "as 'lunatics' and 'idiots', terms, which without any doubt dehumanize and deny them any form of dignity" (§ 59). Remarkably, this branding by itself was found to be a violation of Article 5 of the African Charter, which guarantees "*the right to the respect of dignity inherent in a human being.*" Once branded as "lunatics," the mentally ill were sealed off from the polis by internment at Campana and they became *aneu logou* (without a voice). The patients did not have a voice in the appeals process as Gambian law contained no "provisions for the review or appeal against an order of detention or any remedy for detention made in error or wrong diagnosis or treatment" (§ 71). Their voice was further cauterized in that all patients at Campan,a regardless of the type and extent of their illness, were denied the right to vote in violation of Article 13 of the African Charter. The Gambia was ordered to repeal the Lunatic Detentions Act and to establish a panel to review previous detention decisions. It was also ordered to provide a voice to the mentally ill through representation in the form of legal aid so that patients could challenge their detention and to provide for the right to vote for the mentally ill.

The Commission went further, making general pronouncements on a state's duty to *take* affirmative steps to provide for the health of its citizens, including mental health. The Commission found in Article 16 an "obligation on [the] part of States party to the African Charter to take concrete and targeted steps, while taking full advantage of its available resources, to ensure that the right to health is fully realised in all its aspects without discrimination of any kind" (para. 84). The Commission noted that a lack of resources may be an obstacle to meeting this duty, but "persons with mental illnesses should never be denied their right to proper health care, which is crucial for their survival and their assimilation into and acceptance by the wider society" (para. 85). In response to this decision, The Gambia has taken several affirmative steps to comply with the Commission's ruling, such as drafting a new comprehensive mental health policy and making major improvements at the Campana facility (WHO 2007).

The Commission's redefinition of rights and state duties has inspired other human rights institutions. For example, the Inter-American Court of Human Rights in the *Sawhoyamaxa Indigenous Community Case* ordered "Paraguay to adopt measures necessary to supply the community with potable water, healthcare, food, sanitation facilities, and educational resources" (Schonsteiner 2007, 137). Such rulings open up a host of new responsibilities for the state. No longer must the state merely refrain from infringing on an individual's rights or ensuring that rights are not infringed on by third parties. Now, states can be held accountable for not providing food, housing, adequate mental health facilities, and a healthy environment. The state is increasingly legally culpable for creating and maintaining the structural violence that deprives the Other of his or her rights. These rights are not limited to an Enlightenment understanding of rights, or rights as they were enshrined in mid-twentieth-century documents like the Universal Declaration of Human Rights. The African Commission has established precedents that legally enforceable rights can be expanded to include what Judge Trindade of the Inter-American Court of Human Rights has called the right to life *lato sensu* (in the widest sense) or the *proyecto de la vida*. Indeed, one of the hallmarks of human rights law has been its progressive development with courts fashioning new rights or further expanding the reach of current rights.

A human rights of the Marginalized Other would require that legal institutions go further and define rights and duties, not based solely on their interpretation of the international charter but on the perspectives of the marginalized, that is, to create heteronomic rights and duties. The marginalized should have a right to define their rights from their perspective, including a hierarchy of fundamental rights. As we learned in Chapter 5, this task would require the tribunal to suspend the hegemonic system as much as possible and engage in what Spivak has called a "no holds barred *self-suspending leap into the other's sea*" (Spivak 2004a, 207–208, emphasis added). Further, states found to be violating these rights and courts that oversee these rights would now have heteronomic duties that include working with the marginalized to implement policies to realize their *proyectos de la vida*.[4]

THE RIGHT TO DEFINE RIGHTS IN CANADIAN ABORIGINAL RIGHTS JURISPRUDENCE

Perhaps no legal system has struggled more to define rights from the perspective of the marginalized and the concomitant duties of the states vis-à-vis the marginalized than the Canadian national courts in numerous high-profile aboriginal rights cases. Subsection 35 (1) of the 1982 Constitution Act granted Constitutional status to aboriginal rights, stating, "The existing aboriginal and treaty rights of the aboriginal peoples of Canada are hereby recognized and affirmed." In their attempts to give content to the meaning of aboriginal rights under Section 35(1), the courts often maintain they are giving preference to the rights of indigenous peoples and that these are shaped by the aboriginal peoples' episteme. The courts have also recognized that because of the unique historical relationship between Canada and the aboriginal peoples, the state owes a sui generis duty to the indigenous peoples. As Justice L'Heureux-Dubé summarized:

> Section 35(1) must be given a generous, large and liberal interpretation and *uncertainties, ambiguities or doubts should be resolved in favour of the natives.* Further, aboriginal rights must be construed in light of the *special trust relationship and the responsibility of the Crown* vis à vis aboriginal people. Finally, but most significantly, aboriginal rights protected under s. 35(1) have to be viewed in the context of the specific history and culture of the native society and *with regard to native perspective* on the meaning of the rights asserted. (*R. v. Gladstone* 1996, dissent, emphases added)

However, in practice the Canadian courts have had difficulty in shedding the original violence of the hegemonic system and have allowed politics and economics to trump aboriginal rights. Despite seeing aboriginal rights as sui generis soon after the Constitution Act (*Guerin* 1984), the justices have generally been unable to undertake a "no holds barred self-suspending leap into the other's sea" (Spivak 2004a, 207–208). First Nations legal scholars have subjected this jurisprudence to a withering critique. For example, it is clear that

[4] See Sen 1984, who labels the right to government policies to fulfill rights as "metarights" (cf. Koch 2005, 83, n. 8).

aboriginal peoples and their rights are called to justify their existence before the hegemonic tribunal (just as we saw in Chapter 2 that Muslim girls in France were called to justify their wearing of the headscarf), but rarely, if ever, does the law ask about "the source and content of the legal rights of British settlers" (Metallic and Monture-Angus 2002, § 5, quoting Walters 1993, 358). Instead, the taking of Native lands at least back to the Royal Proclamation of 1763 has been sanctioned by law where "the mere assertion of Crown sovereignty and title is deemed sufficient to establish Crown sovereignty and title" (Christie 2005, 23). Rarely, too, has the long history of cauterizing aboriginal peoples and their perspectives been seriously interrogated by the Canadian courts especially how law continues to aid in this process. The end result is that "contemporary jurisprudence not only borrows from colonial justifications developed and maintained during Canada's overtly colonial period, but actually sanctions, affirms, and strengthens this colonial conceptual framework" (Christie 2005, 21).

The Right to Define Fundamental Rights: R. v. Van der Peet

Defining aboriginal rights was first considered in detail in the infamous *R. v. Van der Peet* decision of 1996. *Van der Peet* gave lip service to the general principles outlined in the previous section but in practice greatly narrowed the aboriginal rights protected by Section 35(1).

Dorothy Van der Peet, a member of the Sto:lo band of the Coast Salish people in British Columbia, sold ten salmon for which she was charged with violating the British Columbia Fishery (General) Regulations that prohibited the selling or bartering of fish caught under the auspices of her Indian Food Fish license. Van der Peet claimed that this prohibition violated her aboriginal rights, guaranteed under Subsection 35 (1), specifically the right "to sufficient fish to provide for a moderate livelihood."

Chief Justice Lamer, writing for the majority, began his analysis echoing the general principles established in earlier aboriginal rights cases. The relationship between the Crown and aboriginal peoples is a "fiduciary one and a generous and liberal interpretation should accordingly be given in favour of aboriginal peoples. Any ambiguity as to the scope and definition of s. 35(1) must be resolved in favour of aboriginal peoples." CJ Lamer stressed that the Court should make special provisions for aboriginal evidence including oral histories: "The courts must not undervalue the evidence presented by aboriginal claimants simply because that evidence does not conform precisely with the evidentiary standards applied in other contexts."

However, when presenting the principles for defining aboriginal rights, Lamer quickly discarded any preferential treatment for the aboriginal peoples and their epistemes. He takes several steps, all rooted in the Crown's perspective, which greatly restrict the rights of aboriginal peoples by freezing their rights to those specific activities undertaken in a bygone era that remained unchanged and were distinct from colonial culture.

Lamer insists that any definition of aboriginal rights "must be directed towards the reconciliation of the pre-existence of aboriginal societies with the sovereignty of the Crown." However, this reconciliation will not be based on the aboriginal episteme or even a meeting of equal world views in which both are similarly interrogated. Instead, the aboriginal perspectives "must be framed in terms cognizable to the Canadian legal and constitutional structure." Aboriginal rights will require the translation of the indigenous episteme into the language of Canadian or Commonwealth law and thus be called to account at the system's tribunal. As we saw in Chapter 5, this translation process will inevitably involve what Conklin has called a judicial *differend* where the victim's episteme will be ignored or corrupted because it is spoken in an idiom unrecognizable in the courtroom. That this is a prima facie irrational method for defining aboriginal rights is described well by aboriginal legal scholar John Borrows:

> It seems unusual that the Aboriginal perspective on the meaning of their rights must incorporate non-Aboriginal legal perspectives. One would think that the Aboriginal perspective is needed precisely because the non-Aboriginal perspective does not effectively reconcile the prior occupation of Canada with assertions of Crown sovereignty. (1997, 46)

With the preeminence of the hegemonic narrative intact, Lamer latches on to a single sentence from the previous *Sparrow* decision to freeze aboriginal rights.[5] In that case, "the Court never doubted the Aboriginal's right to fish for food" because it found, inter alia, that such activity "constituted an integral

---

[5] The unanimous decision of *R. v. Sparrow*, the first Supreme Court case to consider Section 35(1), involved Ronald Edward Sparrow, a member of the Musqueam Indian Band who was cited for fishing with a drift net twenty fathoms longer than allowed by law. He claimed that the governmental regulation violated his aboriginal rights as recognized by Section 35(1). The Court only briefly considered the question of defining the aboriginal right at stake. Mr. Sparrow argued that his right should be "defined as a right to fish for any purpose and by any non dangerous method." The government, on the other hand, argued that the right at stake was the right to fish for food and does not include the right to fish for "ceremonial and social activities." Without much comment the Court held, agreeing for the most part with Mr. Sparrow, that in the case at hand there were no valid limitations on the "existing aboriginal right to fish for food and social and ceremonial purposes."

part of their distinctive culture." Instead of emphasizing that the right to fish for food was assumed to be part of the rights guaranteed under 35(1), Lamer uses the phrase "integral part of their distinctive culture" to erect a test for defining aboriginal rights that leaves the colonial moment intact.

First, aboriginal rights will not be granted when they are *merely a part* of the aboriginal culture, but they must be shown to be *integral* to a distinctive culture; that is, the underlying activity must be "one of the things which made the culture of the society distinctive." Focusing on the aboriginality of the rights, Lamer then insists that the right must have continuity with the distinctive "practices, customs and traditions that existed prior to contact with European society." So, any custom that developed as a result of European contact or since contact will not be considered an aboriginal right. It is clear that the "integral part of their distinctive culture" test, as Lamer develops it, freezes the rights of aboriginal groups to the lives they practiced in some bygone era, for the most part not allowing them to adapt as the centuries unfold even to the traumatic rupture caused by contact itself.[6] His ultimate definition of an aboriginal right is succinct:

> Where an aboriginal community can demonstrate that a particular practice, custom or tradition is integral to its distinctive culture today, and that this practice, custom or tradition has continuity with the practices, customs and traditions of pre-contact times, that community will have demonstrated that the practice, custom or tradition is an aboriginal right for the purposes of s. 35(1).

Lamer then applies this test to the facts of Van der Peet's case. Van der Peet saw the trading of ten salmon as part of her traditional livelihood and defined the right at stake as the right "to sufficient fish to provide for a moderate livelihood." Lamer, on the other hand, defines the right at stake in terms cognizable to a late twentieth-century Canadian court as "trading fish for money or other goods."[7] His definition focuses on the underlying activity while Van der

---

[6] Borrows and Rotman write that this "test draws on inappropriate racialized stereotypes of Aboriginal peoples by attempting to distil the essence of Aboriginality by reference to their pre-contact activities" (1997, 36).

[7] Coyle (2003) writes "the scope of the recognized right in a particular case will frequently depend on what may appear to be an arbitrary process of characterizing the traditional "activity" in question. In Van der Peet, for example, the traditional activity of the Sto:lo Nation for the purpose of s. 35 analysis could have been "fishing for salmon," "fishing salmon for food or for social or ceremonial purposes," "making a modest livelihood from the fruits of the Fraser River" or "taking advantage of the resources of the Fraser River," each of which may appear to be an equally reasonable characterization of the same historical activity, and each of which will lead to a different result if recognized for protection under s. 35" (para. 8).

Peet's definition is based on "the significance of an aboriginal practice, custom or tradition to the aboriginal community in question." To define the right based on its significance to the community would be to suspend the court's episteme and view it from the indigenous perspective. Lamer refuses to take that leap and consider what the activity meant to the Sto:lo people.

Comparing *his own definition* of the activity at stake with *his test* for defining aboriginal rights, Lamer's conclusion is not surprising. The evidence will not support the claim that "trading fish for money or other goods" was an integral part of the Sto:lo's distinctive culture before European contact. Indeed, before the creation of the Hudson Bay Company, the "Natives [in pre-Colonial times] did not fish to supply a market, there being no regularized trading system, nor were they able to preserve and store fish for extended periods of time." Therefore, Van der Peet's selling of ten salmon was not protected by Section 35(1) as there was no aboriginal right to sell fish for money.

By stripping the aboriginal people of the right to define their rights, Lamer is preventing them from realizing their livelihood or *proyecto de la vida* in a manner they see fit. As Borrows writes: "This decision relegated Aboriginal peoples to the backwaters of social development, deprived them of protection for practices that grew through intercultural exchange, and minimized the impact of Aboriginal rights on non-Aboriginal people" (1997, 45).

Justice L'Heureux-Dubé's Dissent in Van der Peet

Justice L'Heureux-Dubé dissented sharply and found an aboriginal right to fish for a moderate livelihood. Her analysis did not translate indigenous rights claims into the episteme of the Court but attempted to discern the meaning the right has for the aboriginal society. She quotes the earlier *Sparrow* decision that "it is possible, and, indeed, crucial, to be sensitive to the aboriginal perspective itself on the meaning of the rights at stake," but she will not subject this perspective to the system's tribunal. "Unlike the Chief Justice, I do not think it appropriate to qualify this proposition by saying that the perspective of the common law matters as much as the perspective of the natives when defining aboriginal rights" (145). Further, aboriginal practices will not be defined as that which is not part of colonial culture, as such an approach "literally amounts to defining aboriginal culture and aboriginal rights as that which is left over after features of non-aboriginal cultures have been taken away."

In defining the right at stake, her focus then is not on the underlying discrete activity at issue but the significance of the activity to the aboriginal people. This method places the aboriginal peoples' distinctive culture or self-defined *proyectos de la vida* at the heart of the analysis. "All practices, traditions and customs which are connected enough to the self-identity and self-preservation of organized aboriginal societies should be viewed as deserving the protection of s. 35(1)." L'Heureux-Dubé is adamant that the *proyectos de la vida* must be defined from the episteme of the aboriginal peoples and not from the perspective of the hegemonic discourse. She writes, "It is almost trite to say that what constitutes a practice, tradition or custom distinctive to native culture and society must be examined through the eyes of aboriginal people, not through those of the non-native majority or the distorting lens of existing regulations." So, if the underlying activity advances the *proyecto de la vida*, it would be protected, but "the same activity could be considered not to be part of their distinctive aboriginal culture if it is done for other purposes – e.g., for purely commercial purposes."

As for the facts of the case, L'Heureux-Dubé argues that the facts do not support Justice Lamer's claim that Van der Peet was fishing "for commercial purposes."[8] "The appellant sold 10 salmon. There is no evidence as to the purposes of the sale or as to what the money was going to be used for. It is clear, however, that the offending transaction proven by the Crown is not part of a commercial venture, nor does it constitute an act directed at profit." Further, the majority opinion didn't consider the views of Van der Peet, who "did not seek the recognition and affirmation of an aboriginal right to fish for commercial purposes."

Beginning from the aboriginal episteme on the meaning of the rights at stake and the underlying activity leads L'Heureux-Dubé to a much different conclusion.[9] For her, it is clear that the Sto:lo have bartered fish for livelihood reasons for a substantial amount of time. Oral histories and expert evidence show clearly that the Sto:lo engaged in trading of fish for centuries for the purpose of their "livelihood, support and sustenance…and, more importantly, that such activities formed part of, and were undoubtedly rooted in,

---

[8]   According to L'Heureux-Dubé, he "not only disregards the above distinction between the purposes for which fish can be sold, traded and bartered but also mischaracterizes the facts of this case, misconceives the contentions of the appellant and overlooks the legislative provision here under constitutional challenge."

[9]   A similar narrowing of rights was done by the Australian courts in *Derschaw v. Sutton*, which concerned Mr. Derschaw catching fish to feed 300 people "for a wake to mark the burial of a prominent Aboriginal man" in a nearby town. The opinion placed great emphasis on the fact that "they were fishing for a multitude of people many of whom did not live in the area. [47]" "According to Heenan J's reasoning if the fish were not consumed by locals of Port Hedland and presumably more particularly, Six Mile Creek, where the fish were caught, Derschaw cannot be regarded as exercising an Aboriginal right (i.e., a native title right)." Of course, providing food and hospitality for such gatherings is an essential part of aboriginal culture, but the court focused its inquiry on how it thought the aboriginal people should manifest their life-project, instead of allowing the indigenous peoples the right to undertake activities that they feel will further their life-projects.

the distinctive aboriginal culture of the Sto:lo." In the terms of this book, L'Heureux-Dubé's analysis begins from the premise that the indigenous peoples have a right to self-ascribe their identities and their life-projects. The rights protected by 35(1) then will be those that advance their life-projects. Of course, individual activities could have many different meanings, and these should be defined by the aboriginal peoples themselves (but cf. *Mitchell v. M.N.R.* 2001, paras. 14–25). Lamer's majority opinion cauterized the views of Van der Peet and affixed his own meaning on her actions just as we saw in Chapter 2 that the French Stasi Commission affixed their own meaning to the wearing of the headscarf by young Muslim women as a form of oppression and did not consult with the young women themselves. In a similar manner, Van der Peet's views, her priorities, and her *proyecto de la vida* were cauterized from the legal analysis. Justice Lamer's analysis is also reminiscent of Judge Arendt's claim that "oppressed minorities were never the best judges on the order of priorities in such matters." The framework developed in this book claims that marginalized Others know what is in their best interest, that rights "must remain under the control of those who are entitled to benefit from them," (Tulkens' dissent in *Sahin*) including determining which rights are most fundamental.

RIGHTS HIERARCHIES AND HETERONOMIC TIERED SCRUTINY

Hierarchies of rights are necessary when courts engage in rights balancing as multiple groups claim competing rights.[10] Many jurisdictions differentiate fundamental rights from other rights and then develop some type of tiered scrutiny, where fundamental rights are given more protection than other rights. For example, in U.S. jurisprudence, if a fundamental right is *not* at stake, the government is only required to show that the infringement of the right is rationally related to a legitimate state interest. The government almost always wins cases that must meet this "rational basis" test. If a fundamental right is at stake or if the government is infringing on the rights of "insular minorities," then the government's interference must meet the strict scrutiny test where governmental policies must be narrowly tailored to address a compelling state interest. It is important to note that rights can be infringed even if they are fundamental rights of marginalized peoples;[11] but for the government

---

[10] Also, see the book on conflicts among fundamental rights.
[11] As the U.S. Supreme Court concluded, "It is not true that strict scrutiny is strict in theory, but fatal in fact" (*Adarand v. Pena* 1995).

to prevail in such circumstance, it would need the most pressing of justifications and the most carefully crafted of policies.

I propose that human rights law should adopt a tiered scrutiny approach; but fundamental rights should be defined, not by a distant tribunal, but by the marginalized Other. In the context of human rights of the Saturated Other, there are two interconnected hierarchies of rights: (1) Some rights will be more fundamental to the Saturated Other; and (2) The rights of the Saturated Other will be more fundamental than rights of non-Saturated Others. This type of heteronomic tiered scrutiny will have a pronounced effect on many cases, including recent cases involving property claims by indigenous peoples. For instance, in *Lansman v. Finland*, the Human Rights Committee that oversees compliance with the International Covenant on Civil and Political Rights approached a claim of the Saami peoples, indigenous reindeer herders, as a weighing of two equal property rights claims, that of a mining corporation and those of the Saami. A heteronomic tiered scrutiny perspective, in contrast, would hold indigenous property claims, in most cases, to be more fundamental than the property claims of businesses or others without such ties to their land.

Fundamental rights of marginalized Others such as the Saami could be infringed but only after the most searching critique of any possible original violence or exclusion. This is because heteronomic rights not only rank higher on the hierarchy of rights, but they are qualitatively different. Such rights claims come from outside the system, from voices that are usually silenced and speak from a different episteme. The court should assume from the start that, in a Levinasian fashion, it is already always not doing enough for the Saturated Other; that it is not only part of the hegemonic system, it serves the hegemonic system.[12] The Court must take special measures to serve the Other. These would include the duty to consult with the marginalized and accommodate their interests, which would necessitate taking positive steps to bring to the table the voices that have been silenced.

These rights are different in another way. They require additional duties. The courts and the state have affirmative duties to work with the marginalized Others to protect their rights, and if these rights are violated they would have affirmative duties to make reparations in order for the marginalized to realize

---

[12]   Levinas writes possibly with some hyperbole: "My being-in-the-world or my 'place in the sun,' my being at home, have these not also been the usurpation of spaces belonging to the other man whom I have already oppressed or starved, or driven out into a third world; are they not acts of repulsing, excluding, exiling, stripping, killing?" (1989b, 82).

their *proyectos de la vida*. All of these duties should be framed from within a prior duty, the duty to learn to learn from below.

FIDUCIARY DUTIES AND THE HONOR OF THE CROWN

The Canadian courts have struggled to develop new ways of conceptualizing state duties for aboriginal peoples, and these have been framed within a tiered scrutiny approach with increased duties mandated when dealing with more fundamental rights as claimed by the aboriginal peoples themselves (See *Delgamuukw v. British Columbia* 1997, para. 162–169). The courts have established two main sets of duties, a fiduciary duty where the Crown is mandated to act in the best interests of the aboriginal peoples and a duty rooted in the honor of the Crown where the Crown has the duty to consult with and accommodate the interests of aboriginal peoples. Both of these are by their nature "other-regarding" and have the potential to move beyond state's affirmative duties developed in recent human rights cases such as by the African Commission in the SERAC and Purohit cases, but they both fail to question the original violence of Canadian sovereignty and fail to rely on the aboriginal episteme.

Mandating a fiduciary relationship, one that is "trust like, rather than adversarial" (*Wewaykum*) between the Crown and aboriginal peoples, was considered a major break from past Canadian policies. First, on the surface at least, such an other-regarding relationship is a clear break from the past colonial mentality; and second, the Canadian courts had previously been reluctant to establish a fiduciary relationship toward one group when it might owe a more general public duty toward other groups. The landmark *Guerin* decision from 1984 argued that the fiduciary relationship with aboriginal peoples stems from the *sui generis* historical relationship, namely that aboriginal peoples had land title and other interests that predate European contact and that the relationship between the Crown and aboriginal peoples "fell somewhere between the kind of relations conducted between sovereign states and the relations that such states had with their own citizens" (*R. v. Sioui* 1990, at 448). As the Crown assumed more and more power over the aboriginal peoples, it "left Aboriginal populations vulnerable to the risks of government misconduct or ineptitude." Thus, the Crown was required to take on more of a responsibility to the point where the Crown serves as a trustee or fiduciary (*Guerin* 1984). As fiduciary, the Crown is required to meet "a high standard of honourable dealing with respect to the aboriginal peoples."

Because the fiduciary duty stems from the vulnerability of the indigenous peoples created by the Canadian government in the colonial moment, one might expect that this would involve a radical responsibility to undo the colonial movement and reverse the increased vulnerability. Instead, by framing this as a *fiduciary* relationship, the Canadian courts relied on a paternalistic framework that, prima facie, does not seriously consider empowering the indigenous peoples.[13] Fiduciaries may be prevented by law from acting in their own best interests, but they are still free to frame the context of the discussion and they need not seek the input of the beneficiaries.[14] Indeed, it is assumed that the beneficiaries are so vulnerable that they are unable to express their best interests. The Crown as fiduciary retains ultimate control of the relationship and "of the legal and practical interests" of the aboriginal peoples (Christie 2005, 37).[15]

In recent cases, especially in *Wewaykum Indian Band v. Canada* (2002), the Courts have substantially watered down this trustee relationship. The Supreme Court ruled that the Crown does not owe a general fiduciary relationship to aboriginal people but only "in relation to specific Indian interests," and these are based on "whether or not the Crown had assumed discretionary control" over the aboriginal interest at stake. In the case at hand, dealing with a bookkeeping error in regard to Native titles that predate the creation of reservations, the Court ruled that the Crown had only minimal "basic obligations" as a fiduciary before the creation of any reservation. These basic obligations are those of "loyalty, good faith and disclosure of relevant information," just the types of obligations that the Crown owes non-indigenous peoples as well. "The Crown can be no ordinary fiduciary; it wears many hats and represents many interests, some of which cannot help but be conflicting." The Crown's duty, then, is to act in a fair and reasonable way in its dealings between beneficiaries. With no special relationship toward indigenous peoples established in this case, the bookkeeping error on the part of the Indian agent, just the type of act of "misconduct or ineptitude" that was meant to be covered by a fiduciary relationship, went uncorrected as it conflicted with other interests that the Crown also was bound to respect.

---

[13] For example, Kant develops fiduciary relationships in the *Metaphysics of Morals*, in the context of the duty that parents owe all children.

[14] Cf. Criddle and Fox-Decent (2009), "Beneficiaries are peculiarly vulnerable in that, once in a fiduciary relationship, they generally are unable to protect themselves or their entrusted interests against an abuse of fiduciary power" (349).

[15] A fiduciary relationship with colonized peoples was also advocated by Edmund Burke and Francisco de Vittoria. Though "other-centered," on balance the historical record appears to suggest that fiduciary doctrine enabled colonialism by lending it a veneer of legality" (Criddle and Fox-Decent 2009, 351).

This same logic undercuts the Court's mandating of a duty to consult with and accommodate aboriginal views in cases where infringements of aboriginal rights are taking place. Consultation and accommodation have been determined by the Court to be "part of a process of fair dealing and reconciliation" necessary to maintain the honor of the Crown. This obligation increases as rights become more fundamental, thus creating a type of tiered scrutiny analysis. The Court envisions a spectrum of duties corresponding to a spectrum of rights claims. Where the right claim is weak, "the only duty on the Crown may be to give notice, disclose information, and discuss any issues raised in response to the notice." When the right claim is "of high significance to the Aboriginal peoples, and the risk of non-compensable damage is high," the Crown may be required to engage in "deep consultation" that might involve formal mediation procedures. If this consultation leads to the realization that the Crown's proposed policy will indeed infringe "in a significant way" on fundamental rights, then the policy will need to be changed to accommodate fundamental aboriginal interests. This accommodation will best be achieved by further "consultation and negotiation."

This procedure for consultation and accommodation is reminiscent of an ideal speech situation or a type of deliberative democracy that Seyla Benhabib has extolled. These deliberations will take place firmly within the context of the hegemonic structure with the Courts as the final arbitrators. The responsibility of the state is not to reach agreement or accommodation with aboriginal peoples but to engage in a "meaningful process of consultation." The aboriginal peoples, for their part, have duties to "not frustrate the Crown's reasonable good faith attempts, nor should they take unreasonable positions." Of course, the Court will be the final arbiter as to whether the indigenous peoples have acted reasonably and whether the government's consultation is "meaningful."

Firmly in control of the fiduciary relationship, with the colonial moment going un-interrogated, the Canadian courts have been reluctant to mandate a governmental duty to learn to learn from below as was seen in *R. v. Van der Peet*. Further, the courts have been reluctant to mandate exceptional measures in order to bring indigenous peoples to the negotiating table.[16] Without such exceptional measures, the duties owed to aboriginal peoples will be defined by a hegemonic court, under hegemonic law, and by hegemonic

---

[16] A unanimous Supreme Court held that the Crown was not required to provide funds for the Native Women's Association to attend constitutional conferences, because attending such conferences was not an aboriginal right under 35(1) and that there was no affirmative duty to ensure participation.

judges. The remedies for such vulnerability must be a comprehensive form of empowerment that addresses the hegemonic structure itself. Without such empowerment, even the expanded duties of the Crown leave "Aboriginal nations...forced to welcome the opportunity to be consulted about how their own lands will be exploited" (Christie 2005, 17) as long as they act reasonably and do not hold unreasonable positions.

The Court's method of reconciling aboriginal and settlers claims by translating aboriginal claims into the episteme of the Crown and the recently crafted paternalistic duties of the Crown should be juxtaposed with the meaning of the Double Row Wampum, which was created to symbolize the agreement of the Iroquois peoples with the Dutch government in 1613 and continues to have much vitality among aboriginal peoples and legal scholars. The belt consists of two parallel rows of purple beads separated by three beads that symbolize peace, friendship, and respect. This wampum represents a radically different potential relationship between indigenous peoples and European descendants, one built on mutual respect and non-interference. This conception of the relationship generally held sway in Canadian law throughout the eighteenth century and into the nineteenth century.[17]

> You say that you are our Father and I am your son. We say, We will not be like Father and Son, but like Brothers. This wampum belt confirms our words. These two rows will symbolize two paths or two vessels, traveling down the same river together. One, a birch bark canoe, will be for the Indian People, their laws, their customs and their ways. The other, a ship, will be for the white people and their laws, their customs and their ways. We shall each travel the river together, side by side, but in our boat. Neither of us will make compulsory laws or interfere in the internal affairs of the other. Neither of us will try to steer the other's vessel. The agreement has been kept by the Iroquois to this date. (Archuleta 2005, 442–443)[18]

---

[17] In *R. v. Sioui* (1990), the Canadian Supreme Court summarized the perspective surrounding a 1760 treaty as follows, "the British Crown recognized that the Indians had certain ownership rights over their land, it sought to establish trade with them which would rise above the level of exploitation and give them a fair return. It also allowed them autonomy in their internal affairs, intervening in this area as little as possible."

[18] Kymlicka (1995) develops a theory to explain how minorities can have self-government within a multinational state. He writes, "The claim is that there is more than one political community, and that the authority of the larger state cannot be assumed to take precedence over the authority of the constituent national communities. If democracy is the rule of 'the people,' national minorities claim that there is more than one people, each with the right to rule themselves" (182). Without such rule, it is questionable whether aboriginal rights will ever be realized (cf. Murphy 2001, 124).

HETERONOMIC RIGHTS AND DUTIES IN
THE INTER-AMERICAN COURT OF HUMAN RIGHTS

Recent rulings of the Inter-American Court of Human Rights have perhaps best exemplified the heteronomic rights and duties that I advocate. The Court, led by its former President Trindade, has been sensitive to its responsibility to the marginalized Other. This responsibility is exemplified and furthered by recent changes in the Court's rules of procedures that give more of a voice to victims and their families in court proceedings in order to better listen to the voice to the Other. Since then, the Court has set new precedents on the rights of indigenous peoples (see Pasqualucci 2006), and it has given special rights to "vulnerable persons" who are "entitled to special protection (*Ximenes-Lopes* 2006).[19] The Court has also given special attention to the perspectives of vulnerable peoples in crafting rights and duties. Most interestingly, perhaps, the Inter-American Court has been at the forefront in empowering the victim through its creative use of non-monetary reparations that often involve the Court working with the Other to realize his or her rights that are defined in context of the life-project of the victim as defined by the victim.[20]

The Court has defined a life-project as "akin to the concept of personal fulfillment, which in turn is based on the options that an individual may have for leading his life and achieving the goal that he sets for himself. Strictly speaking, those options are the manifestation and guarantee of freedom" (*Loayza Tamayo v. Peru* para 148).

Innovative Reparations Ordered by the Inter-American Court

When the Court finds a country in violation of the American Convention or other binding treaty, the Court's reparations orders follow traditional international law standards in that they should aim for full restitution (*restitutio in integrum*), which requires the state to re-establish the previous situation as much as possible.[21] Of course, in many cases, especially with violations of the right to life, full restitution will not be directly possible and the state must be

---

[19] The Inter-American court has paid particular attention to the rights of vulnerable peoples in a series of recent cases (e.g., *Caso de los Hermanos Gomez Paquiyauri v. Peru* 2004; *Bulacio v. Argenitan* 2003; and *Children's Rehabilitation v. Paraguay* 2004).

[20] This method mirrors Justice L'Heureux-Dubé's opinion in the Van der Peet case discussed earlier in the chapter.

[21] Reparations orders are not merely hortatory. The rulings and orders of the Court are binding with the Court often requiring periodic reports on progress toward complying with its reparations orders. States have almost universally complied with the orders of the Court (see Cerna 2004, 203).

ordered to provide alternative damages such as monetary compensation. In its first two decades, the Court was criticized for the modest monetary sums it awarded to victims, especially in cases of disappearances and loss of life (Saul 2004). Recently, the Court has increased the amounts of monetary damage that it has rewarded, and it now far exceeds the amount granted by the European Court of Human Rights in similar cases. The starkest difference between the two courts has been the creative use of non-monetary remedies by the Inter-American Court.

The Court has often used its reparations decisions to develop heteronomic duties in which states have been ordered to work to realize the life plan of marginalized Others.

For instance, the *Cantoral Benavides* decision concerned a twenty-year-old Peruvian biology student who was falsely imprisoned for four years, tortured while in prison, and, upon his release, fled in fear to Brazil. In addition to payments of almost $100,000 directly to the victim, the Court ordered Peru to make a public apology, reverse the verdict, and pay for the costs that the family had incurred during his incarceration and pay for medical treatment and psychological treatment for his mother. When considering Benavides' loss of life-plan, the Court took into account his long-time desire to pursue post-graduate studies in biology. Based on his testimony, the Court concluded,

> [He] had practically mapped out [his] life. From the time [he] entered the University . . . [he] was thinking about graduating, doing a masters degree, a doctorate. . . . [He] studied hard until that problem happened. Now practically nine years have passed and [he] still ha[s] not accomplished that goal. . . . [He] was excited and wanted to continue and complete [his] studies (§ 48).

To restore his life-plan that had clearly been interrupted, the Court ordered Peru to "provide him with a fellowship for advanced or university studies, to cover the costs of a degree preparing him for the profession of his choosing, and his living expenses for the duration of those studies, at a learning institution of recognized academic excellence, which the victim and the State select by mutual agreement" (para. 80).[22]

In cases involving the extrajudicial killing of human rights activists, states have been ordered to continue their work with marginalized populations. In the *Myrna Mack Chang* case, the Court found that Guatemala had violated the right to life, right to fair trial, and right to humane treatment in the assassination of the anthropologist and human rights activist who worked with the

---

[22] Interestingly, from the Court's opinion, it appears that neither the Commission nor the victim's representative requested this form of reparation.

Mayan communities. Guatemala accepted unconditional responsibility for the killing. The state was ordered to investigate the case, prosecute and punish the perpetrators, and publish the results of any investigation. However, what is striking is the extent to which the state was ordered to honor and memorialize the victim, including the establishment of an educational scholarship in the victim's name to study anthropology at a "prestigious national university" (para. 285), which would serve to continue Chang's work. Further, "the State must give a well-known square or street in Guatemala City the name of Myrna Mack Chang and place a memorial plaque alluding to her activities at the site where she died or nearby" (Myrna Mack Chang Case, para. 286). Finally, the state was ordered to pay more than $750,000 in damages and expenses.

These cases should be read in juxtaposition to dozens of substantially similar cases from the European Court of Human Rights. In each case, the European Court only required the state to pay financial damages to the victim(s), and the bulk of the damages are related to pecuniary expenses.

For instance, the *Anguelova v. Bulgaria* case involved a 17-year-old Gypsy/Roma who was taken into custody for allegedly breaking into several cars in Sofia. While in custody, the boy died from blunt trauma to the head and chest. The police claimed that the trauma was either due to his resisting arrest or occurred earlier in the day. After weighing and sifting through voluminous evidentiary records, the Court declared that Turkey had violated his right to life under Article 2, failed to provide an effective investigation (Article 2.1), infringed on his right to liberty under Article 5, and failed to provide an effective remedy as required under Article 13. Strikingly, for reparations the court only ordered a payment of 22,550 euros for non-pecuniary damages and legal expenses to the mother. One wonders if an official apology, in-depth investigations of the police activities toward Roma/Gypsies, or even a memorial might do wonders to quell some of the tensions between majority and minority groups in the country. In more theoretical terms, the hegemonic ideology was not put into question by this court order. In a sense, the government could see the reparations as a cost of doing business. Judge Trindade of the Inter-American Court sees such orders as part of "distorted 'industries of reparations,' emptied of true human values" (*Moiwana Village v. Suriname* 2005).

This stark difference between the two courts can be at least partially attributed to the victim's right to directly address the Court (*locus standii in judicio*). The Inter-American Court changed its rules of procedures in 1997 to allow the victims or their family to directly address the Court during the reparations phase. The Court's awarding of reparations have changed dramatically since, with monetary damages increasing substantially and almost all of the cases involving creative uses of non-monetary damages occurring after 1998. The most recent change to the Court's rules of procedures allows the victims or their relatives to address the Court at all stages of contentious cases. The former president of the Court remarked that this change "marks a major milestone in the evolution of the inter-American system for the protection of human rights" (Trindade 2002, 11), and this granting of increased agency to the victims surely has led to dramatic changes in the Court's jurisprudence.

These reforms in *locus standii* have had a major impact on recent children's rights cases in the Court, especially on how it has defined the *proyecto de la vida* of at-risk children.[23] For instance, *Villagran Morales v. Guatemala* involved claims that the Guatemalan security forces abducted, tortured, and murdered several street children in 1990. This case exemplified a pattern of severe abuse of street children by governmental authorities that has been well documented by several prominent NGOs. It is clear that street children have been routinely cauterized, where they have been branded as inferior and not deserving of legal protection and their voices have been systematically silenced. In this case, two policemen and a civilian were implicated in the crimes, but they were acquitted by domestic courts, in part because the testimony of the victims' mothers were excluded from the evidence for lacking impartiality and several family members and friends feared testifying because of a series of threats.

The Inter-American Court of Human Rights, under its new rules of procedures on *locus standii*, relied heavily on the testimonies of the victims' families and the representatives of the victims, as well as a female street child who was a friend of the victims and had witnessed several parts of the crimes. Other witnesses included a clinical psychologist specializing in trauma studies and experts on the rights of children including the Regional Director of Casa Alianza, an NGO working to educate street children and to represent them in domestic courts. The Court found Guatemala in violation of several articles of the American Convention, including the right to life, the right to physical integrity, right to judicial protection, and the rights of the child, as well as three articles of the Inter-American Convention to Prevent and Punish Torture.

At the reparations stage, Guatemala, arguing from the perspective of the structural violence of the system, held that the children were not particularly close with their families and "with regard to the life plan, the precarious

---

[23] Justice Trindade said that in the Paraguayan children's rights case that "even in the most adverse conditions, the human being emerges as the subject of International Law, endowed with full international juridico-procedural capacity" due to "the high relevance of the IACtHR historical reforms" on *locus standii*.

situation of the victims makes it highly probable that they did not have a life plan to put into practice." The Court saw through this hegemonic view of street children, "preferring to see the children as resourceful micro-entrepreneurs attempting to survive on the margins of an adult world" (Ewelukwa 2006, 108) often attempting to supplement their families' income. The Court found the testimony of the family members and other witnesses extremely compelling. It wrote that "every child has the right to harbor a project of life that should be tended and encouraged by the public authorities so that it may develop this project for its personal benefit and that of the society to which it belongs." Guatemala was ordered to pay more than $500,000 to the families, to substantially modify its national law on children's rights, and "to designate an educational center with a name allusive to the young victims in this case and to place in this center a plaque with the names of Henry Giovanni Contreras, Federico Clemente Figueroa Túnchez, Julio Roberto Caal Sandoval, Jovito Josué Juárez Cifuentes and Anstraun Aman Villagrán Morales." Each of these measures was soon complied with, including naming a school in Guatemala City "Ninos de la Esperanza" after the slain children.[24]

Moiwana v. Suriname

The recent *Moiwana Village v. Suriname* case further shows how the Inter-American Court has been willing to learn to learn from below and reinvigorate its jurisprudence. Although the case has gained some notoriety for its ruling on temporal jurisdiction, what has gone unnoticed is that it breaks new ground in establishing heteronomic rights and heteronomic duties from the episteme of the Saturated Other.

The case involved a massacre of Afro-descendant peoples, the N'djukas, in the village of Moiwana by the national army of Suriname in 1986. In response to the brutality of the Désiré Bouterse regime in the early 1980s, the Maroon people, descendants of escaped African slaves, led by Ronnie Brunswijk, mobilized in an armed insurrection. The army responded to this uprising with an extensive military operation in which hundreds of Maroon villagers were killed and thousands were forced to flee. State agents especially targeted Brunswijk's home village of Moiwana, razing it and massacring at least thirty-nine men, women, and children. Those who escaped the attack fled into the surrounding forest and then into exile or internal displacement. Many years

[24] Ewelukwa (2006) writes, "The case reaffirms the right of street children to personhood by addressing the dominant perception of street children as non-persons and irritants and confirming their status as citizens, persons, and individuals who are capable of making a productive economic contribution. Not only are they full citizens; street children also have a right to the basic dignity to which all human beings are entitled" (110).

later the perpetrators still had not been tried, in part because of a national amnesty law, and the villagers continued to be displaced. The villagers suffered further in that the remains of those killed were not recovered, and without a proper ceremony to honor the dead they would be "unable to return to their traditional way of life."

As a preliminary matter, the Court was faced with the tricky legal question of *ratione temporis* jurisdiction. The massacre occurred in 1986, but Suriname did not ratify the American Convention on Human Rights and accede to the jurisdiction of the Court until 1987 when Bouterse allowed some power sharing and limited democratic elections.[25] The Court ruled that Suriname could be responsible for a series of violations that stemmed from the 1986 massacre but actually occurred after Suriname acceded to the jurisdiction of the Court. These included the ongoing failure to adequately investigate and punish the perpetrators and the continued displacement of the villages. Suriname could be held accountable for the ongoing effects of the past massacre.[26] On the merits, Suriname was found to have violated several articles of the American Convention, including the right to an effective remedy (Articles 8 and 245), the right to humane treatment (Article 5), freedom of movement (Article 22), and the right to property (Article 21). The Court's logic was suffused with cultural sensitivity. For instance, a violation of the freedom of movement was not claimed by either the representatives of the victims or by the Inter-American Commission on Human Rights. However, it was clear from the testimony and the documentary evidence that the N'djukas had been forcefully evicted from their village and were fearful to return until the site had been purified in culturally specific ways. Those that had returned briefly soon after the massacre experienced all sorts of physical and emotional maladies that they attributed to offended spirits. Without the necessary death rituals, the people would not return and were thus denied their freedom of movement, the Court reasoned, under Article 22 of the Convention. Further, because their relationship to their communal land was so strong, their separation from it constituted a violation of Article 5's right to "physical, mental, and moral integrity." The Court's logic mirrored that of Justice L'Heureux-Dubé in the Canadian *Van der Peet* case discussed earlier in this chapter, in that it first started with

---

[25]   However, Bouterse continued to be a very powerful figure throughout the 1990s until finally being brought to trial in Fall 2007. He remained free, and was elected president of Suriname in 2010.

[26]   Such logic could have also applied to the Indian Supreme Court case *NBA v. Union of India* involving the adivasis. Even if the dam had been built, if it could be shown that they were suffering continuous violations of their rights, then the principle of laches would not be relevant.

their definition of the *proyecto de la vida* and then derived the fundamental rights from it. The Court wrote of the N'djukas that "in order for the culture to preserve its very identity and integrity, the Moiwana community members must maintain a fluid and multidimensional relationship with their ancestral lands." As opposed to the *Lansman* case, in which the Human Rights Committee weighed an indigenous peoples' land claim equally with that of a business interest, the Court began its analysis from the fundamental rights as defined by the N'djukas.

Reparations for the Villagers

The Court ordered a panoply of remedial measures that are also notable for considering the villagers' cultural episteme, as revealed by their testimony, in restoring their *proyectos de la vida*. The status of the maroon people as historically disadvantaged and currently marginalized was central to the Court's reasoning with the Court's reparation order seeking to empower them by emphasizing the participation of the villagers in the satisfaction of these remedies and in overseeing the compliance of the state's affirmative duties.

The Court ordered monetary reparations of $3,000 for each of 130 community members for material damages. Moral damages were awarded for $10,000 each to cover the wide range (moral, emotional, and spiritual) and duration of suffering. These moral damages included, inter alia, the inability to bury their loved ones and the "anger in the spiritual world" caused by the continued impunity for the massacre. As the representatives of the villagers said, "angry spirits are avenging themselves on the victims and causing them physical and mental afflictions" (para. 189). The Court also stressed the communal nature of the N'djukas and ordered Suriname to develop a community development fund of $1.2 million to be used for health, housing, and education as "determined by an implementation committee" consisting of representatives from both the village and the state.

As in many other Inter-American Court cases, Suriname was ordered to investigate the massacre, widely publicize the results, and hold the perpetrators legally responsible. Even this routine call for an adequate investigation and prosecution was framed in the context of the villager's episteme. According to the community members, only when justice is accomplished will they be able to appease the angry spirits of their deceased family members, purify their land, and return to permanent residence without apprehension of further hostilities." Similarly, the state was also ordered, as is standard in the Court's jurisprudence, to locate the remains of the dead and return them to the community. It was very clear to the Court that just offering the villagers a chance to return to their land would not, from the episteme of the villagers, meet the international legal standard of *in restituto*. The Moiwana villagers testified that without recovery of the bodies and proper burial including all relevant ceremonies, it would be an injustice to the dead and have lingering negative effects on the living for generations. Without fulfilling the traditional obligations concerning the dead, "it is [as] if we do not exist on earth" (Testimony of Antonia Difienjo). Mrs. Ajintoena also testified that although the Moiwana villagers longed to return to the village, "you can't go back to the place without having arrangements made." As another villager explained, "He needs the support and help of his family members that were killed."

As in other cases, the Court ordered a public apology from the government and the creation of a public memorial. The apology, which includes acceptance of culpability, should be offered to the designated *Gaanman* (leader) of the N'djuka community for the denial of judicial protection and forced displacement. As for the public memorial, its "design and location shall be decided upon in consultation with the victims' representatives."

Finally, even though it could not be shown that the villagers had legal title to their land, Suriname had to guarantee the displaced persons their property rights in the village. Any necessary demarcation of customary land would require working with the villagers as well as villagers from neighboring communities. This should be done through a mechanism chosen by the state, but it should take into account the N'djuka's "customary law, values, customs and mores," including the central place of communal ownership. Once the villagers returned to their land, the state is required to send a representative to consult with them once a month and address any concerns about their safety. The state must also see the "participation and the informed consent of the victims" in deciding these property issues.[27]

Suriname has taken several significant steps to meet the affirmative duties required by this reparations order. Many of the villagers returned for a memorial service where "women of the N'djuka people, dressed in blue and white mourning wraps, wept during the ceremony held on Tuesday near three giant memorial oil lamps while Moiwana dignitaries sprinkled the soil with water to ward off evil" (quoted in Interpretation decision – Trindade, para. 13). The president of Suriname issued an apology to the *Gaanman* (Cairo 2006), and each of the villagers received their monetary compensation. Nonetheless, the

[27] Judge Trindade, in his concurring opinion to the Court's interpretation order, strongly criticizes the Court for "a judicial formalism and a lack of humane sensitiveness" and urges the Court to more fully develop how these property issues will be resolved, especially considering the crucial place that the land plays in N'djuka's spirituality.

villagers have been disheartened that more had not been done to investigate the massacre and prosecute the perpetrators, and much work remains to be done on the demarcation and titling of the villager's land.

Judge Trindade's Concurrence

Judge Trindade, the former Chief Judge of the Court, wrote a separate opinion agreeing in large part with the Court's judgment but adding his own "personal reflections" that stressed the Court's remarkable innovations in establishing the person, especially the vulnerable person, as a subject of international law and establishing new rights and duties from the episteme of the Other. Trindade's concurrence makes clear that such a dramatic innovation in this case was based in large part on the extensive testimony provided by the villagers, especially their suffering of spiritual damage and the importance of harmonious relations between the living and the dead. Their spiritual suffering did not fit the pre-defined categories of human rights law, so the decision, for the first time in international law, "mov[ed] from the right to a project of life (*proyecto de vida*) to the right to a project of after-life (*proyecto de post-vida*)."

In crafting these new rights, he argued that international law had much to learn from the villagers. Establishing a right to a project after life may seem odd at first, but "there is no cogent reason," Trindade argues, "to remain in the world exclusively of the living." This project of an afterlife is clearly a fundamental value for the N'djukas, and thus instead of trying to categorize it into an existing rights framework or cauterizing it completely, Trindade uses their testimony to interrogate the hegemonic system. "Their outlook of life and after-life embodies fundamental values, long forgotten and lost by the sons and daughters of the industrial and the communications 'revolutions'." These fundamental values forgotten by the Enlightenment and its aftermaths as well as by international law can be re-taught by learning to learn from the N'djukas who are "rich in teachings."

In the light of this fundamental right, as defined by the N'djuka episteme, state duties and reparations take on new meanings. Fundamental duties now include the duties of the living toward the dead, of "honouring the dead in the persons of the living." Such honoring must be done by the villagers themselves but necessitates the state and the Court working with the villagers as required by the Court's reparations order.

> The dead need our faithfulness, they are entirely depend[ent] upon it. The duties of the living towards them are thus not limited to securing respect for their remains and to granting them a proper burial; such duties also

encompass perennial remembrance. They need our remembrance today and tomorrow, just as much as we needed their advice and care yesterday. Time, thus, instead of keeping us apart, on the contrary, brings all of us – the living and the dead – together. This, in my view, ascribes an entirely new dimension to the links of solidarity between the living and their dead. Remembrance is a manifestation of gratitude, and gratitude is perhaps the noblest manifestation of rendering true justice.

CONCLUSION

Human rights law differs from most other areas of law in that it consciously strives for progressive development. Indeed, human rights law has been progressively developing rapidly in the past two decades or so. As Judge Trindade has written,

> No one would have anticipated, some years ago, that "street children," and their equally abandoned mothers (and grandmother), would have had their cause brought before, and heard and adjudicated by, an international tribunal such as the Inter-American Court of Human Rights (IACtHR), as in the Villagran Morales and Others v. Guatemala case (1999–2001), with the condemnation of the perpetrated human rights violations. (n16)

> No one would have forecasted, some years ago, that respondent States would publicly apologize to victims of human rights violations, or their relatives, as a satisfaction (as a form of reparation) owed to them as a result of sentences of the IACtHR, as they have done, for example in the cases of Cantoral Benavides v. Peru, Myrna Mack Chang v. Guatemala, and Molina Theissen v. Guatemala. "Individuals indeed count nowadays on international jurisdiction, which has expanded to grant them relief. *The suffering of vulnerable or defenseless individuals no longer falls into oblivion.*" (Trindade 2008, 23–24, emphasis added)

Such a development has required the deconstruction of the original violence embedded in treaties and other founding documents. Examples abound. For instance, the international definition of "torture" now often encompasses acts that were not seriously considered by the drafters of the Convention against Torture, including extreme forms of violence against women and the perpetration of "torture" by non-state actors. Similarly, we saw in Chapter 6 that the definition of persecution on account of being in a "particular social group" in asylum law has widened considerably. Increasingly, international human rights bodies are crafting new rights and duties to better protect marginalized populations, such as the African Commission's groundbreaking rulings on the right to mental health and the right to housing. New rights and duties have also been developed in recent reparation orders of the Inter-American Court of Human Rights, especially in *Moiwana v. Suriname* where the Court fashioned, for the first time, the right to a life-plan after death. Many tribunals, most notably the Inter-American Court, have ordered states to work with marginalized populations to realize their life-plans, that is, their identities and rights based on their own episteme.

This chapter urges that human rights law continue to develop progressively, but the crafting of new rights and duties should not merely be done by progressive jurists, but should be directed by marginalized Others. The crafting of heteronomic rights and duties requires that marginalized populations have a voice in the courtroom and that the face of the Saturated Other confront and bedazzle the system. Tribunals would have a duty to suspend their hegemonic discourse as much as possible and learn to listen to the voice of the marginalized. Such a "no holds barred *self-suspending leap into the other's sea*" (Spivak 2004a, 207–208) will further the creation of new heteronomic rights and duties.

Conclusion

Working with the Marginalized Other to Deconstruct and Reinvigorate Human Rights Law

This book has been an exercise in *de lege ferenda*, what the law ought to be. It explores what human rights law could and should be if an entirely new theoretical approach is taken, an approach that calls into question a vast majority of previous political and legal theory. This book has laid the framework for what Benhabib called a new normative map, a new type of legal judgment, one that is consistent with the underlying fundamental principle of human rights: respect for the marginalized. Concurring with Rene Cassin, I argue that human rights should be "the voice of millions [of] human beings, victims of oppression, misery and ignorance, who aspire to live under conditions of greater justice, freedom and simple dignity" (Cassin 1970).

This concluding chapter first reviews the theoretical argument that I used to develop this "new normative map" based on my phenomenology of the Saturated Other. I will then ask, why law? Is law the proper tool for responding to the Saturated or Marginalized Other? To address this question, I review the examples of judges and others discussed in this book who were able to suspend the hegemonic system and respond to the Marginalized Other. Then I will end with some takeaway points designed for human rights practitioners to consider in their own work. What does it mean to work with the Marginalized Other as recommended in this work?

REVIEW OF THE THEORETICAL ARGUMENT

Much of traditional political and legal theory, including the writings of progressive proponents of concrete universalisms and deliberative democracy such as Arendt and Benhabib, has excluded or, in my terms, cauterized the Other. All too often the victims of human rights abuses are excluded from the polis or unable to express their concerns in its idiom. Theorists like Arendt claim a priori that marginalized Others are *"never* the best judges" when it comes to rights including their own, and she bellowed against parvenus, those like the teenage girl in Little Rock in 1957 who "wanted to push [her] way into a group where it was not wanted." Conversely, this book claims that the Marginalized Other should take center stage in human rights law and self-ascribe their identities and define their rights. At center stage, the Other provides a continuous critique of existing human rights law and a new foundation for a reinvigorated human rights law. To take center stage from previously exclusionary spaces requires extraordinary measures.

These extraordinary measures, I argue in the more theoretical chapters of Part II, will be in response to the appearance of the face of the Saturated Other. Levinas argues that the face of the Other is prior to the ontology of the legal-political system, but in his formulation the appearance of the face only leads to what he called "moments of negation" that will not lead to sustained changes in the system. He writes, "Every disturbance ends up falling back into the order, allowing a broader and more complex order to appear" (Levinas 1998h, 55). Levinas' theory of justice is built on this ethical relationship with the Other, but it quickly moves to the supposedly neutral scales of justice weighing competing rights claims. However, we must constantly ask whether the scales of justice are truly neutral. Those excluded from the system remain cauterized and the original violence of the system remains unless we can theorize some sort of disturbance to the system that is more than a mere "moment of negation."

To theoretically describe an encounter with the Other that leads to more sustained disruptions of the legal-political system, I have developed a phenomenology of the Saturated Other based on the infinitude of the face of the Other, further saturated by the marginalization process. An Other that approaches from outside of the system bedazzles *both* the ego and the system itself, incessantly calling the ego *and* its system into question, and thus calling for a deeper or more saturated responsibility. The phenomenology of the Saturated Other developed here addresses several fundamental questions in current phenomenologies of the Other. For instance, Levinas argues that the Other is non-thematizable and non-knowable – in fact, he argues that one cannot conduct a phenomenology of the Other because the Other is not properly a phenomenon. If the Other is not a phenomenon, it would be impossible to concretize (flesh out) the Other. The Saturated Other in my phenomenology is thematizable and knowable at least to a point but without losing the anti-foundational character of Levinas' formulation. Further, Levinas' account of the Other as stripped of all ontological categories cannot differentiate between the persecutor and the marginalized, between the SS guard and the street children of Guatemala. In my account, the ego is called to an affirmative duty to make just those types of distinctions.

This phenomenology of the Saturated Other must be universalized, at least in a weak sense, in order to be applicable to human rights law. I create a concrete universalism by tying my phenomenology with the insights of deliberative democracy to argue for a new anti-hegemonic concrete universalism. This is the development of a new system, a new concrete universality, a new system of law that begins from the voice of the Saturated Other. It aims toward what Dussel calls a "future 'institutionality,' declared valid, consensually, by the new intersubjectivity" (1997a, 2). To continuously deconstruct the hegemonic system requires access to a different episteme; one that is resistant to appropriation and manipulation, and one that resists becoming the new hegemonic system. This "fundamental epistemic transformation" (Ray 2003, 44), or what Rancière calls "a novel perceptual universe" (1999, 5), is accessed by a patient listening to the voice of the Saturated Other. The voice of the Other interrupts the system in a more sustained way. Without such a sustained interruption, the abusive hierarchy will not be called into question and the testimony of the Other could be used for the purpose of reinforcing the hierarchy. The new system of law, including institutions and democracy and even ideologies and institutions in service to the Other, must continually be called into question by the Saturated Other.

Therefore, human rights law should be based on a patient listening in which the ego does not perpetuate the categorizations or interpellation of the Other. Instead, the Other should self-ascribe their identity and define their rights based on their project of life as they define it. Along with these new heteronomic rights come new heteronomic duties, including an affirmative duty to work with the Marginalized Other to realize his or her life-project. The transcendence of the Marginalized Other deconstructs the original violence in current rights regimes, opening up a space in the law where it can be reinvigorated through the self-ascription of identity and self-ascription of rights by the Marginalized Other.

CAN LAW EMPTY ITSELF OF ITSELF?

The master's tools will never dismantle the master's house.

– Audre Lord

Human rights law, both at the international and the domestic levels, has often been the last bastion for the disenfranchised. For instance, Benhabib in her theory of democratic iterations calls for international norms derived from international law to serve as a check on the democratic processes found in modern nation-states. However, as we have seen in the headscarf affairs in France and Turkey, the norms found in international law are often founded on an original violence that cauterizes the suffering of the Saturated Other. Indeed, all of law, as we saw in Chapter 5, because it is in service to the hegemonic system, cauterizes the Other as it requires the translation of the Other's voice into the language of the courtroom. Justice seems to constantly slip through the hands of justice as "the legal discourse cannot address the aggrieved in the aggrieved's language, the authoritative chains of legal signs cannot be just, for justice is the language of an Other" (Conklin 1998, 228).

Can something as thoroughly hegemonic as law be brought to bear in support of the marginalized? Can law empty itself of the hegemonic discourse?[1] Is it possible for a judge enmeshed within the system to stop the system and to open up a place in the law when exposed to the face of the Other? Such a response is only possible if a judge is willing to question his or her privileged place founded in an original violence and patiently listen to the Other. We need judges who will disrupt the violence, suspend the law, and who will resuscitate the spirit of the laws. We need judges who, confronted with the plight of Mr. Tiede in the German hijacking case discussed in Chapter 2, will conclude "I will not do it."[2]

Can we envision a new rationality, a new anti-hegemonic discourse? This will only be accomplished through a material working with the Other through the Other's eyes as much as possible. There is no formula for such learning, for such exercise of imagination. Spivak (2004) suggests that what is required is "a slow mind-changing process [that] can be used to open the imagination to such mindsets" (533). This is teaching and learning as ethnographic field work, working with materially, in the field, to change the hegemonic system. It must be based on a patient listening, "is never accurate, and must be forever renewed."

In these chapters, we encountered a number of progressive judges who suspended the violence of the law, often by valiantly trying to understand the

---

[1] Countless ethnographies have shown that where the marginalized turn to legal means they are further marginalized. Social movements, such as the adivasis' resistance to the Narmada river project, are neutered by an over-reliance on law (See Rajagopal 2005).

[2] See also the remarkable U.S. district court case of *Builes v. Nye* in which Judge Caldwell overturned an immigration court's order that would have sent Mr. Builes back to Columbia where he would be targeted by drug cartels. As one member of the immigration court wrote, "We appear to have no choice but to order the respondent returned to his likely death in Columbia" (*Builes v. Nye* 2003).

episteme of the Other, such as Judge L'Heureux-Dubé from the Canadian
Supreme Court who patiently listened to the voice of indigenous peoples and
Judge Tulkens of the European Court of Human Rights who saw beyond
the abstract, formal typologies of the Court to try to understand the Turkish
women's perspectives as to why they had chosen to wear the headscarf in universities. Likewise, we encountered a series of progressive tribunals that have
modified their rules of procedures to better give voice to the Other, such as
the Inter-American Court of Human Rights and the Supreme Court of India.
Other tribunals have crafted new rights or given progressive new meanings
to existing rights, such as the African Commission on Human and Peoples'
Rights in two important cases on economic, social, and cultural rights, and
the Ninth Circuit Court of Appeals in the United States when defining particular social groups in asylum law.

These chapters have also presented a number of theorists, judges, and other
legal players who failed to push past varieties of original violence and further
cauterized the Marginalized Other. For instance, both Hannah Arendt, when
judging the Little Rock crisis of 1957, and Seyla Benhabib, in the headscarf
affairs, allow pre-existing theoretical typologies to blind them to the original
violence of the socio-political situations confronting marginalized Others.[3]
Such typologies as original violence are seen in the European Court's ruling on the headscarf affair and the Indian Supreme Court's ruling in the
Sardar Sarovar dam case. Instead of learning to learn from the voice of the
Marginalized Other, these tribunals interrogated the Other in the language of
the hegemonic system. This language is unable and unwilling to understand
the idiom of the Other. Such legal interrogations are perhaps best exemplified
by the verbal berating of asylum seekers by Judge Ferlise in recent infamous
U.S. cases. Theoretically, a similar dynamic is played out in Arendt's analysis
of the Little Rock crisis in which she felt comfortable speaking for, and accusing, the mothers and the representatives of the children, but at no point does
she consider their voices.

CONTINUOUS DECONSTRUCTION AND REINVIGORATION

Human rights law has made great strides and progressively developed in ways
unimagined to its initial proponents in the mid-twentieth century or even

---

[3]   Henry Shue (1996) fittingly wrote, "Typologies are at best abstract instruments for temporar-
      ily fending off the complexities of concrete reality that threaten to overwhelm our circuits.
      Be they dichotomous or trichotomous, typologies are ladders to be climbed and left behind,
      not monuments to be caressed or polished" (160).

since 1999 when I attended the Salzburg Seminar on International Human Rights Law. There, I saw leading human rights scholars, attorneys, and activists seemingly unaware of, or consciously eschewing, philosophical insights, especially those derived from postmodernism and deconstruction. But to be frank, at that point, I was not sure that any philosophical insights could contribute much to the developing cascade in human rights law, except perhaps as a tool to critique predominant ideologies. Now, if I found myself in a similar context, I would make the following points to human rights activists, lawyers, and judges.

I would first argue that human rights law, although experiencing newfound status and institutionalization, needs to be continually deconstructed. The triumph or mainstreaming of human rights is not a cause for exuberance. As Spivak writes, "There is not victory, but only victories that are also warnings" (1995a, xxv in Ray 2003, 47). The challenge of human rights law today is to avoid becoming yet another ideology, one that sets itself up as beyond criticism. Human rights practitioners should be aware of, and vigilant about, the ubiquity and resilience of power relations, especially those embedded in the very operation of human rights law itself. I would present these practitioners with numerous examples of the Marginalized Other being further cauterized by those very institutions designed to help them. Indeed, as I have recently presented this analysis to human rights attorneys and activists in several contexts, they invariably concur that this happens all too frequently, and they often provide even more examples of projects or cases in which they were involved that failed to consider the voices of the Marginalized Other. Such cases of speaking for the Other, or speaking for what Spivak calls a representation of the Other, are sadly not uncommon in human rights law, nor are examples in which the Other's identity and their rights are defined by the hegemonic system with little regard for the *proyectos de la vida* of the marginalized. A human rights law grounded in the phenomenology of the Saturated Other that I develop here would first endlessly interrogate human rights institutions as to whether they are truly just and listening to the voice of the Other.

My recommendations would not end with mere critique, as works of deconstruction all too often do. I contend that recent works by theorists in a postmodern or post-colonial vein have provided a blueprint for how the ongoing progressive development of human rights law can be sustained and even reinvigorated.

I would urge human rights workers to patiently listen to the voice of the Marginalized Other at all stages of their work. I would push for them to take extraordinary measures in their own work to seek out the voice of those marginalized. Even within marginalized communities there are hierarchies and power relations that need to be navigated. Human rights workers should also be conscious of the difficulties of translating the grievances of the marginalized into the idiom of the law. They should bracket or suspend as much as possible any cultural or theoretical presuppositions they have about the marginalized. I would also urge them not to quickly lump individuals into a collective that categorizes them to which they would not recognize, but I encourage the self-ascription of the marginalized. Recall that not all adivasis (discussed in Chapter 5) fit the mold of "ecologically noble primitives" that the mostly transnational activist groups imposed on them. Human rights workers should not decide which rights are most fundamental for the marginalized, but should allow the marginalized to define the rights that are most important to them to realize their *proyecto de la vida* in their own terms.

Instead, human rights workers should work with the Marginalized Other to create an anti-hegemonic discourse that will overturn those invisible ideologies that undergird the system. This will involve working with the Marginalized as social theorists to deconstruct the discourse. It will also involve the Marginalized directing the means to address their marginalization. Too often human rights lawyers reach primarily for legal solutions, even when they may not be most appropriate or desired. Similarly, all too often the law is employed and it leaves the underlying structural violence un-addressed when more comprehensive strategies (social, economic, political, etc.) are needed.

Human rights workers should also advocate for the progressive development of the institutions and organizations with which they work. Human rights tribunals should be pushed to reform their procedures, especially their rules of standing and their procedures for oral hearings and investigative missions, to learn from the aggrieved. Helpful examples of such procedures would include social action litigation in India and the rules of standing in the Inter-American Court of Human Rights. Human rights workers should push definitions in treaties like the Convention against Torture and the Refugee Convention to undo founding violences, such as whether torture can be perpetrated by private individuals and whether persecution on grounds other than the five listed in the Convention could be justification for asylum. Other artificial typologies, such as the privileging of civil and political rights over social and economic rights and the failure to hold states accountable for violations perpetrated by third parties, should also be questioned. Human rights workers should also push to undo artificial typologies created by tribunals such as the margin of appreciation doctrine in the European Court of Human Rights. This doctrine played a useful political function at one time and has been a useful heuristic, but its continued use allows states to unjustly discriminate against minorities. They should push for creative reparations such as the ones awarded by the Inter-American Court of Human Rights. Whereas monetary compensation has an important role for ameliorating human rights abuses, other reparations such as locating and properly burying victims' remains, public apologies, community centers, scholarships, and memorials might be more meaningful and go much further in restoring the *proyectos de la vida* of the victims.

Of course, even the most progressive human rights institutions with the most progressive rules of procedures contain traces of their original violence, and they are inevitably influenced by the structural violence and invisible ideologies in their milieu.

Even the most progressive institutions must be constantly interrogated as to whether they are truly doing justice for the Marginalized Other. As Dussel writes, "When the dreamed 'new' Jerusalem is finally built, it slowly transforms itself into Egypt, the 'second' Jerusalem, the Jerusalem to be deconstructed . . . and the history will continue, never repeating and always renewing itself, as the history of the politics of liberation" (Dussel 2006, 88).

Bibliography

Agamben, Giorgio. 1996. "Beyond Human Rights." In *Radical Thought in Italy: A Potential Politics*, edited by Paolo Virno and Michael Hardt. Minneapolis: University of Minnesota Press, 159–166.

    2002. *Remnants of Auschwitz: The Witness and the Archive.* New York: Zone Books.

    2005. *The State of Exception.* Chicago: University of Chicago Press.

Agarwal, Ranjan K. 2004. "The Barefoot Lawyers: Prosecuting Child Labour in the Supreme Court of India" *Arizona Journal of International and Comparative Law* 21: 663–713.

Ajzenstat, Oona. 2001. *Driven Back to the Text: The Premodern Sources of Levinas's Postmodernism.* Pittsburgh, PA: Duquesne University Press.

Alcoff, Linda. 1991–1992. "The Problem of Speaking for Others" *Cultural Critique*. 20: 5–32.

Aleinikoff, T. Alexander. 2003. "Protected Characteristics and Social Perceptions: An Analysis of the Meaning of 'Membership of a Particular Social Group'." Available at http://www.unhcr.ch/cgi-bin/texis/vtx/publ/opendoc. pdf?tbl=publ&id=419cbe1f4.

Alford, C. Fred. 2002. "Emmanuel Levinas and Iris Murdoch: Ethics as Exit?" *Philosophy and Literature* 26: 24–42.

An-Na'im, Abdullahi A. 1992. "Toward a Cross-Cultural Approach to Defining International Standards of Human Rights: The Meaning of Cruel, Inhuman, or Degrading Treatment or Punishment." In *Human Rights in Cross-Cultural Perspectives: A Quest for Consensus*, edited by An-Na'im. Philadelphia: University of Pennsylvania Press, 19–43.

Arat, Yeşim. 2005. *Rethinking Islam and Liberal Democracy.* Albany: State University of New York Press.

Arat, Zehra F. 1998. "Introduction: Politics of Representation and Identity." In *Deconstructing Images of "The Turkish Woman,"* edited by Arat. New York: St. Martin's Press, 1–36

Archuleta, Elizabeth. 2005. "Gym Shoes, Maps, and Passports, Oh My! Creating Community or Creating Chaos at the NMAI?" *The American Indian Quarterly* 29: 426–449.

Ardizzoni, Michela. 2004. "Unveiling the Veil: Gendered Discourses and the (In) Visibility of the Female Body in France" *Women's Studies* 33: 629–649.

Arendt, Hannah. 1951. *The Origins of Totalitarianism.* New York: Harcourt Brace Jovanovich.

1958. *The Human Condition.* Chicago: University of Chicago Press.

1959a. "Reflections on Little Rock" *Dissent* 6: 45–56.

1959b. "A Reply to Critics" *Dissent* 6 (2): 179–181.

1963a. *Eichmann in Jerusalem: A Report on the Banality of Evil.* New York: Penguin Books.

1963b. *On Revolution.* New York: Viking Press.

1968. *Between Past and Future.* New York: Viking.

1969. *Crises of the Republic.* New York: Harcourt Brace Jovanovich.

1982. *Lectures on Kant's Political Philosophy.* Edited by Ronald Beiner. Chicago: University of Chicago Press.

1990. "Philosophy and Politics" *Social Research* 57: 73–103.

2003. *Responsibility and Judgment.* Edited by Jerome Kohn, New York: Schocken Books.

Aristotle. 1932. *Politics.* Cambridge, Mass: Loeb Classical Library.

1999. *Nicomachean Ethics.* Cambridge, Mass: Loeb Classical Library.

Backhouse, Constance and Donald M. McRae. 2002. Report to the Canadian Human Rights Commission on the Treatment of the Innu of Labrador by the Government of Canada. Available at http://www.chrc-ccdp.ca/publications/ rapport_innu_report/toc-en.asp.

Badiou, Alain. 2001. *Ethics: An Essay on the Understanding of Evil,* translated by Peter Hallward. London: Verso.

2004. "Behind the Scarf Law, There is Fear" *Le Monde,* February 22.

Baker, Liv. 1996. *The Second Battle of New Orleans: The Hundred-Year Struggle to Integrate the Schools.* New York: HarperCollins.

Balibar, Etienne. 2004. "Dissonances within Laïcité" *Constellations* 11: 353–367.

Barber, Michael D. 1998. *Ethical Hermeneutics: Rationality in Enrique Dussel's Philosophy of Liberation.* New York: Fordham University Press.

2000. "Theory and Alterity: Dussel's Marx and Marion on Idolatry." In *Thinking from the Underside of History: Enrique Dussel's Philosophy of Liberation,* edited by Linda Martín Alcoff and Eduardo Mendieta. Lanham, MD: Rowman & Littlefield, 195–212.

Bates, Daisy. 1962. *The Long Shadow of Little Rock: A Memoir.* New York: David McKay.

Baxi, Upendra. n.d. "Random Reflections on the [Im]possibility of Human Rights Education." Available at http://www.pdhre.org/dialogue/reflections.html.

1988. "Taking Suffering Seriously." In *Law and Poverty,* edited by Upendra Baxi. Bombay: Tripathi, 387–415.

1998. "Voices of Suffering and the Future of Human Rights" *Transnational Law & Contemporary Problems* 8 (Fall): 125–170.

2002. *The Future of Human Rights.* Oxford: Oxford University Press.

Beals, Melba Patillo. 1994. *Warriors Don't Cry: A Searing Memoir of the Battle to Integrate Little Rock's Central High.* New York: Pocket Books.

Beiner, Ronald. 1992. "Rereading Hannah Arendt's Kant Lectures" *Philosophy & Social Criticism* 23: 21–32.

Beitz, Charles R. "Human Rights as a Common Concern" *The American Political Science Review* 95:2 (2001): 269–282.

Belelieu, Christopher D. 2006. "The Headscarf as a Symbolic Enemy of the European Court of Human Rights' Democratic Jurisprudence: Viewing Islam through a European Legal Prism in Light of the Sahin Judgment" *Columbia Journal of European Law* 12: 573–623.

Bellil, Samira. 2003. *Dans l'Enfer des Tournantes*. Editions Denoël.

Benhabib, Seyla. 1992. *Situating the Self: Gender, Community and Postmodernism in Contemporary Ethics*. Cambridge: Polity Press.

1996. *The Reluctant Modernism of Hannah Arendt*. Thousand Oaks, Calif.: Sage.

2002. *Claims of Culture: Equality and Diversity in the Global Era*. Princeton: Princeton University Press.

2004. *The Rights of Others: Aliens, Residents and Citizens*. Cambridge, UK: Cambridge University Press.

2006. *Another Cosmopolitanism*. Oxford: Oxford University Press.

Benjamin, Walter. 1996. "Critique of Violence." In *Selected Writings Vol. 1: 1913–1926*, translated by Edmund Jephcott. Cambridge: Harvard University Press, 236–252.

Benvenisti, Eyal. 1999. "Margin of Appreciation, Consensus, and Universal Standards" *New York University Journal of International Law and Politics* 31: 843–854.

Bernasconi, Robert. 1996. "The Double Face of the Political and the Social: Hannah Arendt and America's Racial Divisions" *Research in Phenomenology* 26: 3–24.

Bernstein, Richard J. 1986. *Philosophical Profiles: Essays in a Pragmatic Mode*. Cambridge: Polity Press.

Beverly, John. 1999. *Subalternity and Representation*. Durham, N.C.: Duke University Press.

Bleiberg, Benjamin D. 2005. "Unveiling the Real Issue: Evaluating the European Court of Human Rights' Decision to Enforce the Turkish Headscarf Ban in Leyla Sahin v. Turkey" *Cornell Law Review* 91: 129–169.

Blum, Peter C. "Overcoming Relativism? Levinas's Return to Platonism" *Journal of Religious Ethics* 28, no. 1 (Spring 2000): 91–117.

Blumenson, Eric. 1996. "Mapping the Limits of Skepticism in Law and Morals" *Texas Law Review* 74: 523–576.

Bohman, James. 1997. "The Moral Costs of Political Pluralism: The Dilemmas of Difference and Equality in Arendt's 'Reflections on Little Rock'." In *Hannah Arendt: Twenty Years Later*, edited by Larry May and Jerome Kohn. Cambridge, Mass.: The MIT Press, 53–80.

2005. "Rights, Cosmopolitanism, and Public Reason: Interactive Universalism in the Claims of Culture" *Philosophy & Social Criticism* 31: 715–726.

Borrows, John. 1997. "Frozen Rights in Canada: Constitutional Interpretation and the Trickster" *American Indian Law Review* 22: 37–64.

Borrows, John and Leonard I.Rotman. 1997. "The Sui Generis Nature of Aboriginal Rights: Does it Make a Difference?" *Alberta Law Review* 36: 9–45.

Burggraeve, Roger. 2002. *The Wisdom of Love in the Service of Love: Emmanuel Levinas on Justice, Peace, and Human Rights*, translated by Jeffrey Bloechel. Milwaukee: Marquette University Press.

Burns, Auŝra. 2006. "Moving and Moving Forward: Mushuau Innu Relocation from Davis Inlet to Natuashish" *Acadiensis* XXXV (2): 46–63.

Butler, Judith. 1997a. *Excitable Speech: A Politics of the Performative*. New York: Routledge.

⸻ 1997b. *The Psychic Life of Power: Theories in Subjection*. Stanford, Calif.: Stanford University Press.

⸻ 1999. *Gender Trouble: Feminism and the Subversion of Identity*. New York: Routledge.

⸻ 2005. *Giving an Account of Oneself*. New York: Fordham University Press.

Butt, Leslie. 2002. "The Suffering Stranger: Medical Anthropology and International Morality." *Medical Anthropology: Cross-Cultural Studies in Health and Illness* 21: 1–24.

Cairo, Ivan. 2006. "Suriname Apologizes for Moiwana Massacre." *Caribbean Net News*, July 18. Available at http://www.caribbeannetnews.com/cgi-script/csArticles/articles/000023/002390.htm.

Campbell, David. 1999. "The Deterritorialization of Responsibility: Levinas, Derrida, and Ethics after the End of Philosophy." In *Moral Spaces: Rethinking Ethics and World Politics*, edited by David Campbell and Michael J. Shapiro. Minneapolis: University of Minnesota Press, 29–56.

Canovan, Margaret. 1992. *Hannah Arendt: A Reinterpretation of Her Political Thought*. Cambridge: Cambridge University Press.

Caputo, John D., ed. 1997. *Deconstruction in a Nutshell: A Conversation with Jacques Derrida*. New York: Fordham University Press.

Caputo, John D. and Michael J. Scanlon. 1999. "Apology for the Impossible: Religion and Postmodernism." In *God, the Gift, and Postmodernism*, edited by John D. Caputo and Michael J. Scanlon. Bloomington: Indiana University Press, 1–19.

Carens, Joseph H. 1997. "Liberalism and Culture." *Constellations: An International Journal of Critical & Democratic Theory* 4: 35–47.

Cassin, Rene. 1970. "Speech to the Decalogue Lawyers Society." Available at http://www.udhr.org/history/decacass.htm.

Cerna, Christina M. 2004. "The Inter-American System for the Protection of Human Rights." *Florida Journal of International Law* 16: 195–212.

Chadwick, K. 1997. "Education in Secular France: (Re) Defining Laïcité." *Modern and Contemporary France* 5: 47–59.

Christie, Gordon. 2005. "A Colonial Reading of Recent Jurisprudence: Sparrow, Delgamuukw and Haida Nation." *Windsor Yearbook of Access to Justice* 23: 17–54.

Cogan, Neil H. 1989. "'Standing' before the Constitution: Membership in the Community." *Law and History Review* 7: 1–21.

Cohen, Richard A. 2003. "The Universal in Jewish Particularism: Benamozegh and Levinas." In *Religious Experience and the End of Metaphysics*, edited by Jeffrey Bloechel. Bloomington: Indiana University Press, 135–152.

Conklin, William E. 1997. "The Authoritative Assimilation of the Other within a Master Discourse." In *The Language and Politics of Exclusion: Others in Discourse*, edited by Stephen Harold Riggins. Thousand Oaks, Calif.: Sage Publications, 226–248.

⸻ 1998. *The Phenomenology of Modern Legal Discourse: The Juridical Production and the Disclosure of Suffering*. Aldershot, Vt.: Ashgate.

Cover, Robert M. 1983. "Nomos and Narrative." *Harvard Law Review* 97: 4–68.

Cover Robert M. 1986. "The Bonds of Constitutional Interpretation: Of the Word, the Deed, and the Role" *Georgia Law Review* 20: 815–833.

Coyle, Michael. 2003. "Loyalty and Distinctiveness: A New Approach to the Crown's Fiduciary Duty Toward Aboriginal Peoples" *Alberta Law Review* 40: 841–866.

Criddle, Evan J. and Evan Fox-Decent. 2009. "A Fiduciary Theory of Jus Cogens" *The Yale Journal of International Law* 34: 331–387.

Daud Committee (Committee to Assist the Resettlement and Rehabilitation of the-Sardar-Sarovar Project-Affected Persons). 2001. Government of Maharashtra, Mumbai.

Dawes, James R. 1999. "Language, Violence, and Human Rights Law" *Yale Journal of Law & the Humanities* 11 (Summer): 215–250.

Derrida, Jacques. 1992. "Force of Law: The 'Mystical Foundation of Authority'." In *Deconstruction and the Possibility of Justice*, edited by Drucilla Cornell, Michel Rosenfeld, and David Gray Carlson. New York: Routledge, 3–67.

    1997. "On Responsibility" (interview with Jonathan Dronsfield et al.,) *Warwick Journal of Philosophy* 6: 19–36.

    2001a. *On Cosmopolitanism and Forgiveness*, translated by Mark Dooley and Michael Hughes. London: Routledge.

    2001b. "On Forgiveness: A Roundtable Discussion with Jacques Derrida." In *Questioning God*, edited by Mark Dooley and Michael J. Scanlon, Bloomington, Ind.: Indiana University Press, 52–72.

Derrida, Jacques, et al. 1999. "Hospitality, Justice, and Responsibility: A Dialogue with Jacques Derrida." In *Questioning Ethics: Contemporary Debates in Philosophy*, edited by Richard Kearney and Mark Dooley. London: Routledge, 65–83.

deSouza, Peter Ronald. 2003. "The Struggle for Local Government: Indian Democracy's New Phase" *Publius* 33: 99–118.

Disch, Lisa. 1997. "Please Sit Down, but Don't Make Yourself at Home: Arendtian 'Visiting' and the Prefigurative Politics of Consciousness Raising." In *Hannah Arendt and the Meaning of Politics*, edited by Craig Calhoun and John McGowan. Minneapolis: University of Minnesota Press, 132–165.

Donoho, Douglas Lee. 2001. "Autonomy, Self-Governance, and the Margin of Appreciation: Developing a Jurisprudence of Diversity within Universal Human Rights" *Emory International Law Review* 15: 391–466.

Douzinas, Costas. 2000. *The End of Human Rights: Critical Legal Through at the Fin-de-Siecle*. Oxford: Hart.

Dussel, Enrique. 1985. *Philosophy of Liberation*, translated by Aquilina Martinez and Christine Morkovsky. Maryknoll, N.Y.: Orbis Books.

    1988. *Ethics and Community*, translated by Robert R. Barr. Maryknoll, N.Y.: Orbis Books.

    1997a. "The Architectonic of the Ethics of Liberation" *Philosophy & Social Criticism* 23 (3): 1–35.

    1997b. "Principles, Mediations, and the 'Good' as Synthesis (From 'Discourse Ethics' to 'Ethics of Liberation')" *Philosophy Today* 41 (Supplement): 55–66.

    1998. *Ética de la Liberacíon en la Edad de la Globalizacíon y de la Exclusíon*. Madrid: Editorial Trotta.

    1999b. "Six Theses Toward a Critique of Political Reason: The Citizen as Political Agent" *Radical Philosophy Review* 2: 79–95.

2000. "Epilogue." In Thinking from the Underside of History: Enrique Dussel's Philosophy of Liberation, edited by Linda Martin Alcoff and Eduardo Mendietta. Lanham, Md.: Rowman & Littlefield, 269–289.

2003a. "Ethical Sense of the 1994 Maya Rebellion in Chiapas." In *Beyond Philosophy: Ethics, History, Marxism, and Liberation Theology*, edited by Eduardo Mendieta. Lanham, Md.: Rowman & Littlefield, 167–183.

2003b. "An Ethics of Liberation: Fundamental Hypotheses." In *Beyond Philosophy: Ethics, History, Marxism, and Liberation Theology*, edited by Eduardo Mendieta. Lanham, Md.: Rowman & Littlefield, 135–148.

2004. "Deconstruction of the Concept of 'Tolerance': From Intolerance to Solidarity" *Constellations* 11: 326–333.

2006. "The Politics' by Levinas: Towards a 'Critical' Political Philosophy," translated by Jorge Rodriguez. In *Difficult Justice: Commentaries on Levinas and Politics*, edited by Asher Horowitz and Gad Horowiz. Toronto: University of Toronto Press, 78–96.

Dworkin, Ronald. 1977. *Taking Rights Seriously.* Cambridge: Harvard University Press.

Editors. 1959. *Dissent* 6: 45.

Eisenstadt, Oona. 2007. "Anti-Utopianism Revisited" Paper Presented at the Annual Meeting of the North American Levinas Society, West Lafayette, Ind.

Ellison, Ralph. 1995. *Shadow and Act.* New York: Vintage.

Ewelukwa, Uche. 2006. "Litigating the Rights of Street Children in Regional or International Fora: Trends, Options, Barriers and Breakthroughs" *Yale Human Rights & Development Law Journal* 9: 85–131.

Failinger, Marie A. 1987. "Equality versus the Right to Choose Associates: A Critique of Hannah Arendt's View of the Supreme Court's Dilemma" *University of Pittsburgh Law Review* 49 (Fall): 143–188.

2006. "'No More Deaths': On Conscience, Civil Disobedience, and a New Role for Truth Commissions" *UMKC Law Review* 75: 401–435.

Fanon, Frantz. 1965. *A Dying Colonialism*, translated by Haakon Chevalier. New York: Grove Press.

Finkielkraut, Alain. 2000. *In the Name of Humanity: Reflections on the Twentieth Century*, translated by Judith Friedlander. New York: Columbia University Press.

Fraser, Nancy. 1997. "The Force of Law: Metaphysical or Political." In *Feminist Interpretations of Jacques Derrida*, edited by Nancy J. Holland. University Park: The Pennsylvania State University Press, 157–163.

Freedman, Jane. 2004. "Secularism as a Barrier to Integration? The French Dilemma" *International Migration* 43(3): 5–27.

Fregoso, Rosa Linda. 2006. "We Want Them Alive: The Politics and Culture of Human Rights" *Social Identities* 12: 109–138.

Frey, John Carlos. Director. 2002. "The Gatekeeper." Gatekeeper Productions.

Fullerton, Maryellen. 1993. "A Comparative Look at Refugee Status Based on Persecution Due to Membership in a Particular Social Group" *Cornell International Law Journal* 26: 505–563.

Galanter, Marc and Jayanth K. Krishnan. 2004. "'Bread for the Poor': Access to Justice and the Rights of the Needy in India" *Hastings Law Journal* 55: 789–834.

Gaspard, Françoise and Farhad Khosrokhavar. 1995. *Le Foulard et la République*. Paris: Éditions La Découverte.

Glendon, Mary Ann. 1991. *Rights Talk. The Impoverishment of Political Discourse*. New York: Free Press.

    2001. *A World Made New: Eleanor Roosevelt and the Universal Declaration of Human Rights*. New York: Random House.

Göle, Nilüfer. 1996. *The Forbidden Modern: Civilization and Veiling*. Ann Arbor: The University of Michigan Press.

Gomez, Fernando. 2001. "Ethics is the Original Philosophy; or, The Barbarian Words Coming from the Third World: An Interview with Enrique Dussel." *Boundary 2*: 19–73.

Gould, Carol C. 1976. "The Woman Question: Philosophy of Liberation and the Liberation of Philosophy." In *Women and Philosophy: Toward a Theory of Liberation*, edited by Carol C. Gould and Marx W. Wartofsky. New York: G.P. Putnam's Sons, 8–15.

Griffin, John D. 1995. "The Chinese Student Protection Act and 'Enhanced Consideration' for PRC Nationals: Legitimizing Foreign Policy While Averting False Positives in Asylum Law." *University of Colorado Law Review* 66: 1105–1163.

Grossman, Dean Claudio. 2007. "Reparations in the Inter-American System: A Comparative Approach." *American University Law Review* 56 1375–1468.

Hampton, Henry, Steve Fayer, and Sarah Flynn. 1990. *Voices of Freedom: An Oral History of the Civil Rights Movement from the 1950s through the 1980s*. New York: Bantam Books.

Hanrahan, Maura. 2003. *The Lasting Breach: The Omission of Aboriginal People From the Terms of Union Between Newfoundland and Canada and its Ongoing Impacts*. St. John's, Newfoundland: Royal Commission on Renewing and Strengthening Our Place in Canada.

Hanssen, Beatrice. 2000. "Ethics of the Other." In *The Turn to Ethics*, edited by Marjorie Garber, Beatrice Hanssen, and Rebecca L. Walkowitz. New York: Routledge, 127–180.

Hathaway, James C. 1991. *The Law of Refugee Status*. Toronto: Butterworths.

Helton, Arthur C. 1983. "Persecution on Account of Membership in a Social Group as a Basis for Refugee Status." *Columbia Human Rights Law Review* 15: 39–67.

    1984. "Political Asylum under the 1980 Refugee Act: An Unfulfilled Promise." *University of Michigan Journal of Legal Reform* 17: 243–264.

Herzog, Annabel. 2002. "Is Liberalism 'All we need'? Levinas's Politics of Surplus." *Political Theory* 30: 204–227.

Hook, Sidney. 1958. "Democracy and Desegregation." *The New Leader*. April 13: 3–19.

Hopgood, Stephen. 2006. *Keepers of the Flame: Understanding Amnesty International*. Cornell University Press.

Hosbet, Suresh. 2000. "The Sword against the Poor: Shift in Nature of Public Interest Litigation." *Deccan Herald*, December 22. Available at: http://www.narmada.org/archive/dh/2000dec22.top.htm.

Human Rights Watch. 2006. "Turkey." Available at http://www.hrw.org/english/docs/2006/01/18/turkey12220.htm.

Idriss, Mohammad Mazher. 2005. "Laïcité and the Banning of the Headscarf in France" *Legal Studies* 25: 260–295.

İlyasoğlu, Aynur. 1998. "Islamist Women in Turkey: Their Identity and Self-Image." In *Deconstructing Images of "The Turkish Woman,"* edited by Zehra F. Arat. New York: St. Martin's Press, 241–262.

Inlender, Talia. 2006. "The Imperfect Legacy of Gomez v. INS: Using Social Perceptions to Adjudicate Social Group Claims" *Georgetown Immigration Law Journal* 20: 681–710.

Inter-American Commission on Human Rights. 2009. "IACHR Visits U.S. Immigration Detention Facilities" IACHR Press Release 53/09. Available at http://www.cidh.org/comunicados/English/2009/53-09eng.htm.

Isaac, Jeffrey C. 1996. "A New Guarantee on Earth: Hannah Arendt on Human Dignity and the Politics of Human Rights" *American Political Science Review* 90: 61–73.

———. 1998. *Democracy in Dark Times.* Ithaca, N.Y.: Cornell University Press.

Iyer, Ramaswamy R. 2000. "A Judgment of Grave Import" October 27. Available at: http://www.narmada.org/sardar-sarovar/sc.ruling/iyer.article.html.

Janicaud, Dominique. 2000. "The Theological Turn of French Phenomenology." In *Phenomenology and the "Theological Turn,"* translated by Bernard G. Prusak. Bronx: Fordham University Press, 16–103.

Jay, Martin. 1997. "Reflective Judgments by a Spectator on a Conference That Is Now History." In *Hannah Arendt and the Meaning of Politics,* edited by Craig Calhoun and John McGowan. Minneapolis: University of Minnesota Press, 338–350.

Kassindja, Fauziya. (with Layli Miller Bashir). 1998. *Do They Hear You When You Cry?* New York: Bantam.

Kavakci, Merve. 2004. "Headscarf Heresy" *Foreign Policy* (May/June): 66–67.

Kearney, Richard. 1999. "Desire of God. In *God, the Gift, and Postmodernism,* edited by John D. Caputo and Michael J. Scanlon. Bloomington: Indiana University Press, 112–145.

Keaton, Trica Danielle. 2006. *Muslim Girls and the Other France: Race, Identity Politics, & Social Exclusion.* Bloomington: Indiana University Press.

Khagram, Sanjeev. 2004. *Dams and Development: Transnational Struggles for Water and Power.* Ithaca, N.Y.: Cornell University Press.

Kibreab, Gaim. 2000. "Common Property Resources and Resettlement." In Risks and Reconstruction: Experiences of Resettlers and Refugees, edited by Michael M. Cernea and Chris McDowell. Washington, D.C.: The World Bank, 293–331.

Koch, Ida Elisabeth. 2005. "Dichotomies, Trichotomies or Waves of Duties?" *Human Rights Law Review* 5: 81–103.

Kohn, Jerome. 2003. "A Note on the Text." In *Hannah Arendt, Responsibility and Judgment,* edited by Jerome Kohn. New York: Schocken Books, xxxi–xxxvii.

Kuru, Ahmet. 2005. "Secularism in the United States, France, and Turkey: An Historical Perspective" Paper presented at the Annual Meeting of the American Political Science Association, Washington, D.C..

Kymlicka, Will. 1995. *Multicultural Citizenship: A Liberal Theory of Minority Rights.* Oxford: Clarendon Press.

———. 2001. *Politics in the Vernacular: Nationalism, Multiculturalism, and Citizenship.* Oxford: Oxford University Press.

Laborde, Cécille. 2005. "Secular Philosophy and Muslim Headscarves in Schools" *The Journal of Political Philosophy* 13: 305–329.

Lange, Lynda. 1998. "Burnt Offerings to Rationality: A Feminist Reading of the Construction of Indigenous Peoples in Enrique Dussel's Theory of Modernity" *Hypatia* 13 (3): 132–145.

Latour, Bruno. "La République Dans un Foulard" *Le Monde*, January 17, 2004. Available at http://www.haverford.edu/fren/dkight/Fr105_sec2_Spr04/WeekTwo/LatourContre.html.

Lebeau, Vicky. 2004. "The Unwelcome Child: Elizabeth Eckford and Hannah Arendt" *Journal of Visual Culture* 3: 51–62.

Lefort, Claude. 1986. *The Political Forms of Modern Society: Bureaucracy, Democracy, Totalitarianism*, edited by John B. Thompson. Cambridge: Polity Press.

Levinas, Emmanuel. 1969. *Totality and Infinity: An Essay on Exteriority*, translated by Alphonso Lingis. Pittsburgh, Pa.: Duquesne University Press.

1981. *Otherwise than Being or Beyond Essence*, translated by Alphonso Lingis. The Hague: Martinus Nijhoff.

1987. "No Identity." In *Collected Philosophical Papers*, translated by Alphonso Lingis. The Hague: Martinus Nijhoff, 141–152.

1989a. "Ethics and Politics." In *The Levinas Reader*, edited by Seán Hand. Oxford: Blackwell, 289–297.

1989b. "Ethics as First Philosophy." In *The Levinas Reader*, edited by Seán Hand. Oxford: Blackwell, 75–87.

1989c. "Ideology and Idealism." In *The Levinas Reader*, edited by Seán Hand Oxford: Blackwell, 235–248.

1990. *Nine Talmudic Readings*, translated by Annette Aronowicz. Bloomington: Indiana University Press.

1993. "The Rights of Man and the Rights of the Other." In *Outside the Subject*, translated by Michael B. Smith. London: The Athlone Press, 116–125.

1996. "Meaning and Sense." In *Emmanuel Levinas: Basic Philosophical Writings*, edited by Adriaan T. Peperzak, Simon Critchley, and Robert Bernsasconi. Bloomington, Ind.: Indiana University Press, 33–64.

1998a. "The Idea of the Infinite in Us." In *Entre Nous: On Thinking-of-the-Other*, translated by Michael B. Smith and Barbara Harshav. New York: Columbia University Press, 219–222.

1998b. *Of God Who Comes to Mind*, translated by Bettina Bergo. Stanford: Stanford University Press.

1998c. "Uniqueness." In *Entre Nous: On Thinking-of-the-Other*, translated by Michael B. Smith and Barbara Harshav. New York: Columbia University Press, 189–196.

1998d. "Dialogue on Thinking-of-the-Other." In *Entre Nous: On Thinking-of-the-Other*, translated by Michael B. Smith and Barbara Harshav. New York: Columbia University Press, 201–206.

1998e. "The Rights of Man and Good Will." In *Entre Nous: On Thinking-of-the-Other*, translated by Michael B. Smith and Barbara Harshav. New York: Columbia University Press, 155–158.

1998f. "The Other, Utopia, and Justice." In *Entre Nous: On Thinking-of-the-Other*, translated by Michael B. Smith and Barbara Harshav. New York: Columbia University Press, 223–234.

1998g. "Useless Suffering." In *Entre Nous: On Thinking-of-the-Other*, translated by Michael B. Smith and Barbara Harshav. New York: Columbia University Press, 91–102.

1998h. "A Man-God?" In *Entre Nous: On Thinking-of-the-Other*, translated by Michael B. Smith and Barbara Harshav. New York: Columbia University Press, 53–60.

1999a. "Philosophy and Transcendence." In *Alterity and Transcendence*, translated by Michael B. Smith. New York: Columbia University Press, 3–37.

1999b. "The Rights of the Other Man." In *Alterity and Transcendence*, \translated by Michael B. Smith. New York: Columbia University Press, 145–149.

2001. *Is it Righteous to Be? Interviews with Emmanuel Levinas*, edited by Jill Robbins. Stanford, Calif.: Stanford University Press.

Levinas, Emmanuel, et al. 1988. "The Paradox of Morality: An Interview with Emmanuel Levinas." In *The Provocation of Levinas*, edited by Robert Bernasconi and David Wood. London: Routledge, 168–180.

Levinas, Emmanuel and Richard Kearney. 1986. "Dialogue with Emmanuel Levinas." In *Face to Face with Levinas*, edited by Richard A. Cohen. Albany: State University of New York Press, 13–33.

Lévy, Alma and Lila Lévy. 2004. *Des Filles Comme Les Autres: Au-Delà du Foulard*. Paris: La Découverte.

Lovejoy, C. D. 2006. "Glimpse into the Future: What Sahin v. Turkey Means to France's Ban on Ostensibly Religious Symbols in Public Schools." *Wisconsin International Law Journal* 24: 661–698.

Lutz, Ellen and Kathryn Sikkink. 2001. "The Justice Cascade: The Evolution and Impact of Foreign Human Rights Trials in Latin America." *Chicago Journal of International Law* 2: 1–33.

Macdonald, Euan. 2004. "The Future of Human Rights? Theory and Practice in an International Context." *German Law Journal* 8: 969–984.

MacKinnon, Catharine. 2000. "Points against Postmodernism." *Chicago-Kent Law Review* 75: 687–712.

Magnus, Kathy Dow. 2006. "The Unaccountable Subject: Judith Butler and the Social Conditions of Intersubjective Agency." *Hypatia* 21 (2): 81–103.

Mahoney, Paul. 1998. "Marvelous Richness of Diversity or Invidious Cultural Relativism." *Human Rights Law Journal* 19 (April): 1–6.

Marion, Jean-Luc. 2000. "The Voice without Name: Homage to Levinas." In *The Face of the Other and the Trace of God: Essays on the Philosophy of Emmanuel Levinas*, edited by Jeffrey Bloechel. New York: Fordham University Press, 224–242.

2002a. *Being Given: Toward a Phenomenology of Givenness*, translated by Jeffrey L. Kosky. Stanford: Stanford University Press.

2002b. *In Excess: Studies in Saturated Phenomena*, translated by Robyn Horner and Vincent Berraud. New York: Fordham University Press.

2002c. *Prolegomena to Charity*, translated by Stephen E. Lewis and Jeffrey L. Kosky, New York: Fordham University Press.

Marsh, James L. 2000. "The Material Principle and the Formal Principle in Dussel's Ethics." In *Thinking from the Underside of History: Enrique Dussel's Philosophy of Liberation*, edited by Linda Martín Alcoff and Eduardo Mendieta. Lanham, Md.: Rowman & Littlefield, 51–67.

Mazmanian, Daniel and Paul A. Sabatier. 1983. "One Principle, Two Programs: Desegregation of the Nation's Schools, South and North." In *Implementation and Public Policy*, edited by Mazmanian and Sabatier. Glencoe, Ill.: Scott Foresman, 138–174

McClure, Kirstie. 1997. "The Odor of Judgment: Exemplarity, Propriety, and Politics in the Company of Hannah Arendt." In *Hannah Arendt and the Meaning of Politics*, edited by Craig Calhoun and John McGowan. Minneapolis: University of Minnesota Press, 53–84.

McGoldrick, Dominic. 2006. *Human Rights and Religion – The Islamic Headscarf Debate in Europe*. Oxford: Hart Publishing.

Mendieta, Eduardo. 2005. "Communicative Freedom, Citizenship and Political Justice in the Age of Globalization." *Philosophy & Social Criticism* 31: 739–752.

Mertens, Thomas. 2005. "The Eichmann Trial: Hannah Arendt's View on the Jerusalem Court's Competence." *German Law Review* 6: 407–424.

Metallic, Candice and Patricia Monture-Angus. 2002. "Domestic Laws versus Aboriginal Visions: An Analysis of the Delgamuukw Decision." *borderlands e-journal* 1 (2). Available at http://www.borderlands.net.au/vol1no2_2002/metallic_angus.html.

Mezey, Naomi. 2001. "Out of the Ordinary: Law, Power, Culture, and the Commonplace." *Law & Social Inquiry* 26: 145–167.

Morrow, Derek J. 2005. "The Love 'Without Being' that Opens (to) Distance: Part Two: From the Icon of Distance to the Distance of the Icon in Marion's Phenomenology of Love." *The Heythrop Journal* 46: 493–511.

Moruzzi, Norma Claire. 1994. "A Problem with Headscarves: Contemporary Complexities of Political and Social Identities." *Political Theory* 22: 653–672.

Murphy, Michael. 2001. "Culture and the Courts: A New Direction in Canadian Jurisprudence on Aboriginal Rights?" *Canadian Journal of Political Science* XXXIV: 109–129.

Narayan, Deepa, et al. 2000. *Voices of the Poor: Crying out for Change*. London: Oxford University Press for the World Bank.

Narmada Bachao Andolan. 2000. The Order of the Supreme Court in the Narmada Case Highlights, Comments, and Analysis. Friends of River Narmada. Available at: http://www.narmada.org/sardar-sarovar/sc.ruling/nba.comments.html

Neumann, Iver B. 1999. *The Uses of the Other: "The East" in European Identity Formation*. Minneapolis: University of Minnesota Press.

Norton, Anne. 1995. "Heart of Darkness: Africa and African Americans in the Writings of Hannah Arendt." In *Feminist Interpretations of Hannah Arendt*, edited by Bonnie Honig. University Park: The Pennsylvania State University Press, 247–261.

Oliver, Kelly. 2001. *Witnessing: Beyond Recognition*. Minneapolis: University of Minnesota Press.

Otto, Dianne. 1997. "Content: Rethinking the 'Universality' of Human Rights Law." *Columbia Human Rights Law Review* 29: 1–46.

Özdalga, Elisabeth. 1998. *The Veiling Issue, Official Secularism and Popular Islam in Modern Turkey*. Surrey: Curzon.

Pantea, Maria-Carmen. n.d. "Gender Aspects of Secularism in Today's [sic] French Schools: The Dilemma of Muslim Minorities." In *Gender and the (Post) "East" /*

"*West*" *Divide*. Available at: www.genderomania.ro/book_gender_post/part5/ Maria_Pantea.pdf.

Parasuraman. S. 1999. *The Development Dilemma: Displacement in India*. New York: St. Martin's Press.

Parvikko, Tuija. 2003. "Hannah Arendt and the Arrogance of Judgment" *Alternatives* 28: 199–213.

Pasqualucci, Jo M. 2006. "The Evolution of International Indigenous Rights in the Inter-American Human Rights System" *Human Rights Law Review* 2006 6(2):281–322.

Penashue, Elizabeth. n.d. "A Cry for Future Generations" The International Campaign for the Innu & the Earth (ICIE). Available at: http://webhome.idirect. com/~occpehr/campaigns/icie/index.htm.

Peperzak, Adriaan. 1997. *Before Ethics: Contemporary Studies in Philosophy and the Human Sciences*. Atlantic Highlands, N.J.: Humanities Press International.

Plant, Bob. 2003a. "Doing Justice to the Derrida-Levinas Connection: A Response to Mark Dooley" *Philosophy and Social Criticism* 29: 427–450.

2003b. "Ethics Without Exit: Levinas and Murdoch" *Philosophy and Literature* 27: 456–470.

Plato. 1991. *The Republic of Plato*, translated by Alan Bloom. New York: Basic Books.

Poulter, Sebastien. 1997. "Muslim Headscarves in School: Contrasting Legal Approaches in England and France" *Oxford Journal of Legal Studies* 17: 43–74.

Rajagopal, Balakrishnan. 2005. "The Role of Law in Counter-Hegemonic Globalization and Global Legal Pluralism: Lessons from the Narmada Valley Struggle in India" *Leiden Journal of International Law* 18: 345–387.

Ramji-Nogales, Jaya, Andrew I. Schoenholtz, and Philip G. Schrag. 2007. "Refugee Roulette: Disparities in Asylum Adjudication" *Stanford Law Review* 60: 295–411.

Rancière, Jacques. 1999. *Disagreement: Politics and Philosophy*, translated by Julie Rose. Minneapolis: University of Minnesota Press.

2004. "Introducing Disagreement" trans. Steven Corcoran. *Angelaki: Journal of Theoretical Humanities* 9(3): 3–9.

Ray, Sangeeta. 2003. "Ethical Encounters: Spivak, Alexander and Kincaid" *Cultural Studies* 17: 42–55.

Rediker, Marcus. 2007. *The Slave Ship: A Human History*. New York: Viking.

Reece, Steve. 1993. *The Stranger's Welcome: Oral Theory and the Aesthetics of the Homeric Hospitality Scene*. Ann Arbor: University of Michigan.

Rorty, Richard. 1993. "Human Rights, Rationality, and Sentimentality." In *On Human Rights: The 1993 Oxford Amnesty Lectures*, edited by Susan Hurley and Stephen Shute. New York: Basic Books, 111–134.

Rossiter, Clinton L. 1948. *Constitutional Dictatorship: Crisis Governments in the Modern Democracies*. Princeton: Princeton University Press.

Rothstein, Edward. 2001. "Attacks on U.S. Challenge the Perspectives of Postmodern True Believers" *The New York Times*, September 22.

Routledge, P. 2003. "Voices of the Dammed: Discursive Resistance amidst Erasure in the Narmada Valley, India" *Political Geography* 22: 243–270.

Ruchet, Olivier. 2006. "The Closing of the Republican Mindset: Headscarves, Hegemony, and the Recent Debate on Secularism in France" Paper Presented at the Annual Meeting of the American Political Science Association, Philadelphia, PA.

Sanders, Lynn. 1997. "Against Deliberation." *Political Theory* 25: 347–376.

Saul, Ben. 2004. "Compensation for Unlawful Death in International Law: A Focus on the Inter-American Court of Human Rights." *American University International Law Review* 19: 523–585.

Schonsteiner, Judith. 2007. "Dissuasive Measures and the 'Society as a Whole': A Working Theory of Reparations in the Inter-American Court of Human Rights." *American University International Law Review* 23: 127–164.

Scott, Joan W. 2005. "Symptomatic Politics: The Banning of Islamic Head Scarves in French Public Schools." *French Politics, Culture & Society* 23 (3): 106–127.

Secor, Anna. 2005. "Islamism, Democracy, and the Political Production of the Headscarf Issue in Turkey." In *Geographies of Muslim Women: Gender, Religion, and Space*, edited by Ghazi- Walid Falah and Caroline Nagel. New York: The Guilford Press, 203–225.

Sharpe, Jenny and Gayatri Chakravorty Spivak. 2003. "A Conversation with Gayatri Chakravorty Spivak: Politics and the Imagination." *Signs* 28: 609–624.

Shepherd, Lois. 2006. "Assuming Responsibility." *Wake Forest Law Review* 41: 445–464.

Shue, Henry. 1996. *Basic Rights: Subsistance, Affluence, and U.S. Foreign Policy.* Princeton, N.J.: Princeton University Press.

Simmons, William Paul. 1999. "The Third: Levinas's Theoretical Move from An-Archical Ethics to the Realm of Justice and Politics." *Philosophy & Social Criticism* 25 (6): 85–106.

———. 2003. *An-Archy and Justice: An Introduction to Emmanuel Levinas's Political Thought.* Lanham, MD: Lexington Books.

———. 2006. "Concrete Abstractions and the 'Rights of Man'." *Subject Matters* 3: 113–119.

———. 2007. "Liability of Secondary Actors under the Alien Tort Statute: Aiding and Abetting and Acquiescence to Torture in the Context of the Femicides of Ciudad Juárez." *Yale Human Rights & Development Law Journal* 10: 88–140.

Spivak, Gayatri Chakravorty. 1988. "Can the Subaltern Speak?" In *Marxism and the Interpretation of Culture*, edited by Cary Nelson and Lawrence Grossberg. Urbana, Ill.: University of Illinois Press, 271–313.

Spivak, Gayatri Chakravorty (with Howard Winant). 1990. "Gayatri Spivak on the Politics of the Subaltern." *Socialist Review* 20 (3): 85–97.

Spivak, Gayatri Chakravorty. 1991–1992. "Not Virgin Enough to Say That [S]he Occupies the Place of the Other." *Cardozo Law Review* 13: 1343–1348.

———. 1993. *Outside in the Teaching Machine.* New York: Routledge.

———. 1995a. *Imaginary Maps.* New York: Routledge.

———. 1995b. *The Spivak Reader: Selected Works of Gayati Chakravorty Spivak.* New York: Routledge.

———. 1999. *A Critique of Postcolonial Reason: Toward a History of the Vanishing Present.* Cambridge: Harvard University Press.

———. 2004a. "On the Cusp of the Personal and the Impersonal": An Interview with Gayatri Chakravorty Spivak" by Laura Lyons and Cynthia Franklin. *Biography* 27 (2004): 203–221.

———. 2004b. "Righting Wrongs." *The South Atlantic Quarterly* 103: 523–581.

———. 2005. "Scattered Speculations on the Subaltern and the Popular." *Postcolonial Studies* 8: 475–486.

2006. "Close Reading" *PMLA: Publications of the Modern Language Association of America* 121: 1608–1617.

Steele, Meili. 2002. "Arendt versus Ellison on Little Rock: The Role of Language in Political Judgment" *Constellations* 9: 184–205.

Stern, Herbert J. 1984. *Judgment in Berlin*. New York: Universe Books.

Stevens, Hugh. 1999. "But Words Can Never Hurt Me" *Women: A Cultural Review* 10 (3): 344—347.

Sudgeon, Jonathan. 2004. "A Certain Lack of Empathy" Qantara.de. Available at: http://www.qantara.de/webcom/show_article.php/_c-476/_nr-212/i.html.

Survival International. 1999. *Canada's Tibet: The Killing of the Innu*. London. Available at: http://assets.survivalinternational.org/static/files/books/InnuReport.pdf.

Swanwick, Daniel L. 2006. "Foreign Policy and Humanitarianism in U.S. Asylum Adjudication: Revisiting the Debate in the Wake of the War on Terror" *Georgetown Immigration Law Journal* 21. 129–149.

Talbott, William J. 2005. *Which Rights Should Be Universal?* Oxford: Oxford University Press.

Thomas, Elaine R. 2006. "Keeping Identity at a Distance: Explaining France's New Legal Restrictions on the Islamic Headscarf" *Ethnic and Racial Studies* 29: 237–259.

Trindade, Antônio ACançado. 2002. "Presentation of the Annual Report to the Committee on Juridical and Political Affairs" Permanent Council of the Organization of American States. OEA/ser. G., CP/CAJP-1932/02, published on April 25.

2008. "The Human Person and International Justice" *Columbia Journal of Transnational Law* 47: 16–30.

United Nations. 2005. "France Generally Respects Religious Freedom Despite Areas of Concern – UN Expert" UN News Centre. Available at: http://www.un.org/apps/news/story.asp?NewsID=16059&Cr=france&Cr1=.

UNHCR. 2002. *Guidelines on International Protection: "Membership of a particular social group" within the context of Article 1A(2) of the 1951 Convention and/or its 1967 Protocol relating to the Status of Refugees*, U.N. Refugee Agency, U.N. Doc. HCR/GIP/02/02 (2002).

United States Department of State. 2004. "Annual Report of the United States Commission on International Religious Freedom" May.

2005. "2005 Country Report on Human Rights Practices, Turkey" Bureau of Democracy, Human Rights, and Labor. Available at http://www.state.gov/g/drl/rls/hrrpt/2005/61680.htm.

Urbinati, Nadia. 2005. "The Politics of Immigration and Membership" *Dissent* (Fall): 101–105.

Vandenhole, Wouter. 2002. "Human rights Law, Development and Social Action Litigation in India" *Asia-Pacific Journal on Human Rights & the Law* 3: 136–210.

Villa, Dana. 1998. "The Reluctant Modernism of Hannah Arendt" (Book Review). *Ethics* 108: 817–820.

Walters, Mark. 1993. "British Imperial Constitutional Law and Aboriginal Rights: A Comment on *Delgamuukw v. British Columbia*" *Queen's Law Journal* 17: 350–413.

Warren, Earl. 1977. *The Memoirs of Chief Justice Earl Warren.* Garden City, N.Y.: Doubleday.

Warren, Robert Penn. 1965. *Who Speaks for the Negro?* New York: Random House.

Whitehead, Judith. 2007. "Submerged and Submerging Voices: Hegemony and the Decline of the Narmada Bachao Andolan in Gujarat, 1998–2001" *Critical Asian Studies* 39: 339–421.

Wing, Adrien Katherine and Monica Nigh Smith. 2006. "Critical Race Feminism Lifts the Veil?: Muslim Women, France, and the Headscarf Ban" *U.C. Davis Law Review* 39: 743–785.

Wood, John R. 2007. *The Politics of Water Resource Development in India: The Narmada Dams Controversy.* Los Angeles: Sage Publishing.

World Health Organization. 2007. Effective and Humane Mental Health Care and Treatment for All. The Country Summary Series: Republic of The Gambia. Available at: http://www.who.int/mental_health/policy/country/GambiaSumma ry_11April2007Formatted.pdf.

Yar, Majid. 2000. "From Actor to Spectator: Hannah Arendt's 'Two Theories' of Political Judgment" *Philosophy & Social Criticism* 26 (2): 1–27.

Cases

Adarand Constructors, Inc. v. Peña 515 U.S. 200 (1995).

Airey v. Ireland, 32 Eur Ct HR Ser A (1979): [1979] 2 E.H.R.R. 305.

Albathani v. INS, 318 F. 3d 365, 1st Cir. 2003.

Anguelova v. Bulgaria European Court of Human Rights, Application No. 38361/97, Judgment of June 13, 2002.

Applicant A v. Minister for Immigration and Ethnic Affairs, (1997) 142 ALR 331.

Bandhua Mukti Morcha v. Union of India, 1984. 3 SCC 161. (India).

Benslimane v. Gonzales, 430 F.3d 828, 3rd Cir. 2005.

Builes v. Nye, 239 F. Supp.2d 518, M.D.Pa. 2003.

Bulacio v. Argentina, Inter-Am. Ct. H.R. (Ser. C) No. 100 (Sept. 18, 2003).

Cantoral Benavides Case, Judgment of December 3, 2001, Inter-Am Ct. H.R. (Ser. C) No. 88 (2001).

Caso de los Hermanos Gomez Paquiyauri v. Peru, Sentencia de 8 de julio de 2004, Corte I.D.H., (Ser. C) No. 110 (2004).

Caso "Instituto de Reeducación del Menor" v. Paraguay, Sentencia de 2 de septiembre de 2004, Corte I.D.H., (Ser. C) No. 112 (2004).

Cham v. Attorney General, 445 F.3d 683, 3rd Cir. 2006.

Cooper v. Aaron, 358 U.S. 1 (1958).

Cyprus Case, 1958–1959 Y.B. Eur. Conv. on H.R. 174 (Eur. Comm'n on H.R.).

Dahlab v. Switzerland, 2001-V Eur. Ct. H.R. 447.

Dawoud v. Gonzales, 424 F.3d 608, 7th Cir. 2005.

Delgamuukw v. British Columbia, [1997] 3 S.C.R. 1010. (Canada).

Dudgeon v. United Kingdom, [1981] 4 EHRR. 149.

Fiadjoe v. Attorney General, 411 F.3d 135, 3rd Cir. 2005.

Grupee v. Gonzales, 400 F.3d 1026, 7th Cir. 2005.

Guerin v. The Queen, [1984] 2 S.C.R. 335.

S.P. Gupta v. Union of India, A.I.R. 1982 S.C. 149.

Hernandez-Montiel, 225 F.3d 1084; 9th Cir. 2000.

In Re Fauziya Kassinga, Interim Decision 3278 (BIA); 21 I. & N. Dec. 357.

In Re R-A-, United States Board of Immigration Appeals, 11 June 1999 (Vacated by Attorney General, January 19, 2001).

Klass and others v. Federal Republic of Germany, European Court of Human Rights (Series A, NO 28) (1979–80) 2 EHRR 21.

"The Last Temptation of Christ" Case, Judgment of February 5, 2001, Inter-Am Ct. H.R. (Ser. C) No. 73 (2001).

Loayza Tamayo Case, Reparations (art. 63(1) American Convention on Human Rights), Judgment of November 27, 1998, Inter-Am. Ct. H.R. (Ser. C) No. 42 (1998).

Lopez-Umanzor v. Gonzales, 405 F.3d 1049, 9th Cir. 2005.

Matter of Acosta, 19 I. & N. Dec. 211 (BIA 1985).

McCann v. United Kingdom, 1996, 21 Eur. II.R. Rep. 97.

M.C. Mehta v. Union of India, WP 12739/1985 (1986.12.20).

R v. Mitchell, 2001, S.C.R. 911. (Canada).

Moiwana Village v. Suriname, Judgment of June 15, 2005, Inter-Am Ct. H.R., (Ser. C) No. 145 (2005).

Mukesh Advani v. State of Madhya Pradesh, AIR 1985 SC 136.

Myrna Mack Chang Case, Judgment of November 25, 2003, Inter-Am. Ct. H.R., (Ser. C) No. 101.

Narmada Bachao Andolan v. Union of India, 2000. 10 S.C.C. 664.

New State Ice Co. v. Liebmann, 285 U.S. 262 (1932).

Niam v. Ashcroft, 354 F.3d 652, 7th Cir. 2003.

Qun Wang v. AG of the United States, 423 F.3d 260, 3d Cir. 2005.

Purohit and Moore v. The Gambia, African Commission on Human and Peoples' Rights, Comm. No. 241/2001 (2003).

R. v. Gladstone, 1996, 2 S.C.R. 723. (Canada).

R v. Sioui, 1990, S.C.R. 1025. (Canada).

R. v. Van der Peet, 1996, 2 S.C.R. 507, P 31 (Canada).

Re GJ, 1995, Refugee Appeal No. 13 12/93, New Zealand RSAA, 1 NLR 387.

Regina v. Immigration Appeal Tribunal, Ex Parte Shah.1999. 2 A.C. 629.

Refah Partisi and Others v. Turkey, 31 July 2001. (Application Nos. 41340/98, 41342/98 and 41344/98).

Leyla Sahin v. Turkey, App. No. 44774/98 2005-XI Eur. Ct. H.R.

SG v. France, 347/1988 CCPR/C /43/D347/1988 (November 15, 1991).

Sabuktekin v. Turkey, 2003, 36 EHRR 314.

Sanchez-Trujillo, 801 F. 2d 1571, 9th Cir. 1986.

Scott v. Sandford 60 U.S. (19 How.) 393 (1857).

Center for Economic and Social Rights and Social and Economic Rights Action Center (SERAC) v. Nigeria (155/96) African Commission on Human and Peoples' Rights, Comm.

Shah v. Attorney General, 446 F.3d 429, 3rd Cir. 2006.

Sosnovskaia v. Gonzales, 421 F.3d 589, 7th Cir. 2005.

Ssali v. Gonzales, 424 F.3d 556, 7th Cir. 2005.

Sukwanputra v. Gonzales, 434 F.3d 627, 3rd Cir. 2006.

Velasquez Rodriguez Case, Judgment of July 29, 1988, Inter-Am.Ct.H.R. (Ser. C) No. 4 (1988).

Wewaykum Indian Band v. Canada, 2002. 4 S.C.R. 245 (Can.)

X and Y v. Netherlands, 1985, Application 8978/80.

Ximenes-Lopes Case, 2006, Inter-American Court of Human Rights, Series C, No. 149.

Index

CPSIA information can be obtained at www.ICGtesting.com
Printed in the USA
LVOW01s1041240714

395645LV00011B/229/P